Chicago and Its Botanic Garden

Chicago and Its Botanic Garden

The Chicago Horticultural Society at 125

Cathy Jean Maloney

NORTHWESTERN UNIVERSITY PRESS AND THE CHICAGO BOTANIC GARDEN

Northwestern University Press
www.nupress.northwestern.edu

Printed in Canada

10   9   8   7   6   5   4   3   2   1

Library of Congress Cataloging-in-Publication Data
Maloney, Cathy Jean, author.
    Chicago and its botanic garden : the Chicago Horticultural Society at 125 /
Chicago Botanic Garden and Cathy Jean Maloney.
        pages cm
    Includes bibliographical references and index.
    ISBN 978-0-8101-3095-1 (cloth : alk. paper) — ISBN 978-0-8101-3096-8 (ebook)
    1. Chicago Horticultural Society—History. 2. Chicago Botanic Garden—History.
3. Horticulture—Illinois—Chicago—Societies, etc. 4. Botanical gardens—Illinois—
Glencoe—History. I. Chicago Botanic Garden, issuing body. II. Title.
SB85.I32C476 2014
635.09773'11—dc23
                                                                        2014036190

Contents

Foreword   Sophia Shaw   *vii*

Preface   Robert Finke   *ix*

1   The Early Years: The Gilded Age to the Garden   *3*

2   Building the Garden: Magic from the Marsh   *31*

3   Flower Shows: Days of Mums and Roses   *61*

4   Plants: For Posterity and Progress   *97*

5   Landscape Design: Focus on Excellence   *125*

6   Education and Outreach: Bringing the Garden Home   *171*

7   Plant Science: Save the Plants, Save the Planet   *201*

Acknowledgments   *235*

Appendixes   *237*

Notes   *247*

Image Credits   *257*

Index   *259*

Blue skies are reflected in one of many lakes at the Chicago Botanic Garden.

Foreword

It takes vision, persistence, and a bit of moxie to pull a city out of a swamp. When Chicago's founders decreed *Urbs in Horto* as the motto for the little town, Chicago was hardly the City in a Garden. Years of hard work, planning, investment, and sheer willpower combined to create today's thriving metropolis.

Similarly, when the Chicago Horticultural Society proposed to create the Chicago Botanic Garden on the site of a poorly drained marsh, some doubted if it could be done. But the Garden, like the city of Chicago, and often in tandem with the city, grew robustly as a result of the long-standing efforts of the Society.

The Society's history is much longer than that of the Garden: founded in 1890, the Society celebrates its 125th anniversary in 2015. Today, the Chicago Horticultural Society manages the Chicago Botanic Garden in a model private-public partnership with the Forest Preserve District of Cook County.

When first organized, the Society was instrumental in propelling Chicago onto the global stage by helping to host the World's Columbian Exposition of 1893. The Society's membership was made up of civic leaders, renowned horticulturists and landscape designers, and trailblazers who knew how to get things done. From the world's fair to City Beautiful planning, from the Progressive Era to victory gardens, from World's Flower and Garden Shows to an internationally renowned Chicago Botanic Garden, the Society—as reflected in the Garden's mission statement today—cultivated the power of plants to sustain and enrich life.

Through the Chicago Botanic Garden, the Chicago Horticultural Society reaches millions of people annually. Representing all backgrounds, abilities, and interests, people are attracted to the Garden because its beautiful display gardens and natural areas, and its compelling programs, respond to the human need to connect with nature. Garden educators, in partnership with Garden scientists, train the environmental stewards, urban farmers, plant scientists, and horticultural therapists of today and tomorrow. Garden scientists are helping to conserve, protect, and restore native habitats and the essential benefits they provide.

When the Society created a botanic garden more than 40 years ago in Glencoe, Illinois, near Chicago, it launched a leader in the plant education and conservation movement. On its campus and through its website, publications, and expanding presence at conferences, the Chicago Botanic Garden reaches ever larger audiences, growing its influence as a leading living museum.

This book honors the efforts and vision of the Chicago Horticultural Society's leaders, donors, members, staff, and volunteers who have grown the Chicago Botanic Garden to the international institution it is today.

Sophia Shaw
President and CEO
Chicago Botanic Garden

The Circle Garden comes to life in spring as tulips and weeping Eastern redbud trees burst into bloom. Past the central fountain and boxwood path lined with foxgloves is the Regenstein Center.

Preface

The past 125 years have brought remarkable change to the world of horticulture, and to the role of the Chicago Horticultural Society. From a small group of committed civic leaders and horticulture professionals, the Society has grown to almost 50,000 member households of the Chicago Botanic Garden. Halfway into our ten-year strategic plan, "Keep Growing," we continue to enhance our capabilities to fulfill our mission.

Tangible results of this plan include the Kris Jarantoski Campus, featuring new greenhouses and nurseries and a display garden designed by acclaimed landscape architect Peter Wirtz that will transform the southern part of the Garden into a destination point for visitors and scientists alike. On the north end of the Garden, the comprehensive Regenstein Foundation Learning Campus is under way, expanding on the Society's tradition of outreach and education. The Learning Campus will be surrounded by a new display garden whose concept vision was created by landscape architect Mikyoung Kim, also world renowned for innovative landscape design.

Ambitious plans such as "Keep Growing" make the Garden what it is today: one of the very few botanic gardens in the world recognized not only for captivating display gardens but also for far-reaching scientific research, broad educational opportunities, and innovative urban agriculture jobs-training programs that benefit people in all areas of Cook County.

As the Society's founders knew so well, more than plans are needed. It is my great privilege to work with the dedicated boards, staff, volunteers, members, and friends of the Chicago Botanic Garden whose enduring efforts and support, as well as that of the Forest Preserve District of Cook County, enable us to reach more than one million people who visit the Garden annually or avail themselves of our outreach programs.

The future is bright for the Garden and the people it serves. We invite you to join us in the next 125 years as we cultivate the power of plants to sustain and enrich life.

Robert Finke
Chairman of the Board

Chicago and Its Botanic Garden

1

The Early Years

The Gilded Age to the Garden

Nature does not proceed by leaps and bounds...

...wrote the famed eighteenth-century botanist Carolus Linnaeus. Nor is a garden built in a day. Ground was broken in 1965 for the Chicago Botanic Garden in Glencoe, Illinois, but the Chicago Horticultural Society labored for decades to turn that first spadeful of dirt. In 1890, in a small meeting room at the now-defunct Sherman House hotel in downtown Chicago, a civic-minded group organized the Chicago Horticultural Society[1] for the "encouragement and promotion of the practice of Horticulture in all its branches and the fostering of an increased love of it among the people."[2] The Chicago Horticultural Society, despite world wars and financial downturns, notwithstanding fads and fashions, remained true to its mission, its history intertwining with and contributing to the growth of the city of Chicago and the surrounding region.

A bronze sculpture of Linnaeus, the eighteenth-century Swedish botanist, encourages the love of nature in the Chicago Botanic Garden's Heritage Garden.

Horticulture reaches people in their own backyards, on their dinner table, and at virtually every significant life event. A new baby is welcomed with flowers, brides and grooms pose with bouquets and boutonnieres, newlyweds plant their first tree, the ill take comfort from floral greetings, and mourners sow forget-me-nots in remembrance of lost loves. Since its inception, the Society has enhanced the public and private lives and spaces of the Chicago area through its horticultural programs and partnerships with kindred organizations.

In its early days, the Society orchestrated highly popular flower shows. It participated in the Plan of Chicago of 1909 and the development of the Forest Preserve District of Cook County. Through philanthropic work in school gardens, shelters for disadvantaged women and children, and hospitals, the Society advocated horticulture for health and education. Midcentury, the Society propelled World War II victory gardens into sustained community gardening, resumed the hosting of flower shows, organized garden tours in the city and suburbs, and offered classes throughout the region. Today, the Society serves—at the Garden, online, and at satellite locations—millions of people each year.

Seedling after seedling, flower show after show, garden tour after tour, the Society's mission dovetailed with the projects and people who built Chicago. Its living legacy has created urban farms in the "city that works" and propagated the love of flowers displayed throughout the "city beautiful."

Cuttings from the "City in a Garden"

Despite its frontier beginnings, Chicago has had a long horticultural history. The first mayor of Chicago, William B. Ogden, himself an amateur horticulturist, joined the subcommittee responsible for designing the official seal of the City of Chicago in 1837. Amid the soft palette of blues, greens, and yellows, a brilliantly colored crimson scroll proclaims the city motto, *Urbs in Horto*, which translates as "city in a garden." At that time, the Chicago landscape consisted largely of swamps, barren sand dunes, and sparsely settled prairies. It took vision and more than a dash of optimism to declare the forlorn site a garden city. Yet Ogden and other civic leaders so believed in the restorative powers of nature and of horticulture as evidence of refined taste that they embraced the slogan as integral to the city's growth.

More than a slogan, the garden city ideal prompted Ogden and other civic leaders to form the first incarnation of the Chicago Horticultural Society in 1847. This group comprised patrons of horticulture, such as Ogden, and professional nursery owners whose livelihood depended on growing and selling plants to pioneer homesteaders, farmers, and city window box gardeners. Local nurseries played a critical role in Chicago's growth because many of the plants that had been obtained from established growers on the East Coast simply did not thrive in the Midwest. It became a practical matter of survival to discover trees for fuel, food, and shelter, and vegetables and herbs for sustenance and health.[3]

Each group in the early Society depended on the other. Nursery owners relied on clients for plant purchases, to act as cheerleaders for horticulture, and, indirectly, to help subsidize experimentation that accompanied new planting methods or varieties. Agricultural schools or government-funded experiment stations did not yet exist, and plant trials occurred at the expense of the private grower. The so-called wealthy amateurs, a nonpejorative term of the day that described horticulture patrons, sought new plants for their own greenhouses and to beautify the city in which they had invested their time and money. This public-private partnership of commercial growers and civic leaders would set a successful precedent for years to follow.

In addition to Ogden, early members of this first Society included prominent physician William B. Egan, businessman and library founder W. L. Newberry, and Society president John H. Kinzie, noted son of one of Chicago's first European settlers. Charter member John A. Kennicott, a physician and nurseryman, typified the well-educated commercial grower who joined the fledgling group. Supported with good publicity from the main agriculture and horticulture newspaper of the day, the *Prairie Farmer*, this early Society hosted public exhibitions of fruits and flowers and met to trade tips on growing plants on the prairie.

During these antebellum years, membership in the Society waxed and waned, and other groups such as the Cook County Agricultural and Horticultural Society (1856) and the Chicago Gardeners Society (1858) formed. The new groups included many of the original members of the Chicago Horticultural Society, particularly the commercial growers. As a testament to the stewardship ideals the Society founders held toward the young city of Chicago, often their descendants joined or initiated subsequent iterations of the original Society. The passion they brought to their work and the care with which they tended their own gardens served as exemplars of horticultural possibilities to the citizenry at large.

The W. B. Egan garden, ca. 1860, reflected the horticultural interests of an early Chicago Horticultural Society founder. His son, W. C. Egan, helped revitalize the Society in 1890.

Courtesy Chicago Public Library, Special Collections and Preservation Division, G.P. Smith 566.

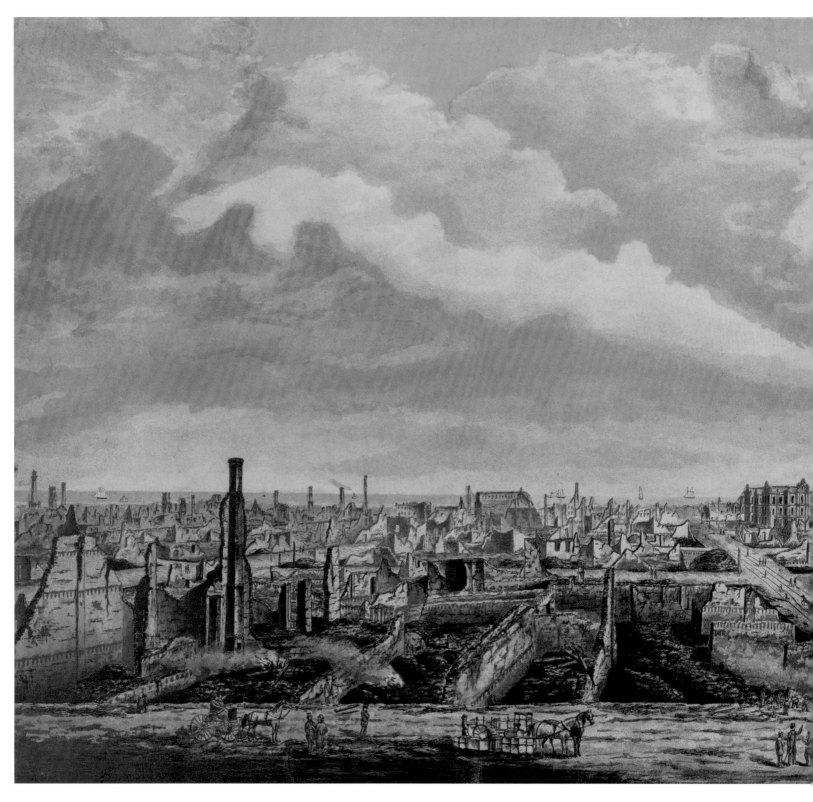

The Great Chicago Fire of 1871 caused massive damage, including the loss of many greenhouses in the burn district. This fire and others like it were among the catalysts for sustainable lumber practices.

Following the Civil War, consensus grew around the creation of public parks for health and recreation, culminating in 1869 legislation that established three park districts for Chicago's North, South, and West Sides. Frederick Law Olmsted, the premier landscape architect of the day, was commissioned to prepare a design for the South Side parks in 1870.

Then came the Great Chicago Fire of 1871. The loss of life and property and the personal tragedies resulting from this calamity evoked a nationwide charitable response. Many influential greenhouses, then located within the city, were destroyed. Horticultural pursuits took a back seat to bricks-and-mortar reconstruction. The logging and timber industry, however, came under scrutiny after it was determined that many frame houses in Chicago contributed to the great conflagration. Ogden was among the many "lumber barons" who lost houses in Chicago and investments in other areas affected by 1871 fires, such as lumber town Peshtigo, Wisconsin. These incidents and others helped spur the conservation movement related to reforesting.

In the rebuilding years after the fire of 1871, many of Chicago's most significant buildings and institutions debuted. William Le Baron Jenney designed the Home Insurance Building, said to be the world's first skyscraper, in 1885. The Chicago Woman's Club formed in 1876 and would soon become a national model of organization. The Chicago Academy of Fine Arts emerged in 1878 (and later became the Art Institute). The Chicago Public Library (1872), Fine Arts Building (1885), Newberry Library (1887), and Hull House (1889) further solidified the city's cultural and philanthropic scene. Many future Society leaders helped organize or manage the development of these bedrocks of culture in Chicago.

Coincident with the development of these cultural icons, this period also saw a growth of horticultural organizations nationally and locally. The national Society of American Florists first organized in Chicago in 1884. Many local horticulturists were among its founding members, and the Chicago Florists' Club (1886) became one of its most influential chapters. The newly built Inter-State Exposition Building (1872) not only was the early home of the Chicago Symphony Orchestra, but its primary function was to host conventions, including displays of floral exhibitors.

The World's Columbian Exposition horticulture and landscape surpassed all previous world's fairs and set the standard for future expositions.

Courtesy Cathy Jean Maloney.

Despite these signs of renewal, Chicago's charms remained unrecognized by many observers on the more established East Coast. Typical is this opinion from an 1884 New York–based *Puck* magazine article: "Chicago is famous for divorces, conventions, trotting horses and the large feet of its women. It is called the Garden City, and a committee of investigation has been sitting for the past six weeks to find out the reason." The article further asserted that there were no museums or art galleries in Chicago and that its citizenry "have not yet got the hang of what is considered etiquette in older places."[4]

To many, Chicago still suffered from its frontier image. Something big was needed to change the world's perception of the City in a Garden.

Chrysanthemums Color the White City

By hosting a world's fair that would eclipse all previous fairs, Chicago's civic boosters hoped to elevate the city's image from that of a backwater village to a modern metropolis. As with any great idea, many claimed authorship of the bold plan to host the 1893 World's Columbian Exposition in Chicago. More likely, the fair resulted from the confluence of many independent minds working together. In 1889, Chicago Mayor De-Witt Cregier formed a committee of 100 to explore the feasibility of hosting the exposition. This executive committee of the task force included several future Society charter members or patrons, such as Andrew McNally, Charles Hutchinson, Samuel Allerton, Harlow Higinbotham, and Victor Lawson.[5] Society president George Schneider served as a commissioner responsible for securing early stock subscriptions for the fair, and Higinbotham, a future Society patron, served as president of the exposition.

In April 1890, Congress appointed Chicago as the host exposition city over arch rival New York City.[6] Great architects with national repute designed the buildings, all of classic white, thus earning the fair's sobriquet of the White City. Horticulture would play a huge role in the fair, and world's fair organizers had commissioned the noted landscape architect Olmsted to design the fairgrounds. Local horticulture and professional groups recognized the fair as an opportunity to feature the city's gardens and floriculture industry. Buoyed by the encouragement of kindred groups that met in Chicago in August 1890, a newly formed national federation of societies, the Columbian Horticultural Association, toured potential fair sites with World's Columbian Exposition vice president Thomas B. Bryan.[7] As with all sanctioned American world's fairs, a national umbrella organization oversaw the horticulture department but depended on local expertise to get the work done.

A flurry of recruiting efforts ensued to create a local organization of sufficient stature to lead the exposition's horticulture efforts. The self-styled "Chicago and Cook County Horticultural Society" (the fledgling group would undergo a number of name changes) distributed a circular inviting anyone interested in horticulture to attend an organizational meeting on September 1, 1890, at the Sherman House. Signed by the temporary Society chairman, the venerable market gardener Jonathan Periam, the circular targeted members of the Chicago Florists' Club and also noted, "It is earnestly desired that as many influential individuals as possible will be present and become charter members."[8] Members of this new group, including many longtime Chicago horticulturists, held their first exhibition in the Inter-State Building from early September through mid-October.[9]

During the September meeting, a subcommittee was tasked to incorporate the Chicago Horticultural Society. Inspired by the energy and the membership of the predecessor groups, the Chicago Horticultural Society was incorporated on October 1, 1890.[10] As with its earlier incarnations, the Society brought together businessmen, professional horticulturists, and the public. In 1891, the Society began a tradition of hosting flower shows that rivaled those on the East Coast and garnered acclaim from first national and then international press. Shows of the 1890s drew from the private greenhouses of Chicago's leading citizenry and from the most prominent florists and nursery owners of the day. The shows anticipated and helped prepare for the spectacular horticultural achievements of the world's fair.

Society members and World's Columbian Exposition horticulture and landscape professionals were mutually supportive. John Thorpe, the exposition's superintendent of floriculture and also a Society member, read a paper at the October 1891 Society meeting on "The Possibilities of Horticulture at the World's Columbian Exposition." Thorpe predicted that the exposition "will advance floriculture twenty-five years" and that "groups of plants of all kinds will not be shown simply in hundreds, but in thousands and tens of thousands." Thorpe asked the Society to raise subscriptions for the fair, and members approved a motion "towards making the Horticultural Department of the World's Columbian Exposition what it ought to be."[11]

Even as the annual shows helped raise awareness of fine gardens and flowers, the Society also fostered strong relationships with the creators of World's Columbian Exposition landscapes. These friendships helped promote the cause of landscape architecture within the Society itself and ultimately throughout the city. Many Society members enjoyed acquaintanceships with Olmsted, as evidenced in letters sent to him from his son, Frederick Law Olmsted, Jr. The younger Olmsted apprenticed at the World's Columbian Exposition construction site during his summer break from Harvard and received the hospitality of his father's Chicago Horticultural Society friends.

Writing about a "very pleasant evening" he had at an intimate dinner party hosted by the Charles L. Hutchinsons, which included fellow Society members the John Glessner family, the younger Olmsted concluded, "They were all entertaining and cultivated people and Mr. Hutchinson in particular attracted me very much."[12] Shortly after this encounter, he called on attorney and longtime horticulture champion Ezra McCagg, who received his visitor very kindly. Young Olmsted wrote of McCagg, "He was much interested in the exposition work and when he said he thought of driving down to the grounds on Sunday I offered him my services as a guide and he at once accepted."[13]

The sophistication of these civic leaders must have reassured the elder Olmsted, who famously and frequently maligned Chicago's landscapes. Typical is this note from the senior Olmsted to his on-site colleague Harry Codman: "Neither public nor private grounds and places are ever kept in America nearly as finely as it is . . . here [in England], and what . . . Chicagoans might regard as creditably clean and neat [and] well-ordered, would here be thought shabby, sluttish and neglected."[14] Putting aside Olmsted's uncharitable remarks, his opinion carried weight in many social and investment circles. Boosters such as Hutchinson and Glessner offered a more favorable impression of the city and its sophisticates to Olmsted and others in his milieu.

World's Columbian Exposition director and Society member James W. Ellsworth negotiated Olmsted's commission, appealing to his sense of patriotism with such entreaties as, "The reputation of America is at stake . . . I know that you will rise to the occasion . . . realizing fully the influence you will have in assisting us to accomplish the great ends in view."[15]

Society members also contributed directly to the displays at the exposition. Society officer J. C. Vaughan commanded worldwide attention with a spectacular show of pansies and, later, cannas at a prime location in front of the Horticultural Palace. The Peterson family nursery provided advice, along with many of the trees and shrubs planted at the exposition. In August 1893, the Society hosted a reception and banquet for those visitors from around the world who attended the World's Columbian Exposition Horticultural Congress, chaired by Vaughan.

According to the *Annals of Horticulture of 1893*, written by preeminent horticulturist L. H. Bailey of Cornell University, "The most striking circumstance of the year in floricultural directions was the chrysanthemum show at Chicago, following the World's Fair, November 4 to 12."[16] This Society-sponsored show, held at the newly built Art Institute, included exhibits from 16 states as well as Canada and England.[17] Cohosted by the National Chrysanthemum Society, the show highlighted mums, with minor exhibits of roses and carnations.

Throughout the 1890s, the Society built on the World's Columbian Exposition momentum by hosting bigger and better flower shows. The group also weighed in on political issues of the day, counseling against efforts in the Chicago Park System to remove park superintendent (and Society member) J. A. Pettigrew. Political wrangling in the parks continued to be an issue such that in 1897, the Society invited member and

J. C. Vaughan and other Chicago Horticultural Society members contributed directly to displays at the World's Columbian Exposition of 1893.

Courtesy Cathy Jean Maloney.

This image, from the Chicago Horticultural Society's 1893 Chrysanthemum Show program, featured flower arrangements at the Art Institute.

Courtesy Center for Research Libraries.

Landscape architect Jens Jensen frequently lectured at Chicago Horticultural Society meetings and became a member and supporter.

Courtesy Sterling Morton Library, Morton Arboretum.

noted landscape gardener O. C. Simonds to read a paper specifying the traits of "The Ideal Park Superintendent."[18] Landscape architect Jens Jensen, who would have his own issues later with the park system, also began his long-term relationship with the Society during this decade, reading a paper on trees at the 1897 annual meeting. Affiliated with the West Side parks, Jensen displayed rare plants at the 1899 flower show and continued to support the Society in future shows.[19]

As the Gilded Age drew to a close, the Chicago Horticultural Society had succeeded in consistently bringing noteworthy flower shows to unprecedented numbers of Chicagoans. Partnerships forged among the Chicago Horticultural Society, professional flower organizations, and philanthropic groups established traditions for decades to come.

Bouquets for the City Beautiful

The turn of the twentieth century coincided with the Progressive Era, when, across America, social reforms aimed to elevate the lives of the poor and working people, resolve class conflicts, and improve the living conditions in urban and rural homes alike. Chicago, with its hordes of newly arrived, impoverished immigrants pitted against a concentration of wealth in the city's expanding industries of real estate, banking, railroads, and commerce, provided a crucible for experimental Progressive programs and policies. From the Pullman strike of 1894 to Upton Sinclair's scalding account of 1904 stockyard life in *The Jungle*, Chicago's business community from railroad barons to meatpackers clashed with the burgeoning labor movement and media reports.

Concurrently, Chicago launched many ground-breaking Progressive initiatives. Jane Addams and her Hull House social settlement brought wealthy donors and poor immigrants together. Many such philanthropic endeavors originated in Chicago between 1900 and the First World War, and the Chicago Horticultural Society participated, as individual members or as a group, in most of them. The Society's own mission, **"the encouragement and promotion of the practice of Horticulture in all its branches and the fostering of an increased love of it among the people,"**[20] emphasized an egalitarian outreach and sought to improve societal conditions through the beauty of flowers. Thus flowers were delivered to invalids, and schoolchildren were taught to garden.

The horticultural arts transcended socioeconomic lines. The City Beautiful movement, which arose from the World's Columbian Exposition, emphasized green space in city planning to improve the crowded, urban environment. Author Carl Smith notes, "The Columbian Exposition as a whole . . . was a cultural milestone that established City Beautiful principles as the standard for urban design . . . Frederick Law Olmsted's ground plan emphasized functionality as well as visual pleasure."[21] Beautiful landscapes and the inherent knowledge of horticulture dovetailed with the City Beautiful ideals.

Chicago Horticultural Society members embraced the City Beautiful movement in Chicago from the outset. In 1903, the Cook County Board established the Outer Belt Commission to identify parcels of land that could be preserved for the public. The executive committee of this group included Society members Charles L. Hutchinson and John J. Mitchell.[22] The Outer Belt Commission evolved into the Municipal Science Club and then later the Special Parks Commission, which also included Hutchinson, Simonds, Clarence Buckingham, and Jens Jensen.

Ultimately, the works of these commissions paved the way for the successful establishment of the Forest Preserve District of Cook County on November 30, 1914.[23] Many individual Society members were intimately involved with the creation and early management of the forest preserves. Jensen created conservation groups, such as the Prairie Club and Friends of Our Native Landscape, that explored and created pub-

lic awareness of the natural treasures in what would become forest preserve land. Peter Reinberg, the first Forest Preserve District president, a city alderman and a professional rose grower, frequently displayed his roses at Society shows. Vaughan, Charles Wacker, and William A. Peterson, all Chicago Horticultural Society members, served as appointed members of the Forest Preserve Plan Committee. A 1918 book commemorating the forest preserves recognized the unique contributions of all three men, hailing Wacker's experience as

The Forest Preserve Plan Committee included Chicago Horticultural Society members Charles Wacker, J. C. Vaughan, Victor F. Lawson, Robert McCormick, and William A. Peterson.
Courtesy Chicago History Museum, ICHi-68452.

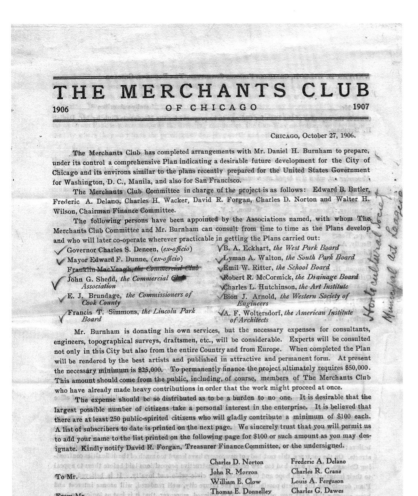

THE MERCHANTS CLUB
OF CHICAGO
1906   1907

CHICAGO, October 27, 1906.

The Merchants Club has completed arrangements with Mr. Daniel H. Burnham to prepare, under its control a comprehensive Plan indicating a desirable future development for the City of Chicago and its environs similar to the plans recently prepared for the United States Government for Washington, D. C., Manila, and also for San Francisco.

The Merchants Club Committee in charge of the project is as follows: Edward B. Butler, Frederic A. Delano, Charles H. Wacker, David R. Forgan, Charles D. Norton and Walter H. Wilson, Chairman Finance Committee.

The following persons have been appointed by the Associations named, with whom The Merchants Club Committee and Mr. Burnham can consult from time to time as the Plans develop and who will later co-operate wherever practicable in getting the Plans carried out:

Governor Charles S. Deneen, (ex-officio)
Mayor Edward F. Dunne, (ex-officio)
Franklin MacVeagh, the Commercial Club
John G. Shedd, the Commercial Club Association
E. J. Brundage, the Commissioners of Cook County
Francis T. Simmons, the Lincoln Park Board

B. A. Eckhart, the West Park Board
Lyman A. Walton, the South Park Board
Emil W. Ritter, the School Board
Robert R. McCormick, the Drainage Board
Charles L. Hutchinson, the Art Institute
Bion J. Arnold, the Western Society of Engineers
A. F. Woltersdorf, the American Institute of Architects

Mr. Burnham is donating his own services, but the necessary expenses for consultants, engineers, topographical surveys, draftsmen, etc., will be considerable. Experts will be consulted not only in this City but also from the entire Country and from Europe. When completed the Plan will be rendered by the best artists and published in attractive and permanent form. At present the necessary minimum is $25,000. To permanently finance the project ultimately requires $50,000. This amount should come from the public, including, of course, members of The Merchants Club who have already made heavy contributions in order that the work might proceed at once.

The expense should be so distributed as to be a burden to no one. It is desirable that the largest possible number of citizens take a personal interest in the enterprise. It is believed that there are at least 250 public-spirited citizens who will gladly contribute a minimum of $100 each. A list of subscribers to date is printed on the next page. We sincerely trust that you will permit us to add your name to the list printed on the following page for $100 or such amount as you may designate. Kindly notify David R. Forgan, Treasurer Finance Committee, or the undersigned.

To Mr.

From Mr.

Charles D. Norton
John R. Morron
William E. Clow
Thomas E. Donnelley
Charles H. Wacker

Frederic A. Delano
Charles R. Crane
Louis A. Ferguson
Charles G. Dawes
Arthur D. Wheeler

Executive Committee

Many Chicago Horticultural Society members belonged to multiple civic and business clubs, such as the Merchants Club. The handwritten notation on this Merchants Club appeal targets the Horticultural Society as a supporter of the Plan of Chicago.

Edward H. Bennett Collection, Ryerson and Burnham Archives, Art Institute of Chicago. Digital File #197301.A000015_1.

Charles L. Hutchinson, philanthropist and business leader, was an early and ardent supporter of the Chicago Horticultural Society.

Courtesy Chicago History Museum, ICHi-68455.

president of the Chicago Plan Commission and Peterson as having a "thorough technical knowledge of horticulture, and one of his chief treasures is a library of some 4,000 volumes." Vaughan was praised as "one of the little band of public spirited citizens who have shown a fatherly spirit towards the Forest Preserve idea since its conception."[24]

The forest preserve movement paralleled the development of the Plan of Chicago, an ambitious, imaginative city-planning project orchestrated by architect Daniel H. Burnham. This comprehensive, daring plan would "stir men's blood," to paraphrase an oft-quoted Burnham axiom. The Commercial Club and its predecessor, the Merchants Club, which both included the city's leading business leaders, hired Burnham in 1906 to prepare the plan. An October 1906 draft of the Merchants Club solicitation letter to prominent businessmen includes a notation targeting the Horticultural Society as potential supporters. Charles L. Hutchinson is listed as an advisor to the plan, representing the Art Institute, and Society member John G. Shedd for the Commercial Club.[25]

The plan itself, published in 1909, listed the following Society members as being instrumental on Commercial Club committees: Chairman of the Plan Commission Charles H. Wacker, John V. Farwell, Jr., Victor F. Lawson, Harold F. McCormick, Cyrus H. McCormick, Martin A. Ryerson, John G. Shedd, John J. Mitchell, and Charles

The Plan of Chicago, a monumental civic planning vision, included the Chicago Horticultural Society and many other groups. This image shows how integrated greenery was woven into the plan.

Courtesy Art Institute of Chicago.

L. Hutchinson. Each of these individuals, through either his professional or philanthropic role, helped further the interests of the plan. Hutchinson, for example, at Charles Wacker's request, agreed to host an exhibition of the plan drawings at the Art Institute, noting, "I need not tell you that the Trustees of the Art Institute will be very glad indeed to do anything in their power to promote the excellent work of your Plan committee."[26]

Throughout the years of the plan development and the movement for the forest preserves, the Society flower shows emphasized Progressive themes. Like many civic improvement groups, the Chicago Horticultural Society also encouraged the *Chicago Tribune's* citywide garden contest with Society leader Edwin A. Kanst's endorsement: "[The contest] will be attended by a general cleaning up of the city, which is of vital importance."[27] The Society uniquely contributed to the success of the effort by encouraging children's gardens with a separate prize category and one-of-a-kind silver medal.[28] E. J. Vlasek of South Central Park Avenue won the children's contest and was awarded the silver medal along with other prizewinners at the public celebration at the Art Institute on August 18, 1908. Opening the award ceremony, Hutchinson pronounced the garden contest a success: "The culture of flowers . . . is not only a pleasure to the individual, but benefits all those who are about us . . . Nothing gives such universal pleasure. Nothing is so democratic and at the same time so aristocratic."[29]

The Progressive Era coincided with the rise of women's garden clubs in the United States. The strength of Chicago's women's club movement had surprised out-of-town visitors during the World's Columbian Exposition, and the clubs grew in number and membership. Many of these women's clubs had included subcommittees on flowers or forestry, and these groups frequently formed the nucleus of new garden clubs.[30] While furthering the cause of beautifying the Chicago area, these new clubs likely offered an attractive alternative to potential Society members. With the emergence of "country estates" in the suburbs, women found avenues for horticultural pursuits closer to home. The Lake Forest Garden Club (1912) and the North Shore Garden Club (1916) were among many that siphoned the women's energies from the Society to various clubs. Often, clubs mounted their own flower shows, which further weakened the attendance at Society shows. Although women had not been elected to board positions, Society flower shows and many philanthropic events depended on the work of women members.

A gradual decline in the Society's momentum became apparent in 1912 with the solicitation to prominent businessmen for pledges to support the flower shows. The *Chicago Tribune* reported that a Society committee had been formed to develop "a plan which would create wider interest in the work of the organization. It was decided to make an appeal to men who own their own estates to join in the work of the Society and to set aside a certain sum each year to be used by the expert gardeners employed on their estates for experiments and for the growing of special flowers and vegetables to be exhibited annually."[31]

The next year, the *Chicago Examiner* headlined, "Women Will Rescue City Flower Society." According to this report, "When the board of directors of the Chicago Horticultural Society met yesterday, its members found for the second time that they were still minus candidates for president and for the executive body. Two weeks ago they arranged to apply to all the women members of the Society to get a list of women candidates. The men are convinced they can no longer run the organization."[32]

With a world war on the horizon and drastic business changes resulting from Progressive legislation, it may be that the men of the Society were too preoccupied to sustain the organization. With their local garden clubs, and, having just obtained municipal suffrage in Chicago in 1913, perhaps women, too, could not devote sufficient time to the Society. The Great Depression also drained resources from many cultural groups. Records are lacking from this period, but from all that remain, it appears that the Chicago Horticultural Society began a hiatus that would last until 1945.

Victory Gardens and the Atomic Age

Although the Society as a whole remained quiescent during the 1920s and 1930s, individual members continued to shape the city's horticultural scene. Many

future and former Chicago Horticultural Society women organized the Chicago Flower and Garden Shows sponsored by the Garden Club of Illinois from 1927 through 1941 at Navy Pier. Chicago's Century of Progress Exposition of 1933 and 1934 tapped the talents of many future and former Society members. But it was the victory gardens in neighborhoods throughout the Chicago area that brought the Chicago Horticultural Society back to life during World War II.

As one of nine cities designated as a regional center for the Office of Civilian Defense in 1941, Chicago participated in many Civilian Defense support efforts. Victory gardens dotted the city with fresh vegetables. "Because of food rationing, and to bring communities together, we had victory gardens," says local gardener Gertrude Gallagher, who lived in the city on South Peoria Avenue at the time. She remembers creating her own backyard garden and that the corners of many blocks were commandeered for community gardens. "Most of the people on our block were city people," she remembers. "They didn't know which end of the seed to plant!"[33]

To teach people about gardening, the Office of Civilian Defense relied on the efforts of horticulturists from

In the 1920s and 1930s, many members contributed individually to significant horticulture events, such as this garden by J. C. Vaughan at the 1933 world's fair.

Courtesy Cathy Jean Maloney.

A Modern Flower Garden. Exhibited at Century of Progress Exposition by Vaughan's Seed Store, 10 W. Randolph street, Chicago; 47 Barclay street, New York City. This house established in 1876, won 28 bronze medals at the Chicago World's Fair in 1893 for horticultural exhibits. Its beautiful fall and spring catalogs, issued annually, illustrate and describe everything a gardener needs.

the Chicago Park District, such as Society member Fred Heuchling. With 18,000 block captains engaged in the effort, Heuchling described the success: "Chicago leads all other large cities in war gardens . . . I have conducted numerous groups of out of town people to inspect war gardens in all parts of Chicago. Almost universally they remarked upon the interesting and often very beautiful block installations at street corners with flagpoles and usually floral decorations."[34]

The Office of Civilian Defense also solicited experienced gardeners to help novices. Among the first were garden clubs such as the Lake Forest Garden Club, which, under the direction of Society members Edith Farwell and committee chair C. Eugene Pfister, hosted open houses for the public to view thriving vegetable plots. In Highland Park, Pfister reported, 650 families started home and community gardens even though "more than half of them had never weeded a potato patch before."[35]

The community-building aspects of victory gardening and the clear need for horticultural education prompted the Chicago Horticultural Society to revitalize. The Society's original charter had lapsed, but according to its rules, any ten members could call a meeting at any time. After some investigative measures, in fall 1943, eleven living members of the old Society lobbied for its renewal. Some no longer lived in the Chicago area, such as Harry Gordon Selfridge, famed retailer then living in London, or Florida resident William A. Peterson of the Peterson Nursery family. Others were venerable local horticulturists, such as August Poehlmann, owner of the expansive Morton Grove greenhouses, and Kanst of the Chicago Parks. Other members, as listed in Chicago Horticultural Society records, were James Burdett, Carl Kropp, Leonard Kill, Clyde Leesley, Jacob Kesner, Philip Schupp, and Mrs. Ernest A. Hamill.[36]

After World War II, the Chicago Horticultural Society helped people plant victory gardens throughout the area including the city parks.

Courtesy Chicago Park District Archives.

Victory gardens extended to the suburbs, such as this backyard garden on the North Shore.

Courtesy Chicago History Museum. HB-07533-A.

In 1945, the reborn Society renamed itself the Chicago Horticultural Society and Garden Center to reestablish its organization and bylaws. Among its stated objectives were the following:

- Crystallize the popular interest in victory gardening and provide the means for perpetuating this interest in Chicago and suburbs after peace comes,
- Conduct garden demonstrations or courses of instruction; to publish a bulletin or periodical; and to operate garden centers or horticultural museums,
- Be active in conserving, protecting and extending the horticultural beauties of Chicago and its suburbs,
- Help popularize gardening in every family in Chicago and its suburbs; and especially to direct these efforts to children.[37]

This set of objectives expanded on but remained true to the original mission of the Society. The newer version updated horticultural pursuits with specific language about conservation and children's education, and it emphasized the community-building aspects of gardening.

The new organization of the Society reflected the democratization of horticulture since earlier days when wealthy amateurs and professional men composed the main groups active in the Society. Now, along with a Board of Trustees, the Society included a Board of Governors with three groups: amateurs; professional and commercial; and governmental, educational, and civic. Marking the changing demographics, the Board of Trustees now included three women: Mrs. Walter S. (Kate) Brewster, niece of early Society founder Charles L. Hutchinson; Mrs. Joseph M. Cudahy, daughter of the Morton Arboretum founder; and Mrs. Albert D. Farwell, author and renowned herb grower. John C. Vaughan II, son of the early Society founder, held a board position, as did Chairman Laurance Armour.

The "amateur" group of the Board of Governors included C. Eugene Pfister, an accomplished rosarian, who also served as the Society president. In a remarkable gender role reversal, amid the throng of women's garden clubs that now proliferated, a national Men's Garden Club had emerged from a nucleus group in Chicago in 1927. Pfister not only led the Men's Garden Clubs of Chicago but also the Men's Garden Clubs of America.[38] Frank Balthis, Garfield Park horticulturist and president of the 1945 Midwest Horticultural Society (which had been launched during the Chicago Horticultural Society's quiescent period), and Fred Heuchling also served as early officers of the Chicago Horticultural Society and Garden Center.

Among the early "professional and commercial" group of the Board of Governors were James Burdett, garden columnist; Otto Clauss, landscape specialist; R. Milton Carleton of Vaughan Seed Company; James Sykora of Amlings; and one woman, Mrs. Bert Schiller McDonald, an internationally known flower stylist.

Governmental, educational, and civic agencies were well represented by such individuals as Kanst and August Koch of the Chicago Parks; Charles G. Sauers of the Forest Preserve District of Cook County; Robert Kingery of the Chicago Regional Planning Association; Anna P. Keller, chair of the Chicago Public Schools' garden project; and Dr. M. J. Dorsey, chief of the pomology department at the University of

Illinois.[39] With these liaisons, the Chicago Horticultural Society and Garden Center resumed its successful partnerships in horticulture.

Society president Pfister observed how the passage of time had shaped the new structure of the Chicago Horticultural Society and Garden Center: "We might well say that we are taking up today where our forefathers left off some twenty or more years ago . . . Times have changed since 1890, when this Society was first chartered . . . In those days there were no garden clubs, there were no suburbs in the present sense of the word, and Chicago was more truly the garden city. Now, industry and commerce, with greater congestion of population, threaten to destroy the garden city."[40]

The new Chicago Horticultural Society and Garden Center did not let any moss grow before acting on its objectives. The first bulletin, *Garden Talks*, published every other month in April 1945, contained hands-on information and growing tips. *Garden Talks*—which became *Garden Talk* in 1961—began the tradition of consistent education through the written word that continues to this day via the Chicago Botanic Garden website and the seasonal magazine *Keep Growing*. On April 16, 1945, the Society opened its first Garden Center at the Randolph Street entrance hall of what was then the Chicago Public Library (now the Chicago Cultural Center). This first center served as a clinic for gardeners to drop in with questions and also as a venue for small-scale flower displays.

The Society recommitted to philanthropy, a consistent component of the Society's mission, in the beautification of the west suburban Vaughan General Hospital grounds from 1944 to 1945. The Chicago Botanic Garden's programs for veterans at the Edward Hines, Jr. Veterans Adminstration (VA) Hospital continue today.

To foster community gardening, the Society and Garden Center cohosted the Victory Garden Round-Up with the Chicago Park District and the National Victory Garden Institute. The all-day event at Soldier Field on September 13, 1945, targeted everyone from amateur gardeners, "seasoned specialists," developers of vacant lot projects, and estate gardeners to join the roundup for information sharing, movies, bountiful harvests, square dance demonstrations, and a Parade of Vegetable Hats.

Achieving all this in such a short time with a membership of just over 130 individuals reflects on the vigor of the reenergized group. Nonetheless, the Society was fortunate to have public-spirited women who proposed the formation of a Woman's Board to assist with member recruitment, to help raise funds, and "to further the goal of the Society: permanent headquarters and a garden center adequate to serve Chicagoland."[41] The Society Board of Trustees approved the creation of the still-vibrant Woman's Board in 1951. The legacy of leadership of the Woman's Board of the Chicago Horticultural Society spans more than six decades—predating the opening of the Chicago Botanic Garden in 1972. The Woman's Board has initiated new

VICTORY GARDEN ROUND-UP!
1945
EXHIBITION HALL

SOUTH END, SOLDIER FIELD

THURSDAY, SEPTEMBER 13, 1945 – 11 A.M. TO 10 P.M.

Great Demonstration of Gardening Accomplishment in all Chicagoland

FOR: . . .

AMATEUR GARDENERS	SEASONED SPECIALISTS	GARDEN CLUBS
ESTATE GARDENERS	COMMUNITY GARDEN GROUPS	VACANT LOT PROJECTS
EMPLOYEE GARDEN GROUPS	PROFESSIONAL ASSOCIATIONS	
COMMERCIAL GROWERS AND DEALERS	ALL OTHER ORGANIZED GARDEN GROUPS	
SPECIALIZED GARDEN SOCIETIES		

For every gardener to display examples of the products of his toil, no matter how humble or how exquisite. No matter whether flowers or vegetables or both. By sheer number and quantity to demonstrate to the world the widespread interest in gardening all over Chicagoland!

NO ENTRY FEES OR CHARGES . . . NO ADMISSION CHARGE

No competition! No worrying about coming off second best! Every exhibitor with a creditable exhibit to receive an award of recognition.

COME TO THE VICTORY GARDEN ROUND-UP

Enjoy the Sights — Beautiful Flowers — Luscious Vegetables and Fruits — Parade of Vegetable Hats — Square Dance Demonstration — Movies — ADMISSION FREE!

Under Joint Auspices of

| CHICAGO HORTICULTURAL SOCIETY AND GARDEN CENTER 78 E. Washington St. Phone Andover 5643 | CHICAGO PARK DISTRICT 425 E. 14th Blvd. Chicago 5 Phone Har. 5252, Ext. 320 | NATIONAL VICTORY GARDEN INSTITUTE 188 W. Randolph St. Phone Dearborn 0941 |

As one of its first significant events, the reinstated Chicago Horticultural Society helped launch the Victory Garden Round-Up.

Courtesy University of Illinois at Chicago Library, Special Collections.

The Fragrant Garden for the Blind, shown in the schematic here, was one of the many philanthropic relationships that have stood the test of time.

Price 10¢ – $1.00 per year

Volume IV - No. 2 - February, 1956

Garden talks

Copyright 1956

—in this issue

Garden Notes for February. . Page 6
Herb Corner. . . . . Page 4
New Officers and Trustees . , Page 5
Plant Breeders Honored. . . . Page 7
Unusual Plant Material. . . . . .Page 3
FRONT COVER:
Artist's Conception of Fragrant Garden for the Blind (see page 2).

horticultural programs and education activities, funded new landscapes, and raised millions of dollars in financial support—all while building awareness of the Garden and its mission.

But when you have no permanent home "adequate to serve Chicagoland," what do you do? The enterprising Woman's Board members opened the doors to their own homes. The early 1950s saw a variety of garden tours conducted at members' homes, from the famed herb garden of Edith Farwell to the Rose Institute at the Pfister garden to the plant sales at the Vasumpaur garden of Western Springs. Garden tours included city as well as suburban gardens, with the Patio Garden Institute conducted in Chicago's Old Town neighborhood in August 1953.

A long-standing philanthropic partnership began in the 1950s with the establishment of the Fragrant Garden for the Blind. Horticultural therapy, while dating to ancient times in its broadest definition, received new attention with the return of so many wounded World War II veterans. This garden, created next to the newly built Lighthouse for the Blind facility on Roosevelt Road in Chicago, was said to be the first in the United States that enabled blind patrons to stroll its paths in the regular course of training. Today, the Society continues its relationship with the Chicago Lighthouse with horticultural therapy programs.

Educational subjects during the 1950s and 1960s in lectures and *Garden Talks* focused on plant recommendations, cultural care tips, and garden design pointers. Topical issues such as "The Atom in the Garden" and "Plastic Flowers . . . Boom or Bust" received attention, with "atomic treated novelties" deemed unlikely to succeed and plastic flowers decried as a fad.[42] Discerning discussions in the Society's publications on the use of mulch and organic methods versus pesticides presaged today's headlines.

In 1959, the Society renewed the tradition of cohosting a flower show by organizing the World Flower and Garden Show. For twenty years, the Society partnered with a blue-ribbon list of kindred organizations to produce shows with international themes and scope. Although most exhibitors hailed from the United States and Canada, many exhibits offered visitors a chance to see gardening techniques and designs from around the world.

The 1960s brought even greater crowds to an expanded flower show relocated to the newly constructed McCormick Place. The Society continued to sponsor lectures, plant shows and sales, and exhibits. The biggest headline of this decade, however, was House Bill 1487, which passed the Illinois state legislature to establish a Chicago Botanic Garden on Cook County land and to be ultimately managed by the Chicago Horticultural Society.

With the 1965 groundbreaking of the Chicago Botanic Garden,[43] a new era of landscape design opened in the Chicago region. The Society commissioned the Pittsburgh-based landscape architecture firm of Simonds and Simonds for a master plan. The firm of brothers John O. and Phil Simonds was known for its pioneering designs that worked in harmony with nature. Over the years, the Society continued to work with prominent landscape architects to design each space within the overall Simonds plan to achieve an environmentally friendly treatment of the entire grounds. With a comprehensive master plan as a guide, each designer offered new vistas, ranging from the Heritage Garden to the English Walled Garden, thus rendering the Chicago Botanic Garden a living museum of landscape design.

In 1972, the Chicago Botanic Garden opened to the public. The idea of a botanic garden, a dream held for decades among Chicago's garden lovers, had finally been fulfilled. The Garden evolved during the next forty years, such that today it comprises 26 distinct gardens and four natural areas. With 50,000 members, the Garden enjoys one of the largest memberships of any U.S. botanic garden—and represents an extraordinary growth from the 130 members on the rolls in the early 1950s.[44]

The establishment of the Garden, long a dream of the Chicago Horticultural Society and garden lovers throughout the Midwest, is a story for the next chapter. Transforming decades of discussion and possibilities into the reality of a botanic garden worthy of the Chicago metropolis required the political will, volunteer effort, funding, and support of the people of Chicago. The Chicago Botanic Garden is living testimony to that spirit.

The World Flower and Garden Shows of the mid-twentieth century were immensely popular.

Courtesy Lenhardt Library of the Chicago Botanic Garden.

The Chicago Horticultural Society has a tradition of philanthropy, education, and outreach. The early Society helped school-children create vegetable plots and worked with community victory gardens. Today, the Chicago Botanic Garden's Regenstein Fruit & Vegetable Garden offers practical tips for homeowners, while Windy City Harvest, a thriving urban agriculture program, offers instruction and job skills to underserved communities.

The Regenstein Fruit & Vegetable Garden

Joseph Regenstein, Jr., a lifelong learner, grew a wide variety of vegetables and fruits as a hobby. On his quarter-acre plot in Barrington, he raised traditional vegetables—beans, squash, and corn—and some novelties, such as round zucchini. On another acre, he grew fruit—even experimenting with apricots in Chicago's temperamental climate. A philanthropist committed to Chicago-area charities, Regenstein emphatically stated the goal of the new garden: "I want it to be a real learning center. And not just another pretty garden!"[45]

True to this vision, the Regenstein Fruit & Vegetable Garden demonstrates the best ways to grow the most ornamental and delicious plants for the Midwest. The nearly four-acre garden is filled in summer with more than 500 varieties of edible plants that grow well in the Upper Midwest. Here visitors will find aromatic herbs, shiny peppers, juicy grapes, and crisp apples in beautifully landscaped beds.

In addition to beds of fruits, vegetables, herbs, and flowers, this garden features unusual and attractive methods of growing edible plants. Design features include compact espalier fruit trees trained to grow against fences, a vertical wall filled with changing displays of greens and edible flowers, and a shaded walkway covered with grapevines.

The garden has decorative features not often associated with fruit or vegetable gardens—restful fountains, shady arbors, colorful containers and borders, and grassy resting places.

Businessman Joseph Regenstein, Jr., had a vision for the Fruit & Vegetable Garden that bears his name: "It should be a place where people learn not only what to do, but why," he explained.

The "backyard bounty" beds of the Regenstein Fruit & Vegetable Garden are filled with herbs and vegetables that can easily be grown at home. Pictured here are fall cool crops.

Mellow fall sunlight illuminates the grape arbor dividing bramble and trained (espalier) fruits at the Regenstein Fruit & Vegetable Garden.

Plants started under a cold frame running along the base of the "glassroom" (classroom) thrive in the Fruit & Vegetable Garden, near other vegetables in small-space beds (left, top). Through season-extension techniques and thoughtful planning, the harvest extends into three seasons, including summer crops (left, bottom).

The centerpiece of Windy City Harvest "incubator farm" program is Legends South Farm, located at the site of the former Robert Taylor Homes project on Chicago's South Side.

The Windy City Harvest Youth Farm at Washington Park in Chicago is reminiscent of the neighborhood victory gardens that flourished in Chicago during World War II.

Windy City Harvest

Windy City Harvest is the Chicago Botanic Garden's urban agriculture education and jobs-training initiative, aimed at helping to create a local food system, healthier communities, and a greener economy. The program has three components: Windy City Harvest Youth Farm, Windy City Harvest Apprenticeship, and Windy City Harvest Corps.

The Garden's Windy City Harvest Youth Farm program works with at-risk teens, teaching them about the food system and good nutrition. Each year, approximately 70 teens from underserved communities are educated and employed at farm sites in Chicago and Lake County. As they move through the program, they learn about growing food, working as a team, being a responsible and accountable employee, and the importance of good nutrition for themselves and their communities. Ultimately, Youth Farm students become better students (all complete high school and many go on to higher education) and are inspired by the belief that their actions can contribute to positive change in small and large ways.

The Garden offers a nine-month accredited certificate and paid internship in sustainable urban agriculture for 15 to 20 adults each year through its Windy City Harvest Apprenticeship program. The program is delivered by Garden staff at the Arturo Velasquez Institute, a satellite campus of Daley College, which is the official

In 2013 the Chicago Botanic Garden launched a new Windy City Harvest program—the largest rooftop farm in the Midwest—atop McCormick Place, the Chicago convention center.

program partner. There are currently six urban farm sites where apprentices learn and practice their production skills. To date, 89 percent of the certificate graduates have found seasonal and full-time jobs in the local horticulture and urban agriculture industry.

The Windy City Harvest Corps program provides opportunities for people with multiple barriers to employment and is intended for both juveniles (ages 17 to 21) and adults who have been involved with the justice system. Specifically, the program provides training in sustainable urban agriculture and transitional employment at Windy City Harvest operation sites for approximately 30 Corps members annually. These participants complete the Roots of Success job-readiness curriculum and are encouraged to apply to the Apprenticeship certificate program.

The Windy City Harvest garden thrives at Arturo Velasquez Institute, where the certificate program in urban agriculture is offered.

In Lake County, participants work as a team at the Windy City Harvest Youth Farm in North Chicago to grow, harvest, and sell vegetables and fruit to underserved urban communities.

2

Building the Garden

Magic from the Marsh

First came the floods, then the fires, then the mosquitoes, then the lawsuits, and ultimately the Nike missiles. The land surrounding and upon which the Chicago Botanic Garden is built, the erstwhile Skokie Marsh, never lacked for interesting times.

The Skokie Marsh once served as a portage for Native Americans crossing between Lake Michigan and the upper Des Plaines River. According to early botanist Herman S. Pepoon, the marsh averaged "a quarter of a mile in width, through the center of which the vegetation-choked waters [of the Skokie River] find a slow run southward."[1] The land supported a wide diversity of plants and animals and was known locally as a wonderful hunting ground for small game and as a popular fishing and hiking destination.

The beauty of the present-day Chicago Botanic Garden rests on land once claimed by the Skokie Marsh.

To Cook County residents, however, the Skokie Marsh often posed problems. Its flatness and low elevation rendered it prone to flooding. With the right combination of seasonal conditions—snowy winter followed by heavy spring rains on frozen ground—Skokie River floodwaters could not be absorbed by the surrounding marshland. Over the years, a variety of drainage methods were employed, with varying degrees of success, to the overall Chicago River watershed.

The soils presented special problems. According to one account, "the topsoil was mostly peat and muck from one to four feet deep, underlaid by glacial clays including an impenetrable rubbery layer. By 1900 a group of Hollanders were raising choice 'Glencoe horse-radish' in rich loamy soils along the eastern border; and 20 years later the marsh had been almost completely drained by speculators who sought, unsuccessfully, to convert it into truck farms . . . In dry autumns the peat beds, ignited by fires in the rank vegetation, burned for months and shrouded the countryside with dense acrid smoke."[2]

As farms and suburbs grew around the marsh in the late 1800s, residents became fearful of the periodic fires. Concerned citizens feared the city of Chicago itself was ablaze in 1898 as the *Chicago Tribune* reported on "the largest fire that ever devastated the Skokie Marsh." According to the *Tribune*, "The dry grass of the swamp burns like tinder, and the bed of the bog has been known to smolder for weeks."[3] By the late 1890s, developers had already attempted to drain portions of the marsh to create celery truck farms, and the devastating fires were often attributed to their disruption of the land.

Mosquitoes and missiles later found their way into the Skokie saga. The former were accused culprits of malaria. The latter headlined in the Cold War of the mid-twentieth century when the federal government identified the Skokie lagoon system—just south of the present-day Garden—as a potential site for Nike missile batteries. How this buggy and martial marsh ever became the exquisite Chicago Botanic Garden we know today warrants a bit of explanation.

Early Botanic Gardens

The Skokie Marsh was not the first choice for a botanic garden in Chicago: there had been several attempts at creating public gardens. Supporters learned from earlier attempts, and when the timing, will, and land became available, the Garden came to be.

Most definitions of a botanic garden specify a curated collection of plants displayed for education and research. Typically, plants are labeled and records are kept on plant acquisition and performance. In the United States, many of the earliest scientific gardens were private, as at Monticello and Mount Vernon, respectively owned by Thomas Jefferson and George Washington. These national leaders also spearheaded the effort to establish the first U.S. Botanic Garden on the National Mall in 1820.[4] Other public gardens opened as cities matured: in Boston, the Arnold Arboretum, affiliated with Harvard University, began with the design assistance of Frederick Law Olmsted in 1872. The New York Botanical Garden opened in 1891, the Buffalo and Erie Botanical Garden in 1900, and, moving farther west, the Matthaei Botanical Garden and Nichols Arboretum in Ann Arbor, Michigan, in 1907. St. Louis, an early rival for Chicago's title as Queen City of the West, opened the Missouri Botanical Garden to the public in 1859.

Where was the botanical garden of Chicago, the so-called Garden City? As with other cities in their formative years, Chicago's exceptional gardens belonged to private citizens. Those of Dr. John A. Kennicott in what is now Glenview and Dr. William B. Egan in Chicago during the 1850s served the physicians not only as physic gardens but also as ornamental landscapes. These prominent horticulturists, as well as other members of the earliest incarnation of the Chicago Horticultural Society, conducted informal research as time and money permitted. While these gentlemen generously opened their gardens to fellow horticulturists and friends, the estates were not by any means public botanic gardens.

Legislation created the Chicago Park System in 1869, and its potential for botanic gardens seemed obvious. Professor Henry H. Babcock, a charter member of the 1860s Chicago Botanical Society, worked with H. W. S. Cleveland, then landscape architect for Chicago's South Side parks, to create a botanic garden therein. Babcock solicited plants and seeds from around the world, and the future for the fledgling garden seemed bright. But, in 1877, the South Parks Board suspended operation of the garden, citing cost constraints.[5]

An early botanic garden in the South Side parks included specimens and seeds from around the world.
Courtesy Cathy Jean Maloney.

ACANTHUS SPINOSUS.

Height 2 ft 6 inches.

BOTANICAL GARDEN,

SOUTH PARK.

Chicago, April 24. 1877.

Drawn by

P. B. WIGHT.

Architect.

HELIOTYPE

As of the 1890s, Chicago's large parks on the West Side and Lincoln Park on the North Side all boasted flower gardens and conservatories. Yet the outdoor display gardens tended toward such floral follies as huge flower sculptures of the globe. These displays flaunted color and fantasy over education. The conservatories typically exhibited exotic tropical plants, which were interesting and informative but not particularly helpful to midwestern home gardeners.

The Society minutes of April 27, 1895, note support for an effort in Union Park on Chicago's West Side to create a botanic garden:

Whereas the Commissioners of the West Side Parks have established at Union Park a Botanical Garden of hardy herbaceous ornamental flowering plants, systematically arranged, combining in groups representative of the flora of the different countries of the world, and especially that of the United States, and have in contemplation, the formation of an Arboretum in one of the larger parks, in which will be placed specimen plants of each tree, shrub and vine that will prove hardy in and adapted to this climate, each plainly labeled with the scientific and common names, whereby those of our citizens interested in such matters or contemplating the improvement of their grounds, can observe the habit, form and other characteristics of the various plants that can be safely used in this section, and thus have a valuable guide to assist them in making their own selections, Therefore be it

Resolved that this Society greets with pleasure the spirit of advancement that has caused the formation of the Union Park Collection, and hereby expresses itself as favorable to the scheme of the establishment of an Arboretum, and promises hearty cooperation in this excellent plan for the diffusion of accurate horticultural knowledge among the people.[6]

This Union Park botanical garden fervor coincided with the year that Jens Jensen was promoted to superintendent of this park. Yet plans for the botanical garden did not gather many newspaper headlines, and it is unclear how much, if any, of the garden actually came to fruition. The West Side parks administration soon became riddled with corruption during this period, and along with Jensen's ouster in 1900, many plans were doubtless scuttled.[7]

The Chicago Horticultural Society, focused as it was in the 1890s on the annual flower show, rented hotel space for its meetings. Still, a more permanent solution was sought. President Chadwick observed in 1897, "Yes, we see how much we need a proper home, and I am thankful to observe that in high quarters there is a feeling that a move may be made before long towards establishing such a centre for this and kindred elevating work on the Lake Front Park grounds, the most suitable spot in or about Chicago."[8]

Following the 1904 flower show at the Fine Arts Building, Society leader Charles L. Hutchinson echoed this thought by proposing a more permanent home for the event; a "portable glass and iron structure to be built on the lake front. . . . [Hutchinson] drew attention to the home provided for flowers in Paris by the municipality, and while he did not argue that the cost should be met by the city of Chicago he said enough money was paid in rental each year to pay the interest on a sum sufficient."[9] The time was not right, however, for a structure to be built on the lakefront.

The battle for the "forever open, free and clear" lakefront in the early 1900s, famously spearheaded by Aaron Montgomery Ward, precluded any further building in Lake Front Park, today's Grant Park. A "proper home" for the Society would have to wait. During this Progressive Era, the Special Park and Outer Belt Commissions identified many natural areas outside and within the Chicago city limits that should be preserved for future generations. In their report of 1904, the Special Park Commis-

sion tagged the Skokee [*sic*] Marsh area as one of those natural areas. Jensen's section of the report argued for preservation of swamps along with forest scenery, describing the Skokee as "meadow scenery." He noted, "Nature has here created one of the prime factors in beautiful landscape, which is unbroken distant view."[10]

As the recommendations of the Special Park Commission folded into those of the Outer Belt Commission, the gritty details of funding and governance created opponents out of natural allies. A 1905 proposal to create "forest preserves" did not pass because some groups thought the hastily crafted bill tendered too much authority in a small group.[11] Put on a referendum in the November elections, the results were so close that dissenting parties sought a court ruling to decide whether the forest preserve act had indeed passed. It would be the first of years-long debates over forest preserve legislation. Even after the forest preserve bill passed, it would be even longer before the Skokie River valley became the Garden's home.

7. A typical view of the edges of the Skokee.

The Skokie River valley, as pictured in this page from the Special Park Commission of 1904, was one of the designated natural areas targeted for conservation.

Courtesy Chicago History Museum, ICHi-68453.

The Forest and the Garden

After many attempts, the Forest Preserve District of Cook County was established on November 30, 1914. An Illinois Supreme Court decision in April 1916 finally resolved continuing legal battles, and the newly created district acquired its first land in the northern suburbs, now known as Deer Grove, in June 1916.[12]

Forest Preserve District agendas frequently included discussion of a site for the study of plants. In 1919, Charles Goodnow, a district commissioner, presented a resolution to create an arboretum in the preserves. The resolution stated that "every specimen of shrub, herb, and tree that will grow in this climate will be planted in such a manner that it may be made a romantic and beautiful spot."[13] That year, the district board approved a botanic garden to be built on 2,000 acres of forest preserve land in south suburban Palos as recommended by a subcommittee including University of Chicago botanist Henry C. Cowles and Northwestern University Professor Charles Atwell.[14]

Although the Palos garden did not materialize, forest preserve commissioners remained optimistic about the possibility of an arboretum. A 1921 forest preserve report promised, "Plans for the greatest Arboretum in the world soon will be disclosed by the Board. This project has been under consideration during the period of two years, but was delayed for reasons of economy."[15] The proposed arboretum was to have "every species of tree and shrub that can be grown in this latitude," a lake shaded by weeping willows, and lily ponds throughout. Members of this arboretum subcommittee included Hutchinson and architect Dwight Perkins.

Little wonder that the Chicago Horticultural Society entered a period of quiescence during this time frame, with so many other initiatives under way. Not only was Hutchinson investigating an arboretum for the forest preserves, but he also served as a trustee for the Chicago Zoological Gardens Project. The latter, which became the Brookfield Zoo operated by the Chicago Zoological Society, would serve as a template for the governance of the Chicago Botanic Garden. Charter members of the Zoological Society Board of Trustees, in addition to Hutchinson, included fellow friends or members of the Chicago Horticultural Society: Charles H. Wacker, Walter S. Brewster, Cyrus H. McCormick, Jr., Harold F. McCormick, Colonel Robert R. McCormick, John T. McCutcheon, and A. G. Becker. This experience

among these leaders would later prove helpful in forming the public-private partnership between the Forest Preserve District and the Society in creating the Chicago Botanic Garden.

The notion of a separate botanic garden might have been perceived as superfluous in the 1920s, with the creation of the Morton Arboretum and the Brookfield Zoo already under way. Zoological gardens of the time combined fauna and flora in outdoor settings. Creators of the Brookfield Zoo, desirous of a "cageless" zoo where the animals seemed to roam in their natural habitat, sought a naturalistic landscape.[16] Achieving the "garden" part of the zoological garden required the landscape talent of the Simonds and West landscape architecture firm. O. C. Simonds himself was busy creating the landscape plan for Joy Morton at his newly established arboretum in Lisle. The Morton Arboretum opened to the public in 1922, and the Brookfield Zoo opened in 1934, both offering new public landscapes.

The Skokie Marsh, on the drawing boards for several years as a Forest Preserve District prospective pur-

Federal Civilian Conservation Corps (CCC) workers dug sloughs to alleviate flooding in the Skokie Marsh.

Courtesy Lenhardt Library of the Chicago Botanic Garden.

chase, became a lightning rod for public discourse on February 4, 1920. The Forest Preserve boardrooms filled with advocates of the purchase, such as the mayors of Kenilworth, Wilmette, and Glencoe and landscape architects Jensen and Simonds. Forest Preserve District president Peter Reinberg, the former florist and rosarian, listened to arguments along with Forest Preserve Plan Commission members Wacker, Perkins, Victor F. Lawson, and J. C. Vaughan. Evanston attorney W. D. Washburne led opposition to the plan, arguing that the land would be better subdivided into truck farms. The *Chicago Tribune* reported that Washburne claimed that "the golf fellows and the dainty dilettantes of the aristocratic ridge" towns would deprive taxpayers of their rights to the land.

Opponents to the Skokie Marsh purchase also claimed that the marsh did not fall into the narrow definition of "forest" which, through its name and charter, the Forest Preserve District protected. Countering the common misconception that a marsh was treeless, chief forester Ransom Kennicott (grandson of charter

Society member John Kennicott) displayed a variety of watercolors depicting majestic trees in the Skokie Marsh. Colonel McCormick, a member of the Forest Preserve Plan Committee and then editor of the *Chicago Tribune*, printed artist Hugo Von Hofsten's *Spring Winds on the Skokie*, a scene that featured a large tree against the sky and marsh.[17]

Finally, on April 23, 1926, the debate, which had turned into a lawsuit, was settled in court in favor of the county. Approximately 2,000 acres of land including the Skokie Marsh would be acquired by the Forest Preserve District of Cook County.

Civilian Conservation Corps Digs In

The Great Depression stalled many expansion projects, but the Civilian Conservation Corps (CCC) federal public works projects, under President Franklin D. Roosevelt, brought work to the Chicago region. In June 1933, 1,000 corps workers began to create the Skokie lagoon system, carving interconnected sloughs out of

CCC workers pause during a day at work in the Skokie Marsh.

Courtesy Lenhardt Library of the Chicago Botanic Garden.

the marsh and constructing a series of dikes, weirs, and drains to improve the flooding situation. By December of that year, approximately 2,400 corps workers labored on-site. According to the Forest Preserve Advisory Committee—which included Burnham and McCutcheon—the federal project saved Cook County taxpayers at least $2 million.[18]

The Skokie lagoon system project was said to be the largest CCC project in the United States. U.S. Secretary of the Interior and Winnetka resident Harold Ickes posted his own personal gardener and estate caretaker as a supervisor on the project.[19] The reconfigured marsh became a favorite outdoor recreation spot for hiking, bird-watching, small boat sailing, and horseback riding. Stocked with black bass and other fish, anglers sought the calm waters. North Shore line trains brought visitors within hiking distance, as they still do today.

The extension of the Skokie lagoon system to include the area between Dundee and Lake Cook Roads, the present site of the Chicago Botanic Garden, appeared on the Forest Preserve District's ten-year plan in 1957.[20] Here is where the interests of the Chicago Horticultural Society and the Forest Preserve District of Cook County ultimately converged.

During the 1950s, the Chicago Horticultural Society, operating from its downtown Chicago location, conducted exhibits of live plants and cut flowers and offered a wide range of educational tours and programs. Yet despite the hard work of many

Nearly 2,400 men worked on the Skokie Marsh lagoon system project—said to be the largest CCC public works project in the United States.

Courtesy Lenhardt Library of the Chicago Botanic Garden.

CHICAGO AND ITS BOTANIC GARDEN

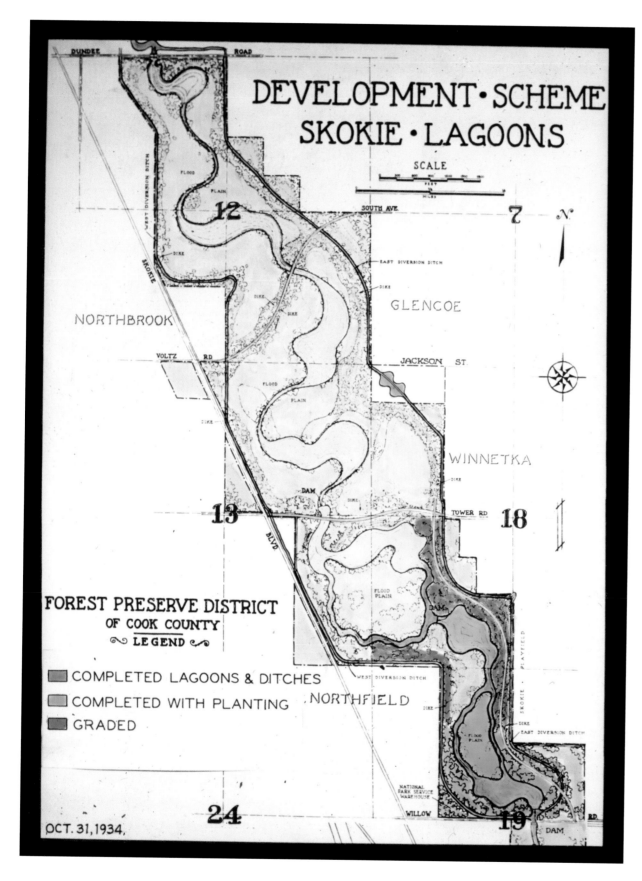

As of 1934, only the southern portion of the Skokie lagoon system, shown on this map from October 31 of that year, was completed with plantings. By the 1950s, work would continue northward to Dundee Road.

University of Illinois at Chicago Library, Special Collections.

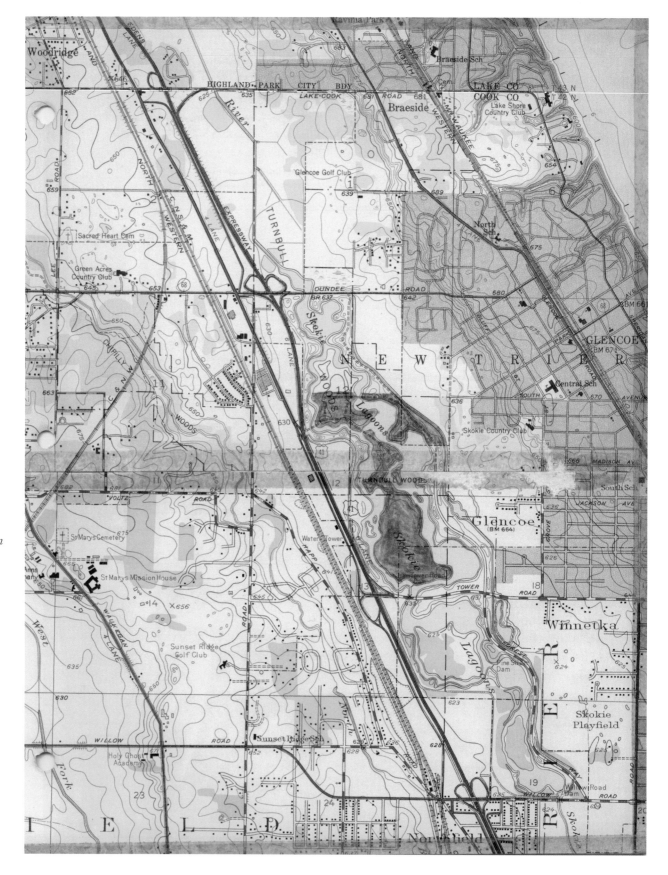

By the 1950s, the Skokie lagoon system, as shown on this map—although complete through Dundee Road—did not include the site of the future Chicago Botanic Garden.

CHICAGO AND ITS BOTANIC GARDEN

Society leaders, membership lagged. The Society tasked a survey committee headed by attorney John Norberg to improve the Society's activities and increase its membership. The committee's 67-page report, released in 1956, and four-volume appendixes included analyses of 18 other horticultural societies across the nation and numerous best practices from other nonprofits.

The survey challenged Society members with these questions: "Is there a real place in metropolitan Chicago for the Chicago Horticultural Society? What can it offer that the Garden Club of Illinois, Inc. and the Chicago Park District do not? Is there really enough interest and enthusiasm for the Society to enable it to survive and grow?"[21] The report recommended a permanent garden to distinguish itself from garden clubs and incidentally reduce the rent paid for a downtown office. "This then should be the long term goal of the Society—a botanical garden operated by the Society, financed in part by the city and affiliated with one of the Universities."[22] As a temporary measure, the report advised securing indoor and outdoor space around the planned McCormick Place convention center in Chicago. The ultimate location, according to the report, should be the forest preserves, or even possibly a colocation at Brookfield Zoo.

Resurrecting its famed flower shows in 1959 and hosting them at McCormick Place, the Society gained visibility and membership. But, as Society president William Allan Pinkerton Pullman later noted, "Once having suggested a botanic garden for Chicago, we found that it was an idea impossible to give up."[23]

Pullman served as the president of the Board of Trustees of the Chicago Horticultural Society from 1959 to 1968 and was instrumental in the creation and founding of the Chicago Botanic Garden. A resident of Lake Forest, he was the grandnephew of George M. Pullman, the developer and manufacturer of Pullman railroad cars, and the great-grandson of the nationally prominent private detective Allan Pinkerton.[24] An avid gardener, William Pullman was the namesake of the Pullman boxwood (*Buxus sempervirens* 'Pullman').[25] Pullman brought both his business acumen and his love of gardening to the campaign to create the Chicago Botanic Garden.

June Reedy, past chair of the Society's Woman's Board, wrote of the excitement when William Pullman announced his plans at the Woman's Board's summer meeting of 1960:

A BOTANIC GARDEN! He might as well have exploded the atomic bomb.
We had heard many grandiose plans before. To name a few: A garden Center in the new underground Grant Park Garage; Garden Centers on the perimeter of Chicago adjacent to the new network of highways; a Horticultural Hall in Grant Park or lakefront; accommodations with some existing established civic enterprises (those asked said NO). Research had proved these and other ideas not only unfeasible but impossible. At first a Botanic Garden seemed the "Impossible Dream."[26]

At about the same time, Pullman and other Society members had been approached for advice from a newly formed business and civic group, the Chicago Central Area Committee, to help identify ways to beautify Chicago, including the then-underused Grant Park. Initially, the Society proposed creating a small botanic garden at this prominent park. "Here is a great cultural potential, a magnificent recreational area, made almost worthless because it is difficult to reach and poorly equipped for public use," said Dr. R. Milton Carlton, prior Board president of the Society, in an April 1961 *Chicago Tribune* article. Carleton also opined that "Chicago is half a century behind the rest of the United States in the development of horticultural facilities."[27]

But the pollution that plagued big cities of the mid-twentieth century also wreaked havoc on urban plantings. Society members reconsidered support for a Grant Park botanic garden—and, in fact, for any urban location, such as the Chicago parks, since they "all suffered from that same smoke pall."[28] Circling back to the original vision of the Forest Preserve District, Society members began to search the outer ring of Chicago for a site.

During the next two years potential sites were scouted, with the assistance of such experts as George Avery, Jr., Ph.D., director of the Brooklyn Botanic Garden and past president of the Botanical Society of America. Charles G. Sauers, superintendent of the Forest Preserve District and a strong supporter of the proposed botanic garden for Chicago, researched parks and gardens across the United States and abroad. By mid-1962, the Skokie Marsh area had been identified as a prime potential site. A Society proposal, "Chicago Needs a Botanic Garden," identified the following reasons supporting the Skokie location:

Size: The generous size of the Skokie site made it superior to any location in the Chicago park system, and being "outside of the smoke area of industrial Chicago" was of great importance.

Access: Visitors could reach the garden by car from Chicago in 30 minutes, a comparable distance from Manhattan to either the New York Botanical Garden in the Bronx or the Brooklyn Botanic Garden. Two rail lines, the Chicago North Shore and Milwaukee and the Chicago and Northwestern, served the area.

Protection: Because of its inherent boundaries (the expressway on the west and the lagoon system on the south), the site "provides better protection than fencing from thievery and vandalism, known problems to botanic gardens."

Filling cultural void: The proposal noted that while Chicago's Loop area supported several museums, the south had the Museum of Science and Industry, and the west enjoyed the Brookfield Zoo and the Morton Arboretum, there was no comparable attraction to the north: "The Skokie Lagoons seem to be the logical site for a botanic garden, an area where no other cultural institution of this nature now exists."

Future membership growth: The location "will become more and more the center of population as the years go by," according to the Society publication.

Natural beauty: The site offered potential for converting the natural beauty of the lagoon system into a "park of the greatest beauty, comparable to the magnificent Keukenhof in Holland." (The Keukenhof, boasting extensive flower gardens, had opened in 1949.)[29]

The proposal included the handwritten signatures of many allied groups and supporters, including representatives from the Civic Federation, the Northeastern Illinois Metropolitan Area Planning Commission, and the Forest Preserve District staff. Thirty Chicago Horticultural Society trustees signed the document, noting their additional affiliation with such groups as the Chicago Community Trust, the University of Chicago, the Garden Club of America, and the Garden Club of Illinois, as well as many of Chicago's leading businesses.

Charles Sauers circulated the Society's draft proposal for comment among his staff, some of whom were concerned about disrupting the rare landscape, the infeasibility of building on peat, and the use of the lagoon system in flood control.[30] By September 1962, internal objections had been addressed, and Pullman, on behalf of the Society, petitioned the president and Board of Commissioners of the Forest Preserve District of Cook County "in arranging a contract, to be almost identical with that of the Chicago Zoological Society, which would include the necessary provisions for leasing, development and maintenance of a Chicago Botanic Garden."[31]

The governance model of the Zoological Society, wherein that Society managed the land owned by the Forest Preserve District, suited the needs of the Chicago Horticultural Society. But members needed to continue their evangelism to garner public support. As Pullman later recalled, "First of all, we obtained the blessing of Mayor [Richard J.] Daley who felt that a botanic garden would be a fine cultural asset for

Why a Botanic Garden for Chicago?

A persuasive proposal for the Chicago Botanic Garden, the cover of which is shown here, listed reasons for supporting the Skokie Marsh location.

Courtesy Lenhardt Library of the Chicago Botanic Garden.

Charles G. Sauers, superintendent of the Cook County Forest Preserve District, was instrumental in gaining support for the land for the Chicago Botanic Garden.

Courtesy Lenhardt Library of the Chicago Botanic Garden.

Robert P. Wintz (left), Bruce
Krasberg, Mayor Richard
J. Daley—who strongly
supported a botanic garden
for Chicago—and William
Pullman attended the World
Flower and Garden Show.

Courtesy Lenhardt Library of the
Chicago Botanic Garden.

Chicago."[32] "By dint of some strenuous telephoning,"
according to Pullman, in June 1963, the state legislature passed House Bill No. 1487 to allow the Forest Preserve District of Cook County to "prepare and maintain
grounds for a botanic garden."

Essentially, H.B. 1487 allowed the Forest Preserve
District to reserve land for the functions of a botanic
garden. Approved by Governor Otto Kerner on August
19, 1963, the bill also provided for an annual tax not to
exceed .0048 percent of the taxable property in the Forest Preserve District of Cook County. The question of
who would manage and operate the garden remained
open. It was back to the telephone, letter campaigns,
public presentations, and personal meetings to finalize
a specific site within the Skokie Marsh and identify the
managing organization. The Society also needed to con-
vince the general public and board of the Forest Preserve
District that the Chicago Horticultural Society had the
wherewithal to manage the soon-to-be botanic garden.

On December 31, 1963, Sauers wrote a formal letter to his boss, Cook County president Seymour Simon,
recommending that

> The Board of Forest Preserve Commissioners enter into an agreement with the
> Chicago Horticultural society whereby
>   The area in the Skokie Valley from Dundee road on the south, Edens Expressway
> on the west, Lake Cook road on the north and Glencoe Golf Course on the east, shall be
> made available for a botanical garden provided that
>   By January 1, 1966 the Society shall have raised $1,000,000 by private subscriptions.[33]

The agreed-upon 300-acre site, today's 385-acre Chicago Botanic Garden, lies just
north of the originally proposed acreage between Tower and Dundee Roads near
a former U.S. Army Nike missile site.[34] The Forest Preserve District had not yet begun to create the lagoon system in the northernmost section, which meant that,
although the Garden could thereby be built on a blank canvas, many hydrologic concerns needed to be addressed. Flood control and filtration systems achieved through
the Skokie lagoon system would need to work seamlessly with the Garden. The
million-dollar subscription hurdle challenged the Society to demonstrate broad-
based support of a highly ambitious project.

The Forest Preserve District of Cook County Board of Commissioners approved
Sauers's recommendations at its meeting on January 6, 1964, and in June of that year,
the Society's fundraising drive officially launched. With a publicity blitz, lead donors,
and a general landscape plan, the Society collected the full $1 million by November
1964, well in advance of the 1966 deadline. The contract with the Forest Preserve
District of Cook County authorizing the Chicago Horticultural Society to manage
the Chicago Botanic Garden was signed on January 27, 1965.[35]

Building the U.S. Army's Nike missile site in the Skokie Marsh north of Tower Road and west of Glencoe. The Chicago Botanic Garden originally was situated close to this old missile site but later was moved farther north.

Courtesy National Archive., U.S. Army Photo (111-SC-589705).

CHICAGO AND ITS BOTANIC GARDEN

Along the Skokie River Corridor, floodplain wetlands, upland prairie, and oak savanna-woodland have been established. Controlled burns help maintain the diversity of native plants and control invasives.

Courtesy Kris Jarantoski.

Today's Skokie River Corridor, as a result of restoration efforts by the Chicago Botanic Garden and its partners, is a beautiful naturalistic area on the western boundary of the property.

Groundbreaking and Garden Opening

On September 25, 1965, ground was broken at the Chicago Botanic Garden. As anyone with a green thumb knows, the secret to great gardens is excellent soil preparation. What a job this entailed—to transform a wasteland of water, polluted from decades of ill-advised drainage, and rubble pits left from the Edens Expressway construction. William Bauer and other engineers from his namesake company spent months in early 1965 surveying the land and analyzing soil conditions.[36] The Society sought additional expertise from Clarence Godshalk and Anthony Tyznik, then of the Morton Arboretum and also from the University of Illinois. As William Pullman observed, "Heavy weights—islands, buildings, bridges, parking areas—can be placed on top of glacial till, but not on peat."[37]

The master plan for the Chicago Botanic Garden addressed not only the load-bearing capabilities and viability of the soil but also the water quality. Tests of the Skokie River during low flow periods showed that the majority of the water was derived from the discharge of an upstream sewage treatment plant and the remainder from natural runoff. By 1960s standards, the water quality achieved an excellent rating, but it was nevertheless unsuitable for recreational purposes. Its excess nitrates

Groundbreaking in 1965 marked the beginning of a new era for the Chicago Horticultural Society.

Courtesy Lenhardt Library of the Chicago Botanic Garden.

and phosphates promoted algae growth and could harm shoreline plantings. Thus, the first construction phase focused on rough grading of the land and building a system of weirs and an underground conduit to divert the polluted water from the visible portions of the garden.

Water, once the persistent problem of the Skokie River valley, became a sparkling, valued feature of the Chicago Botanic Garden. Well before the first shovel bit the earth, the Society had commissioned the renowned landscape architecture firm of Simonds and Simonds to create a master plan for the site. This living document has evolved over the years but consistently features the interplay of water and land. Gardens and natural areas were to be located on or surrounding islands that rose from the erstwhile marsh. Early plans showed two islands, Main Island and Evergreen Island, along with a variety of peninsulas and naturalistic treatments of the shoreline. Over the years, the plan encompassed the nine islands that exist today.

John Simonds and his colleague, fellow landscape architect Geoffrey Rausch, envisioned both practical and poetic reasons for the island concept. "The expansive areas of water had their genesis in the need for earth fill to lift the gardens out of the muck and above flood levels," Simonds wrote.[38] The cut-and-fill process created water basins that reflected sky and sculpted hills for elevated windbreaks and greater vantage points for landscape vistas.

In creating the design concept for the master plan, Simonds found inspiration in the hills and lakes of eighteenth-century Chinese imperial gardens near Peking

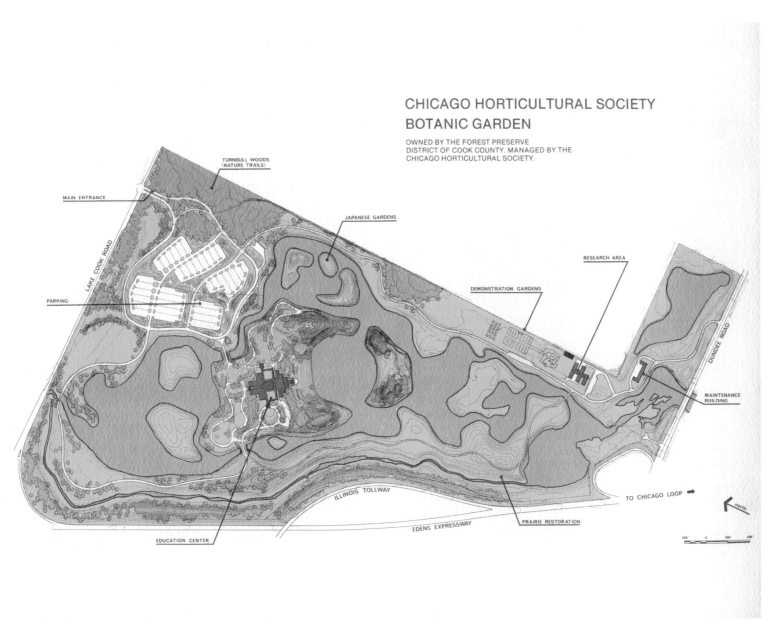

CHICAGO HORTICULTURAL SOCIETY
BOTANIC GARDEN

OWNED BY THE FOREST PRESERVE
DISTRICT OF COOK COUNTY. MANAGED BY THE
CHICAGO HORTICULTURAL SOCIETY.

TURNBULL WOODS
(NATURE TRAILS)

MAIN ENTRANCE

JAPANESE GARDENS

LAKE COOK ROAD

PARKING

RESEARCH AREA

DEMONSTRATION GARDENS

DUNDEE ROAD

MAINTENANCE
BUILDING

EDUCATION CENTER

ILLINOIS TOLLWAY

TO CHICAGO LOOP

north

EDENS EXPRESSWAY

PRAIRIE RESTORATION

*The 1976 early plan of the Chicago Botanic Garden featured
a main island and Evergreen Island (now Evening Island)
and indicated an area for Japanese gardens.*

Courtesy Lenhardt Library of the Chicago Botanic Garden.

The Chinese Garden of Perfect Brightness offered a poetic inspiration for the Chicago Botanic Garden. 40 Scenes of the Yuanming-yuan, *Shen Yuan, Tangdai, and Wang Youdu, 1744.*

Courtesy Creative Commons.

(now Beijing). He wrote, "Scenically, the landforms and waterways would be reminiscent of the fabled garden islands of Soochow [Suzhou] and the Yuan Ming Yuan [Garden of Perfect Brightness] to the west of Peking. When reshaped and provided with freshwater pumped from Lake Michigan, the land-water setting would have few rivals as the site of a fine botanic garden."[39]

Rausch, noting that Simonds was a romantic and a "big thinker," also recognized some practical sources that informed the design. Not only did the CCC efforts in creating the Skokie lagoon system offer tactical solutions, but Simonds's coincident experience in developing the Miami Lakes community in south Florida helped address marshy conditions.

It took several years for the first iteration of this vision to become reality. Rausch did not sugarcoat his assessment of the condition of the land: "I have never seen anything quite as bad as that site," he recalled. "Literally, it was burning."[40] Trash, raw sewage, weeds, and abandoned quarries combined to make the harsh landscape evoke a scene from Dante's *Inferno*. In 1967, the Society's plant collections began with the Garden's first tree, a white fir (*Abies concolor*) sited on the Edens berm.

By winter of 1968, rough grading and water control structures were completed. In 1969, clean water filled the garden lakes for the first time; perimeter fencing was installed, and the Society obtained county and state approval for the entrance road and parking systems. In his progress report for that year, Francis de Vos, Ph.D., the Garden's first director, wrote, "The site with its sculptural earth forms and system of freshwater lagoons and channels is nothing less than magnificent . . . The air is clean. The soil is fertile and deep. Water is abundant."[41]

The Society invited the general public to an open house in October 1969, chartering buses from its downtown headquarters for those who could not drive. By June 1971, the Midwest Bonsai Society hosted its first exhibition at the Garden, the beginning of a long tradition. Lectures, field trips, and workshops, formerly operated through the Society's downtown headquarters, transferred to the Garden. Art Kozelka, longtime garden writer for the *Chicago Tribune*, wrote in October 1971, "Now the terrain has taken on a pleasing stature with the planting of thousands of trees of many species.

Moreover, several demonstration gardens have been planted in a Home Landscape Center, and research buildings constructed."[42]

With the creation of an interpretive nature trail in Turnbull Woods (now a 100-acre section renamed McDonald Woods[43]) and a home demonstration garden, the Chicago Botanic Garden officially opened to the public in the spring of 1972. The Chicago Horticultural Society had finally realized the decades-long dream for a public garden worthy of the Chicago region. In the 1904 Special Park Commission report, Dwight Perkins had advised, "Farm lands now under cultivation west of the Skokee will need some modification according to their possibilities in beautifying the landscape. Here they may be treated as grassy plains and covered with tree growth . . . To change the Skokee from a wet and impenetrable marsh to a dry grass plain may eventually become necessary, yet any drainage scheme that will injure adjoining forests must be avoided."[44] How fitting that the ultimate creation of the Garden respected the land and that the opening events included a walk through the native Turnbull Woods.

It was a milestone in the Society's history, and yet much remained to be done. The master plan for the Chicago Botanic Garden and the Society called for more plantings, more education programs, more research, and relevance to a broad and diverse community. As William Pullman noted a year after groundbreaking, "In developing a budget for the construction of this Garden it must be realized first that it will 'never' be completed—construction and planting will go on for a great many years."[45]

Planting of the first trees in the new Chicago Botanic Garden required a trial-and-error process.

Hills and lakes were carved from the Skokie River valley to create the Chicago Botanic Garden and alleviate the flooding of the Skokie River.

Courtesy Lenhardt Library of the Chicago Botanic Garden.

The Heritage Garden and the Farwell Landscape Garden were among the earliest created at the Chicago Botanic Garden. Both are teaching gardens: the first pays tribute to historic gardens of the world, and the second is the legacy of an early Garden founder, Edith Farwell.

Heritage Garden

The Heritage Garden pays tribute to the botanic gardens of the past and the manner in which they organized and displayed plants.

A large statue of the Swedish botanist Carolus Linnaeus presides over the garden. Linnaeus established binomial nomenclature as the system of naming plants that is still used today. Modeled after Europe's first botanical garden in Padua, Italy (which dates to 1545 and is now a UNESCO site), the Heritage Garden is a circular space, divided into four quadrants.

Fittingly, this garden celebrates the history of gardens from around the globe. Seven perimeter beds display plants according to their geographic origin; 14 additional beds display the several plant families grouped according to their scientific classification.

In the center are found a prominent water feature, with cascading sheets of water, and a classic physic garden devoted to healing, which is planted with medicinal plants from around the world. In the summer, three aquatic pools contain waterlilies, lotuses, and other tropical water plants.

Dawn reveals a beautiful new day at the Heritage Garden.

Displays of small-scale evergreens are suitable for average home landscapes.

Farwell Landscape Garden

The Farwell Landscape Garden displays a cross section of garden types suitable for residential settings and the plants appropriate to these designs.

Specialized garden displays include formal and informal herb gardens, a traditional perennial border, a rock garden, streamside gardens, an easy-to-grow mixed border, and other small-scale landscaping ideas for midwestern gardens.

Tough, low-maintenance, but still quite showy plants have been featured in the easy-to-grow area to inspire armchair gardeners.

Curvilinear paths in the Farwell Landscape Garden invite strolls (this page and next).

A meandering path beckons visitors to take a pleasant stroll through diverse and beautiful settings accented with pools and streams. These garden tableaux offer home gardeners ideas for shade- and sun-loving plants.

Edith Foster Farwell, sometimes called the Dean of Herbalists, frequently opened her Lake Forest garden to the public in the days before the Society's dream of a public garden became reality. She created a knot garden of herbs at the Garden that rivaled that of her award-winning home garden, for which she received the Garden's Hutchinson Medal in 1951. Today, the herb gardens are joined by rock gardens, a pond and stream garden, a traditional bed, and the easy-to-grow bed.

Farwell was said to be fond of the herb rosemary, which in herbal folklore is "for remembrance." Visitors will return for many memories of this garden.

A traditional bee skep anchors one of the garden beds in the Farwell Landscape Garden, while benches beckon visitors to rest and enjoy the setting.

Naughty Faun *by Sylvia Shaw Judson is one of the sculptures adorning the Farwell Landscape Garden.*

59

3

Flower Shows

Days of Mums and Roses

Minnie Wanamaker' was there. 'Mrs. Alpheus Hardy' attended, radiant in yellow. Bertha Palmer, Chicago's leading lady and the scheduled keynote speaker, sent apologies, while the Honorable Thomas B. Bryan ably substituted as master of ceremonies. Chicago's 1891 Fall Flower Show, the first under the auspices of the reinvigorated Chicago Horticultural Society, thus debuted with coveted chrysanthemum varieties such as 'Wanamaker' and the golden-petalled 'Hardy' and the headline-making tastemakers Palmer and Bryan.

Chicago enjoyed a tradition of hosting fairs and conventions, particularly in the latter half of the 1800s when expanded rail lines crisscrossed the city.[1] Beyond the usual regional events—county fairs with tents of pickled peppers next to prizeworthy pigs—Chicago hosted national multidisciplinary fairs such as the 1863 North-Western Soldiers' Fair and many events at the Inter-State Exposition Building in the 1870s and 1880s.

The Chicago Horticultural Society's early flower shows brought fine horticulture to the general public.

Courtesy Chicago Botanic Garden Art Collection.

Showing a well-grown Pot Plant.

'Mrs. Alpheus Hardy' reigned
as a chrysanthemum variety
in the 1890s.

Courtesy University of California
Libraries.

Exhibitions devoted strictly to horticulture, however, tended to be hosted by nursery professionals, and, although they dearly wanted to engage the public, attendance often fell short of expectations.

The *American Florist* reported that low public attendance was common throughout the country in the late 1880s: "As a means of reaching and securing the cooperation of the public, horticultural exhibitions must ever be indispensable; this has long been recognized. . . . While their importance is unquestioned it must be admitted that the public is not yet educated up to the point of contributing reasonably to their support."[2]

Flower shows were more prevalent on the East Coast, where established horticultural societies thrived.[3] Florists in the New England region could also attend many shows in close proximity, whereas travel times between far-flung midwestern cities were much greater. Preparing for a show was costly and laborious in these days without refrigeration, as described by a prominent florist, John Thorpe:

The shipping of cut flowers to exhibition points is always attended with anxiety and to arrive in perfect condition requires great care. . . . All flowers should be cut and placed in water at least twenty-four hours before shipping. . . . In packing wrap each flower carefully in tissue paper just tight enough not to bruise. They should then be placed in either boxes or baskets in tiers so that they do not press on each other. In boxes strips should be nailed far enough apart so as to allow the flowers not to chafe, the stems to be held in place with other strips, using damp paper as a packing between each layer of stems.[4]

Without an appreciative public, or patrons supporting the effort, few nursery owners could afford to exhibit their flowers.

The Chicago Horticultural Society brought fresh ideas and much-needed support to Chicago's flower shows. By partnering with kindred organizations and brokering the talents of professional horticulturists with those of leading citizenry, Society exhibitions drew bigger crowds and gained national recognition. Between 1890 and World War I, Society flower shows elevated horticulture to fine arts status by coordinating with the Art Institute and by providing complementary programming that educated and entertained. After a hiatus between the world wars during which local garden clubs sponsored shows, the Society resumed its organizing role and between 1959 and 1979 conducted 21 flower shows, all worthy of their title, World Flower Show. Today the Society continues to collaborate with leading plant societies to bring flower displays to the public.

World's Fair Flowers

Among the many professional horticulture organizations that proliferated in Chicago during the late 1880s, the Chicago Florists' Club produced the most prominent flower shows open to the public.[5] In 1887, two years after its formation, the Chicago Florists' Club comprised 125 members, including future Chicago Horticultural Society leaders J. C. Vaughan, G. L. Grant, and James D. Raynolds. That same year, the young club had garnered sufficient renown to host prestigious conventions in Chicago, such as those of the American Association of Nurserymen, Florists and Seedsmen in June and the annual meeting of the Society of American Florists in August. These national meetings enhanced Chicago's reputation as a horticultural center.

The eyes of the world focused on Chicago with the highly anticipated World's Columbian Exposition of 1893, and city leaders and nursery professionals recognized the opportunities to demonstrate the city's horticultural sophistication. In August 1890, upon the invitation of the Illinois State Horticultural Society, representatives from more than 20 national and state horticultural societies met in Chicago to brainstorm possibilities for the world's fair. At the meeting's conclusion, delegates prepared a resolution to name this new group the Columbian Horticultural Association. Participants nominated a small executive advisory committee to this association, including Raynolds and Vaughan.[6] National politics forestalled this vote for the Columbian Exposition Horticulture Department, but early Society members secured even more influential positions as Columbian Exposition Board members and officers.[7]

With the incorporation of the Chicago Horticultural Society in October 1890, flower shows in Chicago had the additional backing of leaders in Chicago's business community, many of whom were also avid gardeners. The 1891 Society-sponsored show continued the Florists' Club tradition of inviting socially prominent Chicago women to judge flower arrangements. The judges' rules from the very first show in 1892 emphasized three points: artistic arrangement, adaptability for the purpose intended, and quality of flowers used.[8] At that time, recruiting female judges was a novel concept, as noted in an 1895 newspaper article:

> When this idea was first introduced it met with no little opposition from the growers, who held that they knew all about artistic table decoration. But women have proved most effectually that they are supreme in matters where artistic daintiness and exquisite taste are the principal requirements. A florist is apt to overburden a table with meaningless details thus losing sight of true artistic simplicity, which is so desired.[9]

Ironically, the predominantly female garden clubs that emerged in the early 1900s placed a strong emphasis on flower arrangement judging, with certifications and rule books still prevalent today. Women's ability to compete in art expression in Chicago may well have found acceptance in early flower show judging.

The Society also tapped the expertise of national horticultural experts to judge new plant specimens. Inviting national judges legitimized the flower shows and elevated their status beyond a county fair.

The selection of civic leader Bryan as master of ceremonies for the 1891 show signaled the civic importance of the event. Bryan personally championed horticultural pursuits with his beautifully landscaped Elmhurst estate, Byrd's Nest, and his creation of Graceland Cemetery, which became a landscape showplace as well as the final resting place of many prominent Chicagoans. As commissioner-at-large and board member of the World's Columbian Exposition, Bryan would help generate enthusiasm for an impressive horticultural show at the upcoming world's fair.

National media started paying attention to the growing momentum of Chicago's flower shows. The *Chautauquan* reported in spring 1892, "Boston, New York and Philadelphia have not a monopoly on fine flower shows. The big cities of the West and Southwest have become worthy rivals of the East. Their Florists' Clubs and horticultural societies have their annual chrysanthemum shows and their spring shows which are patronized with the liberality characteristic of the sections."[10]

NOW OPEN. DON'T MISS IT.

Grand Chrysanthemum and Flower Show

OF THE HORTICULTURAL SOCIETY OF CHICAGO

Don't fail to see this magnificent display.

Doors open at 10 a.m. and until 10 p.m.

Classified advertisements such as the foregoing ran in prominent newspapers throughout the duration of the 1892 show as a result of the persistence of the show's press committee.[11] The latter included Society president William Chadwick and secretary W. C. Egan as well as executive committee members Vaughan and Grant and member Edgar Sanders. Newspaper advertisements provided basic logistical information along with teasers about the special programs of the day. The 1892 show, for example, held at the Second Regiment Armory on Michigan Avenue, featured four days of displays including potted and cut chrysanthemums, cut roses and carnations, and baskets of flowers. Each day offered a new attraction: chrysanthemum and plant judging on Tuesday, mantel decorations on Wednesday, table decorations on Thursday, and cut roses on Friday. Adding to the cultural experience, orchestral music programs varied each afternoon and evening, typically opening with a march and closing with finales

ranging from Strauss's "Among the Palms" to Steinhagen's "Christmas Frolics."[12]

Along with the Florists' Club, the Society partnered with the Chicago parks in producing the 1892 show. J. A. Pettigrew, Society vice president and superintendent of Lincoln Park, served as the manager of the exhibition committee, assisted by fellow Society vice president Edwin A. Kanst, the longtime superintendent of Chicago's South Park Commission. Lincoln Park greenhouses supplied cut chrysanthemums and other plants for the show. By pairing with the popular Chicago parks, the Society not only increased the number and quality of exhibits but also attracted those citizens who enjoyed the floral work of the parks.

The 1892 show strengthened the relationship between the Society and the Columbian Exposition horticulture department. New Yorker John Thorpe, who had ultimately won the appointment as Superintendent of the Columbian Exposition's Bureau of Floriculture, served as judge for seedlings and new chrysanthemums at the Society's show. Thorpe, the first president of the newly formed National Chrysanthemum Society, brought additional credibility to the Society show and further secured relationships with Chicago's horticulture community.

The World's Columbian Exposition dominated the news in Chicago during 1893, with its landscape created by Frederick Law Olmsted and the Horticultural Palace designed by Chicago architect William Le Baron Jenney. The Society selected the Palace, an exquisite conservatory topped by a light-filled opalescent dome, as the site of its 1893 Chrysanthemum Show. Slated for November 1893, the show was intended to draw visitors back to the fairgrounds after its closing for a last hurrah.

Such was not to be, however. At the eleventh hour, the Palace was dismantled, thus leaving the upcoming show without a home. Society meeting minutes reflect the consternation of the group upon hearing the news: "On Wednesday we were all plunged into a cave of gloom."[13] However, the business relationships of Society members saved the show. An arrangement was quickly worked out between Society supporters Harlow Higinbotham, World's Columbian Exposition president, and Charles L. Hutchinson, president of the Art

The 1892 World's Flower Show, held at the Second Regiment Armory on Michigan Avenue, built anticipation for the World's Columbian Exposition show to follow the next year.

Courtesy Lenhardt Library of the Chicago Botanic Garden.

Nursery owners and florists from around the world displayed plants in the Horticultural Palace at Chicago's world's fair in 1893. Many of these same professionals displayed at the Society's flower show.

Courtesy Cathy Jean Maloney.

Institute, to accommodate the show in the halls of the latter. This would begin a long-standing association between the Society flower shows and the cultural milieu of the Art Institute.

Despite the national economic depression that surrounded and followed the Columbian Exposition, Society flower shows continued to offer a bright spot in Chicago's cultural scene during the 1890s. Society business leaders helped fund the shows, and local nursery owners executed the logistical tasks. In his January 1897 address to Society membership, President Chadwick acknowledged the nursery owners' efforts: "The Society lays nearly all the burden of the year's work on its Executive Committee." The latter typically comprised Chicago Florists' Club members. Whereas the growers may have done the legwork, it was men like Hutchinson, who, when approached with fiscal uncertainty of upcoming shows, encouraged, "Hold your exhibition and keep expenses down. We will stand by you."[14]

With an expanding list of partnerships, and refreshed with additional programming, the shows drew additional visitors. The 1898 exhibition, for example, introduced the International Color Photo Company with "lantern slides showing the latest marvelous achievement in photography" and also featured the "Grand International Competition in Chrysanthemums, Cut Blooms."[15] Although the international scope might have been exaggerated—Canada appeared to be the only foreign exhibitor—premiums were established for all 48 states and the Oklahoma Territory.

The 1899 show directly linked the Society with other philanthropic causes. Organized by committee chair Mrs. John J. Glessner, booths for a charitable bazaar staffed by Society members and wives displayed items for various Chicago benevolent institutions. Books and stationery were sold to benefit Lying-in Hospital; "old silver, candy, neckwear and ornaments for hair" were sold for the Visiting Nurse Association; and the show's foyer featured a restaurant and booths benefitting the Chicago Exchange for Woman's Work, Margaret Etter Creche, and the Service Club.[16] Partnering with these charitable causes not only drew more of Chicago's leading ladies to the Society but also affiliated the Society name with philanthropic causes—something that may have been missing from the Florists' Club's commercial associations.

The 1898 show promised "brilliant and artistic electrical illumination" by the Chicago Edison Company.

Courtesy Chicago History Museum, ICHi-68236.

Shows at the turn of the twentieth century featured chrysanthemums and were held at the new Auditorium Building on South Michigan Avenue.

Courtesy Chicago History Museum, ICHi-68238, ICHi-68239.

At the *fin de siècle*, the Society flower shows had garnered new audiences and were a highly anticipated tradition in Chicago's fall calendar, with attendance reaching 15,000 visitors by 1899.[17] This decade, which saw much conflict between socioeconomic classes in Chicago, nevertheless brought people from all walks of life to the shows. The shows of the 1890s focused largely on chrysanthemum hybrids—the flower fad of the times—and on cultural excellence of plants and artistic displays of cut flowers. The symbiotic relationship between wealthy amateurs and professional florists, all members of the Society, strengthened as both groups exhibited at the shows.

Progressive Era to World War I

In the years between 1900 and 1915, Chicago and its outlying suburbs absorbed or, in many cases, catalyzed trends affecting the nation. Technology changes, from the emergence of automobiles to the explosion in plant hybridization by California nurseryman Luther Burbank and the like, infiltrated all aspects of gardening and landscape design. Social movements, such as the rising voice for women's suffrage, and the increasing numbers of immigrants affected not only the audiences for floral shows but also their management.

The early 1900s also saw more women directly involved in gardening, with the formation of garden clubs around the nation. Chicago women were always a significant force behind the scenes in early flower shows, serving as judges and organizing charity events. Even as flower hybridizers curried favor with their patronesses by naming flowers after them, Chicago women asserted their roles in more leadership positions within the Chicago Horticultural Society and in civic affairs.

The Progressive Era espoused conservation of natural resources, creation of educational and social programs to nurture the individual, and closing the gaps among socioeconomic classes. Society flower shows of the first decade of the twentieth century furthered all of these goals. By linking many of its shows with Chicago's City Beautiful effort, the Chicago Horticultural Society translated Progressive ideals to hands-on gardening achievable for a wide audience. The 1905 show, for example, featured inspiration for creating beauty in a typical backyard. The *Chicago Tribune* re-

"Surely, dear, the wild brown Bee,
When he sees your ruddy lip,
Flutters near that he may see
If it blooms for him to sip!"

Chrysanthemum
(Intellecto Newyorkae)
Columbo Family

Women were often associated with the beauty of flowers in art nouveau images such as this one from In Love's Garden *by John Cecil Clay.*

Courtesy Lenhardt Library of the Chicago Botanic Garden.

ported, "How ugly backyards may be transformed into gardens of flowers and foliage with slight expenditure of money will be demonstrated by practical experiment at the annual flower show . . . Someone suggested the idea that the 'city beautiful' could be obtained only by the obliteration of the untidy and unadorned back yards, and now this idea is to be presented in tangible and simple form."[18] Six model gardens created by early landscape designers offered visitors suggestions on disguising utilitarian features of gardens, such as fences and laundry poles, and how to properly combine flowers for visual effect. Lecturers included C. B. Whitnall of Milwaukee's County Park Commission and Evart G. Routzahn, a significant figure in public health.[19]

The Coliseum, a large auditorium (no longer extant) on South Wabash Avenue became the new venue for the 1905 and 1906 shows, so chosen to provide more people with the opportunity to visit the show in its cavernous hall. As in 1905, demonstration gardens in 1906 offered show visitors pointers on improving their own backyards. Further extending a welcome to small-space gardeners, the show dates were extended to include Sundays, and admission was reduced by half so that shop workers and clerks could afford to attend. Appealing to the public's desire for lavish gardens, the hall decorations followed a Hanging Gardens of Babylon theme with colorful flower baskets and draped ropes of laurel hanging from the ceiling, along with rows of shrub standards along the aisles.

The 1907 show instead emphasized naturalistic gardens and marked a departure from displays of exotic plants. "Formal decorations will be abandoned for the 'naturalistic' method on the advice of Jens Jensen," explained the *Chicago Tribune*.[20] Jensen, rehired in Chicago's West Side park systems in 1905 after a politically motivated firing in 1900, had been building his résumé with landscape design work on the North Shore. Seeking a designer in 1901 for his Lake Geneva estate, Society President Edward G. Uihlein had selected Jensen. Other commissions from Society members and patrons soon followed, with Jensen building a loyal North Shore clientele base.[21]

Although formal gardens inevitably crept into some displays, Jensen's naturalistic precepts could be seen in informal garden displays, such as a farm home tableau with old-fashioned garden, and dried arrangements including pine boughs, colored leaves, corn, and shrubbery. A rustic summer house overlooked a scene of winter beauty, encouraging Chicagoans with the potential of midwestern gardens even in the grip of February.

So successful was the 1907 show that the Society of American Florists decided to host its national show in Chicago in 1908. Grower Willis N. Rudd, executive committee member of the Society of American Florists and manager of the 1908 show, effused, "This was the first time a national flower show was ever attempted in this country. Chicago, which is the world's greatest flower market, and where the most successful flower shows in this country have been held, was chosen as the place to hold a national flower show and to show the way to other cities."[22]

Probably to feature Society of American Florist hothouse specimens, the naturalistic gardens from 1907 gave way to an Italian garden theme with subtropical and exotic plants. The national character of the 1908 show drew more entrants from around the country—including the presumed "largest chrysanthemum in the world" sporting 500 blossoms and sent by rail car from the New Jersey estate of the Twombly-Vanderbilt family.[23] This "war of the roses" pitted prizewinning flowers named after Chicago's leading ladies, such as 'Mrs. Potter Palmer' and 'Mrs. Marshall Field', against similarly eponymous East Coast entrants, such as the bloom 'Mrs. J. Pierpont Morgan'.

Attendance at the 1909 flower show reached similar record heights of nearly 30,000, attesting to the impact of the prior year's national spotlight. The Chicago Horticultural Society continued to promote its civic improvement theme, with city forester J. H. Prost presenting stereoviews in a lecture titled "The City Beautiful." Based on popular vote, children's school gardens received awards of collections of shrubbery.[24]

The amateur and professional floral displays were so successful, the *Chicago Examiner* wrote, "Each year for eighteen years . . . there has been a flower show in Chicago and gradually these displays have gained the place of the largest and best in America. Boston and Philadelphia have horticultural societies with large endowments and beautiful halls, but nowhere can a flower count on such enthusiastic support as the Chicago public gives the show. So, without any endowment, the Chicago Society is enabled to offer prizes and conduct a show that excels all others."[25]

Support for the Society shows had certainly grown. The 1909 show program listed 78 patrons and patronesses including the Allerton, Armour, Blackstone, Bowen, Buckingham, Dickinson, Dupee, Egan, Glessner, Higinbotham, Hutchinson, Lathrop, Lawson, Lowden, McCormick, Mitchell, Palmer, Rosenwald, Ryerson, Uihlein, and Wacker families. Horticulture professionals also supported the show either monetarily or by serving in Society leadership positions (for example, George Asmus, Jens Jensen, Edwin Kanst, August Poehlmann, Peter Reinberg, Willis Rudd, and J. C. Vaughan). Helping with publicity, Society shows received donations from eight Chicago newspapers, and journalist James H. Burdett and editor James Keeley served as Society officer and director, respectively. By 1910, no fewer than 18 committees worked throughout the year to ensure the show's success; these committees ranged in focus from Inside Decorations, including members Jensen and Asmus, to Audit and Admissions, with members Vaughan, Hutchinson, and Poehlmann.[26]

The 1906 flower show in the Coliseum evoked the Hanging Gardens of Babylon.
Courtesy Cathy Jean Maloney.

Masterpiece paintings formed the backdrop behind ferns in 1912 at the Art Institute of Chicago.

Hutchinson, who had served in a variety of leadership and sponsorship positions with the Society throughout the years, assumed its presidency in 1910. The Fall Flower Show, significantly scaled back, nonetheless returned to the Art Institute in September 1911, with a display of indoor and outdoor blooms. In 1912, under Hutchinson's leadership, the Society decided to host a spring show, on the theory that most gardeners, inspired by the show, could put ideas immediately to practice in their backyards. "The lessons on gardening for promotion of the 'City Beautiful' idea which the Horticultural Society has endeavored to teach will be more timely in the Spring," prophesied the *Chicago Examiner.*[27] With the chrysanthemum out of season, tulips, hyacinths, lilies, and roses starred in this experimental show.

An open appeal published through Chicago's newspapers in May challenged the city's elite to pledge support for the flower shows by encouraging their private gardeners to experiment with raising new varieties.

Quoted in the *Chicago Tribune*, Vaughan said, "Chicago already has made a name for Itself in the horticultural world, but we have paid most attention to the commercial side of the matter. We are merely asking the cooperation, *of public spirited men* who know that we are doing a good work."[28]

The outreach to businessmen and the modified show season paid off. The first successful spring show prompted a return to the Art Institute in 1913 with an April show opening with Rose Day. This show set a record for a single weekday attendance with 16,000 visitors. The Society not only sponsored a spring show but also the traditional Chrysanthemum Show at the Art Institute that year with longtime partners the Chrysanthemum Society of America and the Chicago Florists' Club.

The last significant show of the Progressive Era commenced November 9, 1915, at the Coliseum. Under the presidency of Rudd, the Society sponsored the naming of the best chrysanthemum. Fittingly chosen

Cut and potted flowers were displayed in settings framed with paintings at the Art Institute of Chicago.

Courtesy Institutional Archives of the Art Institute of Chicago. AIC_00146321-01.

The 1915 show was one of the last significant shows of the Society's early period.

Courtesy Chicago History Museum, ICHi-68242.

Flower Show

COLISEUM

CHICAGO

NOVEMBER 9th to 14th, Inclusive

1915

by daughter of reformer Chicago mayor turned Illinois governor Edward Dunne, the yellow seedling 'Illinois' was christened while a 25-piece band played and 8,000 visitors sang.[29]

The Society suspended its larger flower shows indefinitely amid concerns over World War I and the rising influence of local garden clubs, which assumed a greater role in hosting shows. But the Progressive Era left a tradition in Chicago flower shows that would endure, including the following:

Partnerships: Collaboration between wealthy amateurs and nursery professionals predominated in the Society shows of the 1890s. The Progressive Era shows included a more wide-ranging palette of partnerships with national flower societies, the Art Institute, civic groups such as the Chicago Park Commissions, and Chicago newspapers. By working with other like-minded groups, the Society amplified the focus given to horticulture by reaching larger audiences.

Community beautification: The City Beautiful movement was interwoven among many Progressive Era efforts, and the Society contribution included flowers and greenery in the urban environment. In its shows, the Chicago Horticultural Society encouraged displays of beautiful backyard gardens, which helped bring the lofty goals of the City Beautiful to one garden at a time.

Charitable efforts: By donating a portion of show funds and encouraging booths for nonprofit activities, the Society's early shows fostered the democratic spirit of horticulture. Horticulture was not just for wealthy amateurs or professionals but was accessible to everyone.

Education: Hosting flower shows with an educational component—lectures, model gardens, dramatic programs—became a hallmark of the Society. Commercialism often crept into shows hosted by other organizations promoting plant sales or landscape design. But the Society endeavored to include new ideas in the arts and sciences for all visitors, whether or not a profit could be made.

Horticulture as art: From the outset, the Society has promoted the work of new or emerging talents. During the earliest flower shows, the Society commissioned up-and-coming artists to design the program covers. Many of these artists went on to successful careers. The J. Manz & Co. engravers, who then employed painter Joseph Pierre Birren and illustrator Joseph Christian Leyendecker, produced the 1896 cover. Graphic illustrator Anita Parkhurst produced the 1912 cover.[30] The 16th show cover was created by illustrator Cyrus Leroy Baldridge, who, while at the University of Chicago, called his studio the College Shop. All of these fledgling artists took classes during this period at the Art Institute. Other covers were created by Barnes-Crosby Co., whose talent included that of Maginel Wright Enright Barney. Evanston artist Edna Lee Rogerson (Cook), who drew the 1910 cover, went on to become a well-known California artist. Recognizing and patronizing such early artistic talent not only introduced these young artists to possible clients but also suggested the artistic possibilities of gardening to visitors.

Society programs themselves became sought-after collectibles. Newspapers recognized the art value of the programs even as early as 1899: "The poster decided upon by the Horticultural Society is the most striking it has ever gotten out. The design used for the show last year, which was a novel departure drawn by Mr. Buehr

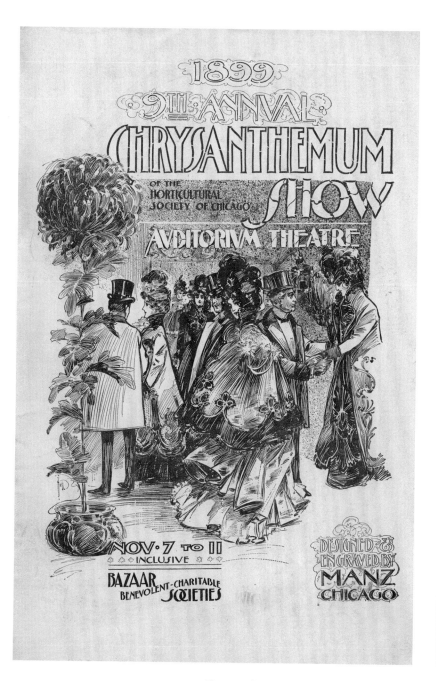

The 1899 flower show cover became a sought-after collectible.

Courtesy Chicago History Museum, ICHi-68237.

Cyrus Leroy Baldridge, who produced this cover for the 1907 show, became a well-known illustrator.

Courtesy Chicago History Museum, ICHi-68244.

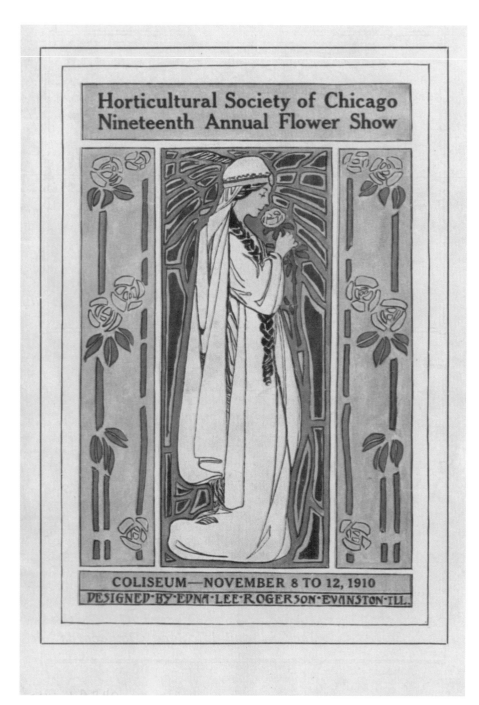

Changing art styles and print technologies can be seen by comparing the pen-and-ink drawing of 1899 with the art nouveau style of the 1907 cover and finally the transition into this colorful Arts and Crafts cover of 1910.

Courtesy Chicago History Museum, ICHi-68240.

of the Art Institute, has been adopted this year by the managers of the Philadelphia chrysanthemum show."[31] By 1906, the *Chicago Tribune* ran announcements alerting collectors when the programs and posters were available.[32]

Post–World War II Shows

How the world had changed in the 44 years since the Society staged its last significant show in 1915! In 1959, the revived Chicago Horticultural Society and Garden Center took on an ambitious goal of hosting the World Flower Show at the Chicago International Amphitheater near the Stockyards. Built in 1934 coincident with Chicago's Century of Progress Exposition, the amphitheater represented the city's past and future as a convention city. Air-conditioned and outfitted with the latest broadcasting equipment, the amphitheater hosted international livestock shows; 1952 Democratic and Republican primaries, following which the winning ticket of Eisenhower-Nixon ultimately defeated Stevenson-Sparkman; and a live appearance by gold lamé-clad Elvis Presley in 1957.

The St. Lawrence Seaway opened in 1959, and the international scope of the flower show paid homage to this historic event. Continuing the tradition from the Progressive Era flower shows, the 1959 show sought to raise funds for charitable purposes, including assistance for the handicapped and the blind, key projects of the Society's Woman's Board. As with all earlier shows, and setting the stage for future events, the World Flower Show of 1959 included a host of partnering organizations including the Illinois State Nurserymen's Association, the Allied Florists Association of Illinois, the Chicago Parks, the Men's Garden Clubs of America, and the central western zone of the Garden Club of America.

One notable misstep occurred with this first show, timed in close proximity with another flower show run by the Garden Club of Illinois at Navy Pier. The latter group, a consortium of local clubs that reflected the popularity of women's garden clubs during the past four decades, had mounted a Chicago Flower Show since 1927. The *Chicago Tribune* fanned the flames of this supposed dispute with its headline, "Two Flower Shows

Loaded with Thorns." Reporter Eleanor Page wrote:

> *Chicago's own "Battle of the Flowers" which has been simmering along for months, comes to a head Saturday with the opening of the Garden Club of Illinois' flower show on Navy Pier, held in conjunction with the Modern Living exposition.*
>
> *Cries of stealing each other's thunder, to say nothing of show dates, judges, and publicity are being flung back and forth between the women running this effort and those running the World Flower Show, which opens March 14 in the Amphitheater in the stockyards.*[33]

The *Tribune* philosophically advised readers to attend both events. The dual shows mirrored overlapping jurisdictions felt at the national and local levels of the Garden Club of America (founded 1913) and the National Garden Club (founded in 1929), the latter comprising the groups affiliated with the Garden Club of Illinois.[34] Many garden clubs aligned with one or the other national umbrella group, and occasional skirmishes were inevitable.

Navigating the shoals of these potential conflicts, the Society strove to be an independent "horticultural conscience of the community," as self-described in the 1961 flower show guide.[35] The 1961 show relocated to the newly built McCormick Place because, according to Society officials, "progress and constant effort to improve this event have always been their policy."[36] While retaining traditions of philanthropy and partnering, the 1961 show also embraced modern ideas of garden design.

As a "world" flower and garden show, many of the exhibit gardens displayed international themes, such as *The Fashions of France*, with its multihued parterres and château-style fountain; *Kyoto Comes to Chicago*, including 15-foot-tall, 100-year-old Tanyosha pines; *A Bit of England*, with grassy paths leading to an elevated garden pool built from English stone and slate copings; and the *American Garden with Foreign Influences*. This last garden, according to the show guide, demonstrated how "English, French, Italian and Japanese elements leave their mark on the modern American garden."[37] Palatine landscape architect Harold O. Klopp brought the mélange of foreign themes together in a pleasing composition.

Klopp, also a Society trustee, served as the official landscape designer for the show and contributed his expertise to many future shows. Landscape design exhibits had evolved from the Society's early model garden

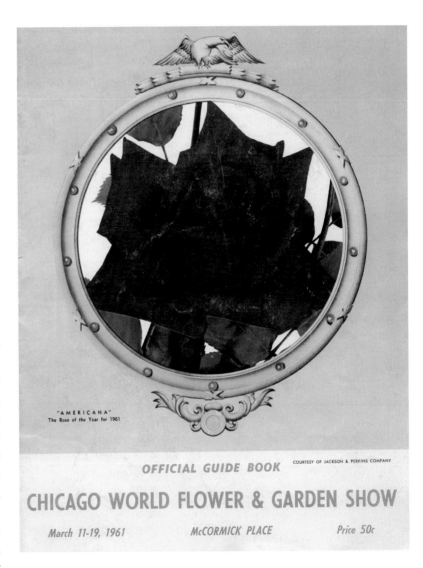

"AMERICANA"
The Rose of the Year for 1961

OFFICIAL GUIDE BOOK   COURTESY OF JACKSON & PERKINS COMPANY

CHICAGO WORLD FLOWER & GARDEN SHOW

March 11-19, 1961   McCORMICK PLACE   Price 50c

Mid-twentieth-century flower shows, such as the 1961 Chicago World Flower and Garden Show at McCormick Place, emphasized a "world" focus and featured design and educational events.

Courtesy Cathy Jean Maloney.

displays of the 1900s to holistic compositions meant to inspire visitors' yards. Flower arrangements and individual specimens still commanded attention and prizes at the show—particularly in exhibits from specialized plant societies and professional growers—but designed gardens consumed nearly one-half of the floor space.

In other ways, the 1961 show retained traditions of past shows, updated for the midcentury. Musical entertainments, instead of the orchestral sounds of the past, were provided by 17 Chicago-area choral groups including the DePaul University Choir, the Chicago Fire Department Glee Club, and the Mello-Aires of Glen Ellyn. The Society's consistent art tradition was reflected in the show guide's welcome letter: "A flower show should and can be a work of art. It should and can be a product of both great mechanical skill and superb taste." The show should be about teaching by example, offering a "great uplift of spirit," the letter continued, and a "chance to meet old gardening friends."[38] Included in the midcentury shows were ideas for floral decoration in fashion and interior design.

LET'S TOUR THE FLOWER SHOW (Continued)

One exhibit from the 1961 World Flower Show highlighted design changes— from a Victorian summer house on the left to a "modern" patio scene on the right.

Courtesy Cathy Jean Maloney.

Inspiring and informative shows continued for the next two decades. Shows hosted at McCormick Place drew record crowds in 1962 and included a theme celebrating the twentieth anniversary of the United Nations in 1965. When McCormick Place suffered extensive damage from a fire in 1967, the show relocated to the amphitheater with a Chicago Salute theme.

Shows in the late 1960s and early 1970s brought a mix of both tradition and innovation. The 1968 show included a tribute to the Girl Scouts, an organization founded by the great-great-granddaughter of Chicago Horticultural Society founder John Kinzie. In 1969, overtones of the psychedelic era colored the theme of the show, Power of Flower. Contemporary issues further surfaced in the 1970 show, which included exhibits warning against the imminent dangers of air and water pollution.

Fashion shows featuring floral-inspired dresses and floral decorations in a formal setting were among the attractions at midcentury flower shows.

Courtesy Lenhardt Library of the Chicago Botanic Garden.

Amid the great construction project under way to create the Chicago Botanic Garden, the Society continued to host Chicago-based flower shows throughout the 1970s. The show returned to the rebuilt McCormick Place in 1971, and, until the last event in 1979, included new gardening events such as Horti-Court, a judged competition of plants for amateurs.

The 1979 show attested to the long-standing ability of the Chicago Horticultural Society to bring together different groups in Chicago's gardening community. Both the Garden Club of Illinois and the Garden Club of America contributed to this show. With 300 members participating, the former displayed an extensive exhibit showing imaginative uses of flowers inside a typical home. The GCA displays, titled *Miracle of Water*, highlighted designs for various water gardens as well as an educational exhibit on water quality. Individual garden clubs also joined in the show, including the Lake Forest, Winnetka, and Kenilworth clubs. Businesses, nonprofits, and nursery professionals joined in the event.

But with so much energy and effort expended in developing the new Chicago Botanic Garden, it became difficult to muster the resources to continue the show. Citing declining attendance and rising costs, Society President Roy Mecklenburg, Ph.D., explained that "finances were the primary reason for ending the show." Bruce Krasberg, longtime chairman of the later shows, faulted the recent brutal winters—1979, for example, had a record snowfall. "After the cold, cold weather, people got used to sitting on their duffs and they didn't want to get out and look at anything but the television," he said.[39]

Program covers continued to reflect the art and graphic trends of the day, as this cover from the 1975 World Flower Show demonstrates.

Courtesy Lenhardt Library of the Chicago Botanic Garden.

The Show Must Go On

After so many decades of hosting flower shows in downtown Chicago, how would the Society continue to inspire gardeners with exhibits of landscape and beautiful plants? The answer seemed obvious, as headlined in the *Chicago Tribune*:

THE BIGGEST GARDEN SHOW OF THEM ALL

From the Chicago Horticultural Society, the folks who for so many years gave you the giant indoor Flower and Garden Show, comes an invitation to visit the outdoor flower show—300 acres of gardens, shrubbery, trees, lawns, ponds not to mention greenhouses and exhibits.

So wrote Art Kozelka, longtime garden writer for the *Chicago Tribune*, in 1979, the year of the last significant Society garden show.[40] Indeed, with its ever-changing exhibits, the Chicago Botanic Garden could be perceived as a year-round, enormous flower show.

Even when the Chicago Botanic Garden opened, the tradition of hosting flower shows continued, albeit on a smaller scale. "The first show on the Chicago Botanic Garden property was in July of 1973. Because the Education Building did not yet exist, the show was held in the garage of the Maintenance Building," explains Stephanie Lindemann, who manages the shows at the Garden today. Neither 'Minnie Wanamaker' nor 'Mrs. Alpheus Hardy' will be there, but you are sure to see a wide variety of new or tried-and-true favorite plants.

With the acres of plants on continual display at the Chicago Botanic Garden, can there be room for flower shows? Yes! Plant connoisseurs can enjoy specialized flower shows and public programs every month, and the Garden's Bonsai Collection is among the best of its kind.

Bonsai Collection

One of the most unique "shows" hosted by the Society is its specialty collection of nearly 200 exquisite bonsai—dwarfed, shaped trees that have been cultivated to grow in pots or trays using the artistic method of the same name.

The Society has had an abiding interest in bonsai, with many of the flower shows of the early and mid-twentieth century featuring bonsai displays or lectures. Although Japanese bonsai had been introduced to the American public at the 1876 International Exposition at Philadelphia, most Chicagoans had never seen live examples. At the 1905 Society flower show, for example, a star attraction was the 3-foot tall, 300-year-old "strange plant . . . of the property J. Rosenwald and is valued at $500," according to the *Chicago Tribune*. "The Japanese gardeners have a method of confining the leaves of the tree to small bunches so that it is far different from the natural species."[41] This prized arborvitae introduced many Chicagoans to the art of bonsai.

The first bonsai donated to the Garden in 1971 included three lacebark elms. Donations such as these from individuals and groups such as the Midwest Bonsai Society and Prairie State Bonsai Club helped increase the collection to about 45 trees in 1995. In 2000, Japanese bonsai master Susumu Nakamura donated 19 of his favorite trees to the Garden, elevating the collection to a new level.[42]

These miniature works of art receive meticulous attention and care from the Garden's bonsai curator and more than 25 skilled volunteers. Through a careful process of pruning branches and roots, pinching back new growth, wiring and shaping tree forms, and monitoring each plant's individual need for fertilizer, soil mix, water, and sunlight, they have been transformed into living sculptures. These azaleas, maples, junipers, ginkgoes, and pines have achieved an idealized form of botanic beauty, quite apart from the trees in our backyards.[43]

There are 27 styles of bonsai in this collection, with each officially recognized style intended to enhance or call attention to certain characteristics of the plant when grown in the wild. Pines are a favorite specimen because they grow abundantly in Japan and have adapted to Japan's rocky coastlines, higher elevations, and extreme wind that bends branches and trunks naturally, with no need for guide wires.

Trees selected from the Bonsai Collection are displayed morning and night, three seasons a year—spring, summer, and fall—in the Searle and Runnells Courtyards of the Regenstein Center. Pictured in the foreground is trident maple (Acer buergerianum).

Japanese wisteria (Wisteria floribunda 'Kyushaku')

The oldest bonsai by far, a limber pine (Pinus flexilis), is estimated to be between 700 and 1,000 years old.

Ponderosa pine (Pinus ponderosa)

Today's Flower Shows and Public Programs

The Chicago Botanic Garden is now the venue for a wide variety of flower shows and public programs. Appealing to diverse audiences, the Garden hosts a number of special events, exhibits, and other public programs. Beginning in 1998, Big Bugs by artist David Rogers featured oversize insect sculptures placed in Garden settings. The 2003 Chapungu exhibition, cohosted with the Garfield Conservatory, introduced Garden visitors to the sculpture of Africa. A favorite since 2000, the Antiques & Garden Fair —now called the Antiques, Garden & Design Show—offers a matchless pairing of timeless treasures and floral favorites. By expanding the Garden venue to host these events, thousands more visitors are introduced to the possibilities of horticulture.

The American Flower Show series at the Garden currently includes multiple shows per month in the growing season, such as displays from the Midwest Fruit Explorers, Bromeliad Society of Greater Chicago, Ikenobo Ikebana Society–Chicago Chapter, Mid-America Bonsai Society, American Rhododendron Society–

The Midwest Daffodil Society Show includes cut blooms, floral design, and photography competitions inspired by the display gardens at the Chicago Botanic Garden.

Chicago Chapter, and Garden Clubs of Illinois District IX. The lineup sometimes changes, and some shows are judged whereas others are displays only.

The Garden introduced a major new Orchid Show, an exhibition of more than 10,000 orchids, in 2014. The Illinois Orchid Society teamed up with the Garden during this time by having experts on hand and offering repotting services. Early spring shows continue with the Northern Illinois Gesneriad Society, the Midwest Fruit Explorers, the Midwest Daffodil Society, the Central States Dahlia Society's annual plant and root sale, and the Midwest chapter of the American Rhododendron Society show.

Summer begins every other year with the popular Show of Summer, cosponsored by Chicago-area garden clubs affiliated with the Garden Club of America. Other shows often include the Wisconsin–Illinois Lily Society, the North Shore Iris and Daylily Society, and the Cactus & Succulent Society of Greater Chicago. The Ikebana International Show is a summer favorite, with an annual exhibition of traditional Japanese flower arranging.

Harvest season frequently features displays from the Gardeners of the North Shore, the Midwest Bonsai Society, and the Illinois Gourd Society. A longtime Society tradition, the Roadside Flower Sale Workshops are held in early fall. At these workshops, Garden volunteers and other participants transform dry flowers, grasses, and pods into beautiful arrangements for purchase at the Society's later Roadside sale. This event is followed later in the season by the Illinois Mycological Association Mushroom Show & Sale. A venerable Illinois group, the Illinois Mycological Association exhibits from 50 to 100 varieties of mushroom foraged from area forests.

The Central States Dahlia Society Show features hundreds of dahlia blooms ranging in size from a silver dollar to a dinner plate, judged and on display.

The popularity and longevity of these shows proves that flower shows have not lost their appeal. Lindemann describes the invaluable opportunity provided by shows to "talk to a live person" one-on-one to share information and the joy of gardening.

"One thing remains the same since 1891," says Lindemann. "A flower show is a special event and attracts hundreds of thousands of attendees."[44]

Six Chicago-area garden clubs affiliated with the Garden Club of America present a competitive exhibition at the Chicago Botanic Garden every three years. In 2014, this arrangement won Best in Show.

Big Bugs (including this 25-foot-ant) were first exhibited at the Chicago Botanic Garden in 1998. The natural sculptures returned to amaze visitors again in 2002.

In 2003 the Chicago Botanic Garden hosted Chapungu, an exhibition of contemporary African stone sculptures drawn from the collection of the Chapungu Sculpture Park of Zimbabwe, Africa.

The inaugural Orchid Show in 2014 featured more than 10,000 orchids in dramatic displays within the Regenstein Center and the Garden Greenhouses.

The annual Antiques & Garden Fair (which became the Antiques, Garden & Design Show in 2015) was introduced in spring 2000 and features beautifully designed indoor gardens amid antiques, vintage décor, and botanically themed items offered by leading vendors.

Visitors of all ages are delighted by Butterflies & Blooms,
which opened at the Chicago Botanic Garden in 2012.

Wonderland Express has become a winter holiday tradition at the Chicago Botanic Garden.

Area chefs offer cooking demonstrations as part of the summer Garden Chef Series at the Garden.

A fall highlight at the Chicago Botanic Garden is Trains, Tricks & Treats, when the Model Railroad Garden is decorated for Halloween and children are encouraged to visit in costumes.

The Flower Show Series includes ikebana, the art of Japanese traditional flower arranging, by the Ikebana International Society and the Sogetsu School of Illinois.

More than 50 daylily varieties are in bloom at the Northshore Iris and Daylily Society Show & Sale.

The Evenings music series has become a summer tradition for many Garden visitors, who picnic on the Esplanade while enjoying live music.

The annual Fall Bulb Sale, presented by the Woman's Board of the Chicago Horticultural Society, offers more than 225 varieties of bulbs, along with potted mums and pansies. Staff are on hand to answer questions and offer tips.

First hosted by Chicago Botanic Garden volunteers in 1980, the annual Roadside Flower Sale features beautiful dried arrangements made of plant materials from the Garden. Professional floral designers lead volunteers in creating the items at special workshops, and proceeds benefit the Garden.

Deciduous bonsai are highlighted in the Three Friends of Winter bonsai silhouette show. These living sculptures have a special beauty during their dormant phase, when their branch structure can be admired without foliage.

4

Plants

For Posterity and Progress

From its first chrysanthemum show, the Chicago Horticultural Society has introduced Chicagoans and the world to new plants, various ways of growing plants, unique plant combinations, and plants for particular habitats. Through the Chicago Botanic Garden's research programs, scientists are helping to conserve, protect, and restore native plants and the essential benefits they provide.

In the 1800s, plant hunters, botanists, scientists, and pioneer farmers studied the plants of the Chicago region—still considered a frontier by the more settled East Coast. Many of Chicago's early institutions focused on the economic and scientific value of plants: the Chicago Academy of Science and Illinois Natural Survey sponsored botany field trips throughout the state, and the Illinois Horticultural Society shared technical information about plants. The Chicago Horticultural Society, in addition to sharing scientific data among professionals, extolled the splendor of nature to the citizenry of the Chicago area. Thus inspired, it was hoped that the city itself could be made more beautiful and its residents more uplifted through the power of horticulture.

Plants of every color, shape, and size captivate the senses at the Chicago Botanic Garden today—such as the tower of jewels (Echium wildpretii) *in the English Walled Garden.*

At the outset, the Society promoted excellence in plants by growing them in private greenhouses and gardens. Members collaborated with professional growers and hired European gardeners well trained in the horticultural arts. Society flower shows displayed the finest of these specimens, and competitions and prizes encouraged continuous improvements. By opening the shows to the public and heavily publicizing the events, the Society stimulated widespread interest in better flower culture. Society members such as William C. Egan, Jens Jensen, and O. C. Simonds wrote essays on the best plants for the area in popular books and newspapers aimed at a wider audience, as well as writing for the trade journals favored by other Chicago institutions. In the 1940s through 1960s, Society members opened their gardens to public tours, displaying plant possibilities *in situ*.

When the Chicago Botanic Garden opened, the Society created a living museum of plants best suited to the Midwest. The new Garden affords many continued possibilities: partnering with leading growers, displaying only the best plants, and sharing information with the general public. Plant evaluations are no longer conducted in individual Society members' greenhouses but rather through rigorous trials by Garden professional horticulturists. Plant acquisitions no longer rely on members' backyard donations but can be obtained through global plant-hunting expeditions, from growers throughout the world, or from the Garden's own greenhouses. The modest number of plants on view from the Society's early days is dwarfed by the Garden's growing collection of more than 2.6 million specimens.

Some plants have remained consistent favorites from the Society's early days to today. The stories of these plants—chrysanthemums, roses, and orchids—in some ways mirror the history of the Society itself: from a small group of stalwarts to a thriving, robust collection of "best in class" individuals.

Chrysanthemums made headlines and captivated gardeners' hearts for decades.
Courtesy Chicago History Museum, ICHi-68243.

Profiles of Popular Plants

Chrysanthemum: "Queen of Autumn"

Throughout the years, certain plants have always been in favor. The chrysanthemum has appealed to gardeners for centuries. Popularity of this Asian native plant spread across the United States in the early nineteenth century with the arrival of the florist flower 'Old Purple' (*Chrysanthemum sinensis × indicum*). The United States soon superseded Europe in developing new strains, and by the early twentieth century, outdoor, fall-blooming chrysanthemum varieties tempted gardeners.[1] Especially when faced with impending winter gloom, horticulturists in northern cities such as Chicago clamored for new and better chrysanthemums.

Little wonder, then, that the Society's earliest flower shows starred chrysanthemums. Beginning with the first show in 1891, according to the *Chicago Tribune*, "Chrysanthemums occupy all the room . . . Chrysanthemums of every known color or combination of color; chrysanthemums big and chrysanthemums little; chrysanthemums with long, ragged, straggly petals; chrysanthemums with dense, closely-curled, woolly petals."[2] J. C. Vaughan, nurseryman and Society leader, swept most of the judging categories, with fellow Society members Willis Rudd and William H. Chadwick ranking a close second.

Subsequent shows sought a variety of ways to display and inform the public about chrysanthemums. Each year a substantive prize was offered for the best new seedling, thus promoting innovation and excellence in plant breeding. Society members such as Martin A. Ryerson and John J. Mitchell were well-known competitors in raising chrysanthemums in their own greenhouses.[3]

To help popularize the flower, the Society showed artistic ways to display the blooms. In 1897, for example, a Professor Choyo arranged three vases of chrysanthemums in the Japanese style. The vases themselves, hundreds of years old, were of simple design to better feature the plants. Two vases were arranged for a wedding. The groom's vase held red flowers underneath white, with a half-opened flower at the top indicating hope. The bride's arrangement reversed the color layers but did not include the symbol of hope. Through the authentic arrangement of flowers, the Society aimed to expose the public to cultural traditions and art from outside the United States.

Flower show program covers glorified chrysanthemums for the next several years. When the Society re-formed in 1945, one of its earliest events that year spotlighted a lecture by botany professor and renowned breeder of the so-called Chicago strain of frost-hardy mums, Ezra Kraus, Ph.D., of the University of Chicago. The Society hosted chrysanthemum exhibits at its downtown Garden Center[4] in the early

Martin A. Ryerson (center front), shown here touring French artist Claude Monet's garden at Giverny, cultivated chrysanthemums, roses, and many other plants in his private greenhouse.

University of Chicago Photographic Archive, apf7-01162, Special Collections Research Center, University of Chicago Library. Courtesy *Chicago Maroon*.

NEW CHRYSANTHEMUM MRS. W C. EGAN.

Chrysanthemums were named after prominent members of the Chicago Horticultural Society, such as the Egan family.

Courtesy Cathy Jean Maloney.

As shown in Gardening *magazine, the 1897 flower show included a display of cut chrysanthemums in authentic Japanese style. A groom's vase is on the left, and his bride's is on the right, with a third adding a balanced composition.*

Courtesy Cathy Jean Maloney.

CHRYSANTHEMUMS ARRANGED IN JAPANESE STYLE BY PROF. CHOYO.

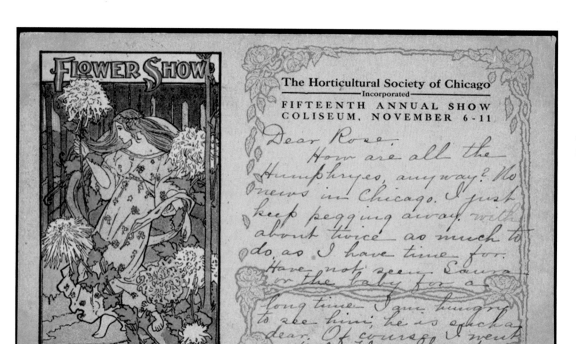

The 1904 show revisited Japanese chrysanthemum culture.

Courtesy Special Collections of the Lenhardt Library of the Chicago Botanic Garden.

1950s and continued to team with the University of Chicago to host a chrysanthemum conference with keynote address from Professor Paul Voth.[5] The Society's mid-twentieth-century publications often featured articles on chrysanthemums. Typical essays included proper care and planting of mums with suggestions on spring dividing, pinching for fuller plants and blooms, and disbudding for long-stemmed incurved and Japanese cultivars (dubbed "football" mums for their traditional use in homecoming corsages).

Chrysanthemums received a renewed interest in the mid-1960s, according to *Garden Talk*, due to the "application of scientific knowledge of heredity and plant responses to day-length and temperature control."[6] On June 17, 1966, the City of Chicago adopted the chrysanthemum as its official flower, based on recommendations from Chicago's City Beautiful committee. This single yellow mum with a bronze center was developed by the Chicago Park District. John A. Lundgren, park district chief horticulturist and 1971 Society Hutchinson Medal winner, noted that although this first flower was not winter-hardy, his "mum experts" would develop a new variety that could survive Chicago winters.[7]

An article in the April 1972 issue of *Garden Talk* described mums' continued popularity as staples in gardens and ceremonies: "Why are chrysanthemums so popular; you see them in estate gardens and in the 'front yards' of us common folks; people who scarcely garden at all are apt to have a few clumps stuck against the foundation or in the border shrubberies. Even commercial plantings often blossom out in late summer with beds of chrysanthemums. They can't all have been brought home from the hospital or a funeral."[8] This mention of mums in the "flower power" era as important symbols in health and mourning rituals attests to the enduring favor toward the plant.

Today, the Chicago Botanic Garden presents visitors with annual displays of chrysanthemums. Chrysanthemum "towers" have become a recent favorite, with hundreds of mums planted in pillars and cascading from arbors. From the handful of winter-hardy chrysanthemums available in the 1890s, the Chicago Horticultural Society, in tandem with kindred organizations, helped popularize the flower in the Midwest.

Rose: A Favorite by Any Name

While forsythias and daffodils brought hope to winter-weary Chicago, the rose beguiled its citizenry. Rose displays accompanied, and sometimes eclipsed, those of chrysanthemums in the Society's early flower shows. Society president Chadwick opined of the 1895 show, "We gave as good a rose show, probably, as ever was seen in America, some think even England where the rose luxuriates."[9]

The "war of the roses" between 'Mrs. Marshall Field' and 'Mrs. Potter Palmer' varieties receded with the introduction of the 'Mrs. Aaron Ward' rose at the 1912 show, held at the Art Institute. Roses displaced chrysanthemums on center stage at this show, the first held by the Society in spring rather than fall. According to the *Chicago Tribune*, "The reason for the popularity of the Ward rose is the charming and unusual color. It is a deep golden orange, shading to a creamy lemon."[10] In addition to politically current roses such as 'Theodore Roosevelt' and 'William Taft,' the show promised blue roses, a horticultural feat never achieved then or now. It was the German-bred climber 'Violet Blue' (*Rosa* 'Veilchenblau') that garnered the media attention, warranted or not, with its purplish hue.

Overleaf: *Bold planting ideas are front and center in the Crescent's annual beds, while hundreds of evergreen boxwoods give shape to their curves. Here, abloom with chrysanthemums, the Crescent shows its fall colors.*

Named for its circular boundary, the Circle Garden features a central dancing fountain. Trees, shrubs, and perennials provide an attractive backdrop to the changing display of showy annuals.

Hanging seasonal displays greet visitors as they cross the bridge connecting the Visitor Center to the main island of the Chicago Botanic Garden.

The Mrs. Wm. H. Taft rose was among many with political connotations featured at the 1912 show at the Art Institute.

Courtesy Institutional Archives of the Art Institute of Chicago. AIC_00146320-01.

As with chrysanthemums, roses were often exhibited at the Society's downtown Garden Center when the group re-formed in the 1940s. Hybrid tea roses, while available since 'La France' was introduced in 1867, garnered renewed enthusiasm in the two time periods that coincided with the Society's initial heyday and subsequent rebirth. The discovery of the hybrid tea rose 'Soleil d'Or' in 1900 jump-started the "war of the roses" at the Society's turn-of-the-century flower shows, and the introduction in the United States of 'Peace' after World War II reignited rose fever.

The extraordinary success of the Society's Rose Festival in 1951 inspired the formation of the Woman's Board. Building on that success, the Society's Pageant of Roses at Eugene Pfister's estate Rosebrae in June 1952 displayed three acres of roses ranging from old-fashioned species no longer commercially available through modern roses. Woman's Board members dressed in costume to interpret a living exhibit of roses throughout history. Five themed areas contained species roses representing the Italian Renaissance, damask and cabbage roses from the French Empress Josephine era, antebellum Victorian moss roses, hybrid teas of the late nineteenth century, and floribundas suggesting the modern roses.[11]

This embrace of the diversity of roses found its way into 1950s Society publications, which celebrated old-fashioned roses along with new introductions. Even as a *Garden Talks* article of November 1956 headlined "New Rose Selections," a June article of that same year featured "Old Rose Friends." The latter celebrated the fragrance and the disease resistance of old-fashioned roses, recommending 'Harrison's Yellow', 'Old Blush', 'Maiden's Blush', 'Madam Hardy', and 'Rosa Mundi'.

In 1985, one year before the rose was designated the official flower and floral emblem of the United States of America, the Krasberg Rose Garden opened at the Chicago Botanic Garden. Bruce Krasberg, a rosarian and Society Board member, had often evangelized the beauties of the rose, as in his October 1973 *Garden Talk* article, "Roses: The Best All-Around Flowers."[12] As Kris Jarantoski noted, "The Rose Garden was one of the gardens we created in response to public demand."[13] Roses are now among the 11 specialized collections of the Chicago Botanic Garden.

Heirloom roses such as Old Blush China rose (Rosa 'Old Blush') merit a special section in the Chicago Botanic Garden's Krasberg Rose Garden.

La France hybrid tea rose (Rosa 'La France')

Damask rose (Rosa damascena)

Rosa mundi (Rosa gallica 'Versicolor')

Sweetbriar rose (Rosa rubignosa)

Indoor gardening lent Chicago winters a bit of cheer, and parlor gardens at the turn of the twentieth century featured the latest novelties. While many houseplants such as ferns and the occasional palm could commonly be found, orchids represented the pinnacle of indoor gardening.

Society members strove to demonstrate that orchid culture could be mastered even with the modest window gardens of the average Victorian homeowner. Society president Chadwick wrote, "The public occasionally reads of great sums paid for orchid plants and it is true that individual orchids have commanded a thousand, twelve hundred, fifteen hundred . . . but these are rare and extreme instances. You can get good ones from 1–3 dollars."[14] Chadwick may have been commenting on the "orchidelirium" of the Victorian era wherein wealthy patrons sent orchid hunters into the jungles to collect prize specimens. He praised the orchids at Lincoln Park, Washington Park, and the West Side parks as well as several private and commercial collections. The former could be seen daily by the public, and the latter, thanks to the Chicago Horticultural Society, could be viewed at its flower shows.

Edward Uihlein's orchids were frequently shown at Society flower shows.

Courtesy Cathy Jean Maloney.

ORCHIDS IN THE CONSERVATORY OF MR. E. G. UIHLEIN. CHICAGO

In his 1894 book *Chicago the Garden City*, Andreas Simon singled out the conservatory and orchids of Edward Uihlein: "Foremost among these friends of the children of Flora stands Mr. Edward Uihlein, one of the vice presidents of the Chicago Horticultural Society. . . . The greatest interest is awakened by the superb collection of orchids that are partly suspended from the glass roofs of the greenhouses, partly found in pots along the tiers below."[15] Uihlein's Wicker Park residence was surrounded by a "large park-like garden" and more than 1,900 square feet of greenhouse space. The earliest Society flower shows included orchids from Uihlein's conservatories and those of other Society members.

Throughout the first decade of the twentieth century, several Society members raised orchids in friendly competition. Mr. and Mrs. Selfridge hunted orchids themselves on trips to Cuba, and, assisted by their gardener at their Lake Geneva estate, successfully hybridized the plant themselves.[16] When Selfridge left Chicago for business pursuits in London, he was said to have left his orchid collection to the Lincoln Park Conservatory.[17]

After the Society's reincorporation, *Garden Talk* articles and flower shows explored the world of orchids. One cranky 1961 article headlined, "Orchids are not houseplants!" and cautioned that the orchid was "ungainly rather than pretty and it is a nuisance to care for."[18] This alternate viewpoint revealed the Society's willingness to publish controversial opinions—in the interest

of unbiased education. More typically however, *Garden Talk* extolled orchids for "even the most average house plant enthusiast." In articles from the early 1980s, *Phalaenopsis*, *Cattleya*, and miniature *Cymbidium* hybrids were recommended along with visits to the Illinois Orchid Show hosted at the Garden. The Garden has continued this relationship with the Orchid Society, and today, visitors can enjoy the many genera of orchids in the Garden's permanent greenhouses along with the exhibits of plants during the Orchid Society shows and the Garden's Orchid Show.

Orchids can be seen today at the Chicago Botanic Garden either at the orchid shows or any day in the Garden's greenhouses.

× Maclellanara *Yellow Star 'Golden Gambol'*

Through these examples of chrysanthemums, roses, and orchids, the Chicago Horticultural Society continued to educate the public on proper plant care and introduce new plants to the public. With the enhanced capabilities of the Chicago Botanic Garden, the Society's role has evolved. Chrysanthemum flower shows developed into an annual fall display at the Garden. From a few rose sports such as 'Mrs. Marshall Field' visible at the Society's shows, hundreds of roses can now be viewed at the Garden. Similarly, plants such as orchids, once available only to the privileged members of society, are now on display for everyone to view every day in the Garden Greenhouses within the Regenstein Center.

By cultivating flowers and exhibiting them in public shows and then by sponsoring tours and lectures, the Society's leadership offered homeowners personal hands-on experiences with plants. Later publications such as *Garden Talk* disseminated plant information even more widely. Frequently, Society members made outright donations of plants to public institutions such as the Chicago Park District or, later, the Chicago Botanic Garden. When the Garden finally opened, the possibilities for plant research, education, and information multiplied as quickly as did the plants themselves.

In the case above:

Paphiopedilum *Via Figaro 'Star Command'* × *'Star Wars'* (left)

Paphiopedilum *(Moy Lin Gum* × *Via Quatra)* × *Red Pepper 'Green Jade'* (right)

Paphiopedilum *After Dark* × *James Watson 'Giant Plum'* (center)

Burrageara *Living Fire*

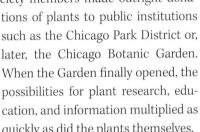

Paphiopedilum *Golden Emporer 'Sunshine'* × *Crazy Jolly 'Butterscotch'*

The Garden Opens

Leaders of the Chicago Horticultural Society, in conjunction with the renowned environmental planning and design firm of Simonds and Simonds, studied the existing horticultural collections of the Chicago area to identify the needs and gaps. Because the Morton Arboretum had already acquired an extensive collection of woody plants from around the world, the Society's planning committee decided in 1970 that "the display or educational plantings [for the Garden] should be restricted to the best species and cultivars for this area." The committee also recognized that the "excellent seasonal displays at the Garfield and Lincoln Park Conservatories should not be duplicated at the Garden."[19] The Society determined that, rather than acquire an exhaustive list of every plant, the Garden would display only the best plants for the Chicago and Midwest region.

At the Chicago Botanic Garden construction site, heavy clay soil filled up planting holes and required trenching and draining.

Courtesy Lenhardt Library of the Chicago Botanic Garden.

Landscape architect Geoffrey Rausch recalled the early planting efforts while the Garden was just a rubble-filled construction site. "That first winter we sat around a wood stove in this frigid tin building and planned lush and wonderful things for the future." The first plantings, seven large white pines, did not go well, according to Rausch: "We eagerly dug that first tree hole dreaming about beautiful things to come. We were brought back to reality quickly as the hole slowly filled up with water. We ended up having to trench and drain every plant in the garden."[20] The heavy clay soils and one of the worst winters in Chicago—that of the 1967 blizzard—wreaked havoc on the plantings. None of the pines survived, and the director of the Garden, Dr. Francis de Vos, "started getting phone calls about the trees with the unique golden-brown color." Lore has it that de Vos and staff painted the trees green until they were replaced with new, extremely hardy Scots pines.

Despite this inauspicious start, with the talents of the horticultural staff experts, the Chicago Horticultural Society acquired and maintained the collection of what would become more than 2.6 million plants today. Representing nearly 10,000 plant varieties of about 250 plant families, the collection, well documented with labels, maps, and detailed database records, has earned the Garden's museum status by the American Alliance of Museums. The collections program has been cited as a best practice in case examples for other public gardens.[21] Visitors can learn about the plants by exploring the well-labeled gardens or by searching the online databases.

The Living Collections

According to Executive Vice President and Director Kris Jarantoski, the Chicago Botanic Garden has one of the largest collections of documented and labeled hardy herbaceous perennials on display in any public garden in North America. They range from 1-inch-tall thyme to 8-foot-tall compass plant (*Silphium laciniatum*) and are displayed as specimens, as ground cover, in mixed borders, and integrated into sweeps of thousands of plants.[22] Herbaceous perennials (including bulbs, grasses, aquatics, and ferns) compose the vast majority of the Garden's plant collections. Almost half of these are ornamental perennials (as opposed to those plants in the native habitats at the Garden).

The Chicago Botanic Garden's collection of woody plants in the Dwarf Conifer Garden is one of the largest displayed in an ornamental setting of any public garden in North America.

The woody plants, while less diverse than the perennials, were the first permanent plants in the Garden. Trees and shrubs ranging from miniature bonsai to mighty oaks are incorporated into beautiful landscapes. At the Garden, visitors can enjoy one of the most extensive woody plant collections displayed in an ornamental setting in any public garden in North America. The Garden continues to expand its woody plant collection as older trees planted for windbreaks and structure succumb to disease. In particular, more species and cultivars will be added of horse chestnuts and buckeyes (*Aesculus*), hornbeam (*Carpinus*), cotoneaster (*Cotoneaster*), daphne (*Daphne*), deutzia (*Deutzia*), beech (*Fagus*), hydrangea (*Hydrangea*), peony (*Paeonia*), mock orange (*Philadelphus*), cinquefoil (*Potentilla*), oaks other than red (*Quercus*), stewartia (*Stewartia*), lilac (*Syringa*), linden (*Tilia*), elm (*Ulmus*), and weigela (*Weigela*).[23]

Deciduous trees, evergreen shrubs, and bulbs are just some of the ornamental plants on display at the Chicago Botanic Garden.

Today, Garden staff members continuously work to offer the best plants for the Midwest through plant-hunting expeditions, plant trial research, and partnerships with kindred organizations to create new cultivars best suited for the region. Whereas the earliest plant recommendations came from personal evaluations from a few Society members, now the full resources of the Garden—from plant trials to extensive research—stand behind the suggestions.

Between 1994 and 2012, the number of taxa at the Garden increased from just under 7,000 to almost 9,500.[24] To maintain this growth trend, the Garden plans to continue a robust acquisition program that draws from four sources: commercial firms, natural ecosystems, home garden enthusiasts, and other botanical institutions. Collecting from commercial firms—especially the plant originator—is a pri-

Woodland ephemerals, such as these shooting stars (Dodecatheon meadia) in the Native Plant Garden, herald the start of spring at the Chicago Botanic Garden.

mary method because these plants are most often accessible to homeowners. Wild collecting from natural ecosystems—typically taxa growing outdoors in temperate regions between the 35th and 55th parallels—is used for breeding, evaluation, and conserving species from around the world.

It is instructive to see how some hybrids fall to fashion. For example, early rose cultivars came and went with fads—from the early fame of 'Louis Van Houtte' to the fin-tailed fancy of the mid-twentieth century 'Chrysler Imperial'. It is equally interesting to note how other plants' popularity changes as their ecological impact is discovered. Some plants are not endorsed by the Garden when growing experience reveals their weaknesses. Still others, such as winged euonymous (*Euonymus alatus*), European cranberry bush viburnum (*Viburnum opulus*), or Japanese barberry (*Berberis thunbergii*), may have been popular in the mid-twentieth century, but new information about the invasive nature of these plants now recommends against them. The Garden's website offers detailed recommendations for homeowners as well as *Plant Evaluation Notes*, which compares the relative successes of plant trials. In the Regenstein Center, the Garden's Plant Information Service helps share this knowledge with the public.

Aquatic plants, seen here in the Waterfall Garden, also adorn the Chicago Botanic Garden's many water features.

Within the Living Collections, the Garden has designated several specialized collections. Specialized collections are collections of distinction, recognized nationally and internationally. These genera were chosen because they provide an opportunity to address research issues; include areas where the Garden is already strong; can be supported by curatorial staffing to acquire, develop, study, and disseminate information; are adaptable to the growing conditions of the Midwest; add interesting color or texture to the Garden; or are relevant to the Garden's visitors and consumers.

Sweeps of woodland and shoreline plants help create the natural style of Spider Island. In winter, the bark and branches of trees and shrubs provide color and texture.

A panoramic landscape features a broad hillside lawn between a perennial drift and backdrop of deciduous and evergreen trees on Evening Island. In the background is an iconic feature of the Chicago Botanic Garden, the 48-bell Theodore C. Butz Memorial Carillon.

*Brookside geraniums
(Geranium 'Brookside')
bloom in summer, providing
a colorful ground cover near
one of the Garden lakes.*

The Garden's specialized collections include hardy kiwi (*Actinidia*), buckeye (*Aesculus*), serviceberry (*Amelanchier*), dogwood (*Cornus*; nonbracted), geranium (*Geranium*), ginkgo (*Ginkgo*), oak (*Quercus*), rose (*Rosa*; landscape), willow (*Salix*; under 6 feet), spirea (*Spiraea*), and arborvitae (*Thuja plicata*).

Three of these Chicago Botanic Garden specialized collections have been accepted as collections of the North American Plant Collections Consortium (NAPCC): geranium, oak, and spiraea. The NAPCC works with a network of North American public gardens to preserve taxa of plants in living collections and also works to improve curatorial practices.[25]

Beyond chrysanthemums, roses, and orchids, the Chicago Horticultural Society has expanded the palette of the backyard gardener and urban planner alike to thousands of tested plant specimens. Millions of plants are on display at the Chicago Botanic Garden, but even more can be discovered through the information services available through classes, plant sales, publications, and online resources. From orchids at Lincoln Park to Farwell's herbs, many of today's plants owe their roots to the work of the Society and Garden.

Fall views across the Great Basin toward the Arch Bridge highlight the hues of the season, including brilliant tree foliage (above) and the bright colors of late-season perennials, such as these purple asters (right).

The Krasberg Rose Garden, offering hundreds of roses hardy to the Chicago area, attracts rosarians and plant lovers alike. The Dwarf Conifer Garden specializes in small evergreen plants that retain their color through the long midwestern winters.

Krasberg Rose Garden

For plant lovers, and particularly for rosarians, the Krasberg Rose Garden displays the best roses for the Chicago area. Three acres are dedicated to more than 200 varieties, with more than 5,000 roses chosen for their outstanding performance, hardiness, and disease resistance.[26] The garden is named after rosarian Bruce Krasberg, longtime Chicago Horticultural Society Board member and former national president of the Men's Garden Clubs of America.

The Krasberg Rose Garden is more than a great collection of roses; it is also a garden in which these elegant flowers are incorporated into the landscape. Graced with informal curving lines and myriad shrubs, trees, perennials, and ground cover, the garden captivates visitors even when roses are not at their peak. The roses themselves are arranged so that pale colors can be seen nearer the fountain and darker shades toward the main entrance. Landscape architect Geoffrey Rausch designed a broad lawn panel, contemporary in style, as a counterpoint to the strolling paths. The lawn terminates with a focal point of a fountain and arbor. The fountain is "based on a plan-view of an old-fashioned rose," according to Rausch.[27]

Garden beds east of the cedar arbor include many reliable roses that have withstood the test of time. Since old garden roses are intermittent bloomers or bloom just once in the season, the bed includes roses that have the look and fragrance of old garden roses but the repeat blooming of the modern shrubs.

Near the entryway to the garden, the History of Roses Bed presents rose development from the earliest wild rose to the modern hybrids. All the roses are in pink tones to better enable visitors to detect differences in fragrance, shape, size, and other characteristics independent of hue.

In addition to thousands of roses along the sides of its graceful, curving path, the Krasberg Rose Garden features a fountain on its lawn and a myriad of shrubs, trees, and perennials.

Though it's always beautiful, one of the best times to visit the Krasberg Rose Garden is in the morning, when the roses are the most fragrant—the warming effects of the early sun help release fragrant oils from the dewy petals. Find a bench in the shady cedar arbor, near the bubbling foundation in the shape of a Tudor rose, for the best seat in the house.

The gentle hillside setting and attractive stone hardscape of the Dwarf Conifer Garden enhance the conifer display.

Dwarf Conifer Garden

Another garden devoted to particular types of plants is the Dwarf Conifer Garden. In the Midwest, plants with winter color are especially valued, and dwarf conifers are particularly suited to small-space gardening. One of the best of its kind in the country, the Dwarf Conifer Garden features more than 230 different kinds of the smaller members of the conifer family. Originally designed by Environmental Planning and Design and renovated in 2008 by Doug Hoerr of Hoerr Schaudt Landscape Architects, the garden includes a grand staircase entrance, views to the Elizabeth Hubert Malott Japanese Garden, and an accessible-to-all path.[28]

Conifers

Conifers are plants that bear cones. Mostly native to the Northern Hemisphere, conifers have skinny needle-like or scale-like leaves that help reduce moisture loss and allow snow to be shed easily. The conifer family includes both the oldest living thing on earth, *Pinus aristata*, or bristlecone pine, known to exceed 4,000 years in age, and the largest, *Sequoia sempervirens*, or coast redwood, nearly 400 feet tall.

Dwarf Conifers

Dwarf conifers are trees that do not reach the size that is typical for their species. Dwarfism occurs naturally in various ways, such as through witches'-brooms (clumps of branchlets) or seed mutation. The Dwarf Conifer Garden offers visitors inspiration for incorporating small-scale evergreens into the landscape.

All hardy in the Midwest, the dwarf conifers in this garden delight the eye with interesting shapes, textures, and colors.

The Dwarf Conifer Garden includes a broad staircase entrance invitingly interplanted with conifers.

The inspiring landscape design of the Chicago Botanic Garden underscores its core value that beautiful gardens and natural environments are fundamentally important to the mental and physical well-being of all people.

5

Landscape Design

Focus on Excellence

The Chicago Botanic Garden today is a living museum of plants arranged in award-winning compositions of landscape design. Yet, when the Chicago Horticultural Society formed in 1890, the term "landscape architecture" had yet to be coined, and few gardens in the city garnered acclaim for design excellence.

Landscape design in the United States lagged behind more established countries in Europe and Asia. In the seventeenth century, struggling colonists at Jamestown, Virginia, scratched out furrows for root crops, and Plymouth pilgrims learned from the Wampanoag tribe how to grow flint corn in Massachusetts. Meanwhile, across the Atlantic Ocean, André Le Nôtre was designing palatial gardens at Versailles in the 1660s, and, in the 1700s, Lancelot "Capability" Brown introduced curves and pastoral views to London's Kew Gardens. These European landscape designers and others would ultimately influence garden design in the fledgling United States.

As author Ann Leighton documents in her three-volume garden history, America's gardens evolved over two centuries from a focus on "meate and medicine" to "comfort and affluence."[1] After utilitarian needs were satisfied, property owners could devote resources to ornamental gardens. U.S. Eastern Seaboard estate owners began hiring landscape designers to adorn their gardens even as midwestern gardeners planted trees for shelter, fuel, and fences and derived basic food from their gardens.

In the Chicago area, as in many nineteenth-century American cities, the notion of landscape design expanded with the rural cemetery movement and subsequent creation of public parks. Chicago's Rosehill Cemetery, designed by Philadelphian William Saunders, and Calvary Cemetery started the local trend in 1859. Graceland Cemetery (1860) and Mount Greenwood Cemetery (1879) also featured accomplished landscape designs.

Chicago Horticultural Society members helped launch all these efforts. William B. Ogden served as charter member and investor in both Rosehill and Graceland. Florist and early Society member Edgar Sanders helped design Calvary. Landscape gardener and Society member O. C. Simonds is credited with much of the naturalistic design at Graceland, and Society president Willis Rudd supervised Mount Greenwood and established greenhouses to supply its floral needs for years.

For a while, cemeteries served Chicagoans as the primary examples of landscape art. Then, with the establishment of the Chicago Park System in 1869, the general public witnessed the latest trends in garden design as conceived by some of the most prominent American landscape designers. Frederick Law Olmsted and Calvert Vaux prepared a plan for the South Side parks in 1871, and several disciples of their firm followed, including H. W. S. Cleveland and Jacob Weidenmann. William Le Baron Jenney's designs shaped the West Side parks, followed by Jens Jensen's artistry in the 1880s and later.

Individuals in the Chicago Horticultural Society first promulgated the ideals of good landscape design by creating elegant gardens themselves, as did Jensen and O. C. Simonds, or by commissioning landscape architects in work on residential estates. Landscape architecture became a focus in Society classes, flower shows, tours, and ultimately the 385 acres known today as the Chicago Botanic Garden.

Tours and Teachings

Landscape design figured among the agenda topics at many early Society meetings, where members explored the national debate over carpet bedding versus naturalistic garden styles. An 1891 meeting, for example, focused on a paper from J. A. Pettigrew, then Lincoln Park's superintendent. Pettigrew advocated a style sympathetic with Olmsted's designs: "The object of this paper is the encouragement . . . of natural gardening and the endeavor to curb within reasonable limits the mad race after florid and artificial effects as depicted in the 'bedding out' style of some modern flower gardens." He praised aquatic gardens with "wild outlines and irregular shores" and generally advised members to "avoid formality; plant species or varieties in clumps of size to show the plants in their individuality and not dotted and repeated frequently throughout the border."[2]

Among converts to this naturalistic style was Society secretary William C. Egan. Egan described how he refined his own design sensibilities at his Highland Park estate, Egandale. He shared his experiences in an essay, "How I Built My Country Home: A Concrete Example of Landscape Gardening," replete with before-and-after photographs. Egan detailed how he had improved his landscape by massing plants and removing artificial ornamentation such as fanciful rockwork and other "clutter." Nonetheless, Egan also confessed to a soft spot for popular fashion:

Geometrical beds, clipped trees, and sheared hedges are giving place to the tasteful and natural commingling of flowers and shrubs and the planting of trees for their untrammeled beauty. In my planting I have endeavored to follow the teachings of [William] Robinson of England and Elliott [sic] of this country, and a formal vase or flower stand on my grounds would be as much out of place as a wash tub in a parlor even if the hoops were gilded and the soap-suds made from Cologne water. . . . Still I wanted to be in fashion, and grow some flowers "above ground."[3]

Egan compromised and placed an oversize rattan basket of annuals within a flower bed. He typically proposed a more restrained landscape style and wrote, "My garden is open to all who will love and appreciate its contents, be they from the mansion in the park or from the cottager's home."[4] Like other Society members, Egan helped popularize landscape design through writings and tours of personal gardens.

Olmsted's exquisite grounds plan for the World's Columbian Exposition of 1893 highlighted the possibilities for thoughtful landscape design. Well attended by Society members along with regional and international visitors, the exposition featured a variety of styles, from the naturalistic Wooded Island to the formal Court of Honor. The success of the world's fair design inspired Society members to commission landscape architects to design their own grounds. Their personal tastes mirrored the diversity of fashions at the turn of the twentieth century. Society members Harriet and Cyrus McCormick, Jr., for example, worked closely on their residence, Walden, with Warren Manning, Olmsted protégé and plantsman for the world's fair. Much more formally designed, the nearby Villa Turicum estate of Harold and Edith Rockefeller McCormick featured an elaborate terraced watercourse leading to Lake Michigan below.

Society member and landscape architect Jens Jensen often bridged many communities and social strata within the Chicago area. Even as his clientele included North Shore estate owners, he also founded conservation groups such as the Prairie Club and Friends of Our Native Landscape, which raised environmental awareness within many social circles. Through Jensen's connections, members of the general public were invited to visit properties that had been designed by various prominent landscape architects, which helped expose more homeowners to the possibilities of landscape design.

Early Society flower shows, limited by indoor venues, nonetheless tried to emphasize the benefits of landscape design. The 1907 show designed by Jens Jensen, who had prevailed over six competitor designs, divided the exhibit space into a winter and summer landscape. *Park and Cemetery* magazine hailed the idea of combining landscape design with a show: "No previ-

A BASKET FLOWER BED AT EGANDALE.

Society member W. C. Egan experimented with landscape design at his Egandale estate. As shown in this Gardening *magazine image, an oversize basket of flowers is a compromise between naturalistic design and floral follies.*
Courtesy Cathy Jean Maloney.

Jens Jensen facilitated tours of North Shore landscapes such as the McCormick estate as visited by members of the Prairie Club of Chicago.
Courtesy Prairie Club of Chicago.

ous show has been systematically designed to do justice to gardening as a whole."[5] Later shows of the early twentieth century included lectures on landscape design. The 1910 show, for example, featured pieces on "Landscape Architecture," by former Chicago Park System landscape designer Mrs. A. E. McCrea; "The Ornamentation of the City Lot," by Howard Evarts Weed; and "The Use of Native Trees and Shrubs for the Home Grounds," by Jensen.[6] In 1912, landscape gardening warranted its own exhibit with photographs and plans of home grounds, school grounds, railroad stations, parks, and cemeteries.

When the Society was quiescent between the world wars, individual members opened their homes to tours such as the Garden Club of America meeting in the Chicago area in 1919. After the Chicago Horticultural Society reincorporated, and before the Chicago Botanic Garden opened, Society members often hosted tours of their personal landscapes. The 1950s saw a daylily institute at the Fischer home in Hinsdale, and Elmer A. Claar's Northfield garden featured peonies. At the Rose Institute at the Pfister Mundelein residence, Rosebrae, Woman's Board members dressed in costume and explained lore of more than 700 roses.[7] The Woman's Board also sponsored a plant sale and tour of the Vasumpaur garden in Western Springs.[8]

Individual Chicago Horticultural Society members such as Kate Brewster opened their gardens for tours even when the Society was not active.

Smithsonian Institution, Archives of American Gardens, Garden Club of America Collection, IL003002.

Future Chicago Horticultural Society president William A. Pullman frequently offered tours of his garden, shown here ca. 1926.

Smithsonian Institution, Archives of American Gardens, Garden Club of America Collection, IL005001.

The Chicago Horticultural Society sponsored tours of member landscapes, such as Elmer A. Claar's Northfield garden, pictured on the cover of a 1955 Garden Talks.

Courtesy Lenhardt Library of the Chicago Botanic Garden.

Society members visited the Hubert A. Fischer private garden in Hinsdale, pictured on the cover of a 1955 Garden Talks.

Courtesy Lenhardt Library of the Chicago Botanic Garden.

The herb garden at Edith Farwell's estate was featured on the cover of a 1957 Garden Talks.

Courtesy Lenhardt Library of the Chicago Botanic Garden.

In addition to tours and lectures, some of the early issues of the Society publication *Garden Talks* offered tips on landscape design. Bruce Krasberg, rosarian and Society Board member, wrote an article on "Front Yard Gardening" in 1954, noting, "For a number of years, I have been putting on a one-man campaign to get home gardeners to put more color in their front yards."[9] Over the years, American backyards had become the family's private sanctuary, with front yard design relegated to foundation shrubs and monotonous lawn. Author Christopher Grampp notes of this period, "One could literally drive for hours through American subdivisions and see the same front yards almost anywhere one looked."[10] Krasberg's ideas presaged the resurgence in front yard gardening that reemerged in the 1990s and continued into the following decades.[11]

Smaller city gardens also began to receive more attention in the 1950s. As predicted by Eugene Pfister, encroaching industrialization and the postwar suburban boom left the city of Chicago in need of beautification. The January 1954 issue of *Garden Talks* noted, "Various influences . . . have arisen of late years to overshadow the idea of keeping our city horticulturally attractive as visioned in its original slogan 'The City in the Garden.'" Citing rapidly expanding industry and population and the "voracious maw of superhighways," the writer opined, "In the face of the demands of the atomic age, Chicago may well become a mere aggregation of steel, glass, stone and concrete, all gracefully designed and molded by man to meet functional needs but bare of those rich landscape beauties of nature, without which no community can happily exist."[12] Partnering with the University of Illinois's Department of City Planning and Landscape Architecture, the Society sponsored a demonstration of how small homes in the city could be beautified with gardens. Selecting 30- to 50-year-old homes and apartment houses, the Society offered a garden makeover wherein students designed landscape plans for typical city lots.[13]

Another early design idea promulgated by *Garden Talks* incorporated edible gardens into the landscape. Vegetable gardens had followed utilitarian formats in the victory garden years, but contributors Mr. and Mrs. Kurt Melzer proposed that "City Kitchen Gardens Go

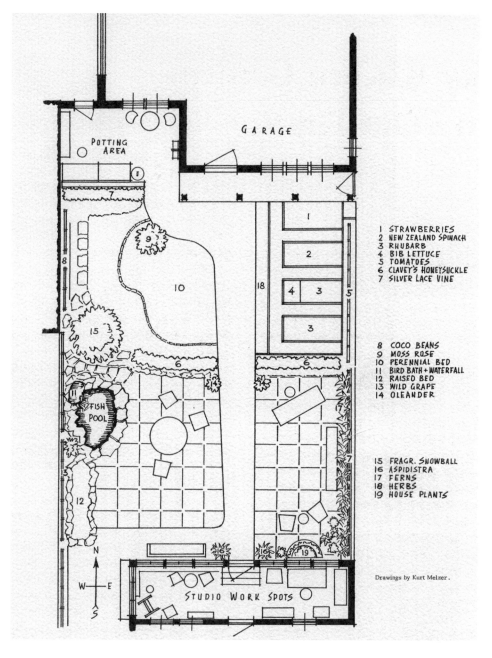

1 STRAWBERRIES
2 NEW ZEALAND SPINACH
3 RHUBARB
4 BIB LETTUCE
5 TOMATOES
6 CLAVEY'S HONEYSUCKLE
7 SILVER LACE VINE

8 COCO BEANS
9 MOSS ROSE
10 PERENNIAL BED
11 BIRD BATH + WATERFALL
12 RAISED BED
13 WILD GRAPE
14 OLEANDER

15 FRAGR. SNOWBALL
16 ASPIDISTRA
17 FERNS
18 HERBS
19 HOUSE PLANTS

Drawings by Kurt Melzer.

Garden Talks espoused innovative landscape design ideas, such as incorporating edibles into the perennial border.

Courtesy Lenhardt Library of the Chicago Botanic Garden.

Formal." Their article and accompanying plan diagram showed how spinach and beans coexisted harmoniously with a perennial bed and fish pool.[14]

Harold O. Klopp, the Palatine, Illinois, landscape architect and Society member who would later design many of the Society's tableaux at the flower shows, offered timely advice for garden renovations. In his *Garden Talks* article "Improving the Old Garden," Klopp tackled the common problem of redesigning a 20-year-old overgrown landscape. He depicted the state of many post–Depression era gardens:

> *Most back yards of the vintage of '20s or '30s are now entirely enclosed with a screening of lowering shrubs or small trees with a large expanse of open lawn in the center. . . . Probably there is a shade tree or more in the open lawn. Probably there are a few flower beds at various points along the shrub planting.*
>
> *But the shrubs, now probably 20 to 40 years old, have grown very thick and tall and are probably crowding each other. . . . They have an untidy appearance and form a considerable band of shaded area in which it is difficult to grow grass or most flowering plants.[15]*

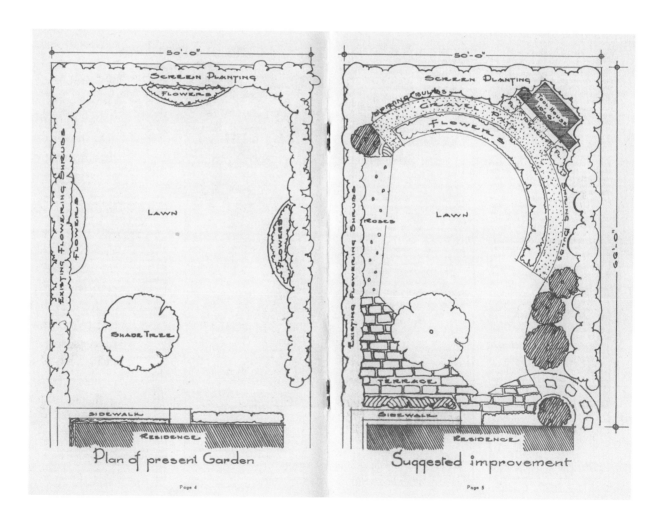

Landscape architect Harold O. Klopp proposed a much-needed renovation of old 1930s-style gardens in his 1956 Garden Talks *article.*

Courtesy Lenhardt Library of the Chicago Botanic Garden.

Klopp's proposed plan preserved many of the existing trees and shrubs while adding a curved perennial border and gravel walkway separated from the shade of the perimeter shrubs. With so many neglected "grandmothers' gardens" of perennial borders, this plan offered a refreshing option for the midcentury backyard.

Klopp, and other designers from garden clubs and regional garden centers, created a variety of landscape designs for the Society's revamped flower shows of the mid-twentieth century. In the World Flower and Garden Show of 1959, Klopp described the philosophy of the show's garden designs:

These gardens have been planned with the average home owners' problems in mind: How to get interest in the garden during the winter months with colorful building materials and how to pick up this color in the summer with flowering plants; how to take advantage of grade changes through the use of various retainers; how to ease maintenance problems by using as many permanent materials as possible.[16]

No longer were the shows devoted to cut flowers or prize potted specimens. Models of landscaped gardens highlighted the shows of the 1960s and 1970s. In 1961, for example, in addition to the foreign-influenced garden themes, the flower show featured "Fourteen Practical Gardens" by members of the Better Gardening Association. These design models, intended for any 10-by-15-foot garden, ranged from "Barbecue Patio" by Burger Nursery and Garden Center of Elgin to "Rocks in a Garden" by Harold's Garden Center and Nursery in Homewood. The Ornamental Growers Association of Northern Illinois sponsored an exhibit showing the maturation of a garden design by using various sizes of plant material in two similar garden designs. Amlings and Carson Pirie Scott sponsored two mirroring exhibits showing "Flowers 'N' Fashions 1870–1961" in which one garden featured a Victorian gazebo and all its trimmings and the other a "modern" barbecue with patio umbrella table.

Through its shows, publications, lectures, and tours from 1890 through the 1970s, the Chicago Horticultural Society inspired homeowners to embrace landscape design. To this arsenal of educational tools the Society added perhaps its most influential demonstration capability—the living landscape designs of the Chicago Botanic Garden.

The "Fun in the Sun" patio display by Sears Roebuck at the Chicago Horticultural Society's 1966 flower show emphasized outdoor entertaining.

Courtesy Lenhardt Library of the Chicago Botanic Garden.

The Chicago Botanic Garden—Pioneering Architecture and Landscape

The Chicago Botanic Garden offers a permanent place to explore landscape design. By the time of the Chicago Horticultural Society's 125th anniversary in 2015, the Garden contained more than 2.6 million plants on 385 acres. Displaying plants in a cohesive design that accomplishes the Society's mission has involved years of master planning, thoughtfully fine-tuned for new opportunities or contingencies.

In the very early planning stages, Society leadership considered several design options for the Garden. Many arboreta and public gardens of the day were organized by genus and species, such as Harvard's Arnold Arboretum, or were former pleasure gardens of prominent individuals, such as George Washington's Mount Vernon. Five approaches to plant arrangement for public gardens were considered: systematic (groupings by evolutionary order or scientific classification), synoptic (best representative plants of a range), landscape garden (for general landscape effect), demonstration garden (how-to examples for homeowners), and public display garden (seasonal shows of flowering plants).

The Society's Board decided to incorporate the best of all design types, as noted in a 1969 report by Francis de Vos, vice president of the Society and director of the Garden:

> *While the scientific program and concern for accuracy must never be compromised it is felt that a purely "botanic" arrangement of the collections is not desirable. Instead the plan layout should be more free. The larger landscape should be subdivided into garden spaces of many types each suited to its own special purposes and each with its own unique landscape quality. Even the parking and service areas should be of garden character.*
>
> *There should be synoptic gardens, there should be demonstration gardens, and there should be seasonal displays.* [17]

Balancing these garden types with the Society's mission, and with other demands such as the education and research value of plant collections, can involve many experts. Kris Jarantoski, currently the Garden's executive vice president and director, has worked at the Garden since the 1970s. "Every ten years we do a strategic plan," he explained. "Out of that comes a master site plan." [18] Potential initiatives consistent with the Society's mission are articulated and then prioritized by the Garden staff; the initiatives are approved by the Society's Board; and the new or revamped gardens follow.

An early design concept that continues today, according to Jarantoski, is to have more intensive gardens in the center islands, with a gradual shift to more native plants and naturalistic designs on the periphery. Thus, the Heritage Garden, the Krasberg Rose Garden, and the Regenstein Fruit & Vegetable Garden on the main island are planted with many plant varieties—native and nonnative—while the outlying Dixon Prairie focuses on Illinois natives.

A significant and prevailing influence on the design of the Garden is the choice of architectural style for the buildings. The Garden's Board wanted a modernistic style for the Garden's buildings, beginning with the choice of architect Harry Weese for the first structures, the maintenance building and the research and production facility. Modernism was again preferred in the selection of architect Edward L. Barnes for the Education Building (renamed the Regenstein Center).

Edward Larrabee Barnes (1915–2004) had already received national acclaim for his work along with fellow Harvard colleagues Henry Cobb, Ulrich Frazen, John Johansen, Philip Johnson, and I. M. Pei. His master plan for the Haystack Mountain School of Crafts, developed at about the same time as the Garden, shows a similar respect for the environment and won the American Institute of Architects' prestigious Twenty-Five Year Award.[19] Barnes's style also showed a modernistic flair. The master plan conceived by Barnes has been continued through the work of architect Laurence Booth, whose firm,

Booth Hansen, has completed several projects in the new millennium.

True to form, Barnes's design of the Garden's Regenstein Center defied classification. *Inland Architect* magazine described the building as "non-pop, nonhistoricistic, non-ironical, non-post-modernist that succeeds by virtue of its designer's subdued but firm and unmistakably personal style."[20] Barnes, a New Yorker, noted, speaking of himself, "This architect likes clarity; the clear separation of man and nature, Maine lighthouses, Wisconsin barns and silos and crystalline forms in nature. Perhaps this building has such clarity."[21]

The single-level, cruciform Regenstein Center featured courtyards on the east-west axes and a cluster of pyramidal-roofed greenhouses on the south. The elegant tree-lined walkway leading to the north entrance, ultimately redesigned by Dan Kiley's landscape architecture firm, visually extended into the interior main gallery with narrow reflecting pool and skylit ceiling. The building, despite Barnes's self-proclaimed desire for distinction between "man and nature," is tailored to blend into the landscape.

The Regenstein Center set the forward-looking tone for future construction at the Garden, both in the landscape design and in new facilities, but it was not without controversy. William Pullman and some Board members had desired a more traditional, formal building. A schism developed within the Board, with the majority vote favoring the contemporary Barnes building. Pullman, convinced that the Board had set the wrong direction for the Garden, resigned in 1968. Although the Board disagreed with his stance, it acknowledged his significant contributions by awarding him the Society's 1968 Hutchinson Medal.

Seeking a landscape architect with a compatible design sensibility, the Board chose John O. Simonds (no

The modernistic style of architect Edward L. Barnes's Education Building, now the Regenstein Center, set the tone for the buildings and future landscapes at the Garden.

known relation to O. C. Simonds) of Pittsburgh. The landscape architecture firm of Simonds and Simonds, later renamed Environmental Planning and Design, created the original master plan for the Chicago Botanic Garden and designed many of the individual gardens.

Simonds is widely hailed for his early influence in integrating environmentalism with landscape design. His style is described as modernist and romantic.[22] Geoffrey Rausch, Simonds's successor to the firm, continued to design landscapes for the Garden for many years. These innovators in environmental design helped shape the Garden—which itself grew from conservation efforts of the Forest Preserve District of Cook County.

John O. Simonds prepared the first master plan for the Chicago Botanic Garden.

Courtesy Chicago Botanic Garden Photo Archives.

Geoffrey Rausch, Simonds's successor to the firm, worked with the Chicago Botanic Garden for decades to develop individual gardens from the master plan.

Courtesy Chicago Botanic Garden Photo Archives.

While each garden is unique to the site and program requirements, the Society's design process is consistent. The Garden's philosophy was spelled out in 1996: "One of the single most important activities that is carried out at the Chicago Botanic Garden is the designing and planning of its gardens. This includes the development of major new gardens such as the Waud Circle Garden, the planning of smaller new gardens like the Betty Brown Meadow, modification and improvements to existing gardens, such as the Lavin Plant Evaluation Garden, and the seasonal designing of annual flower beds and container plantings."[23]

According to this thinking, larger gardens would be designed by "nationally recognized landscape architects/planners" with substantial experience in large public gardens. "The best local landscape architects" would be selected for smaller gardens, and Garden staff and planners, also involved in any garden design, would create seasonal displays and plant replacements. The Society articulated specific criteria for

The Home Landscape Center was among the first gardens installed.

Courtesy Kris Jarantoski.

evaluating new garden concepts; it stated that a proposed garden should "fit with the Society's mission and strategic plan; meet aesthetic and quality standards; reinforce and complement existing designs, and the desired sense of place, space and vistas; meet requirements for the American Disabilities Act; increase scope and strengthen content of plant collections; be appropriate for the Society's conservation ethic; respond to sustainable maintenance; [and] provide opportunities to educate the public about the people/plant connection."[24]

But in the 1970s, having just opened the Garden, the Society had not had the time to consider all the complexities of designing a botanic garden from scratch. Geoffrey Rausch recalled the learning experience involved for all: "Nobody at that time was thinking about botanical collections." In its early plans, the Society had considered collections in a designed landscape, but few real-life examples existed. He credited Francis de Vos for orienting the compass toward creating designs with educational underpinnings. De Vos recognized that a proper design could not be developed without understanding the Garden's program requirements. Therefore, "John [Simonds] and Francis sat down for a week in a cottage in Michigan and developed a program," Rausch said.[25]

This program has evolved with the Society's mission statement and all the strategic planning efforts and operational programs to date. But in the 1970s, busy with construction and planting, the Society opened just two gardens: the Home Landscape Center and the Learning Garden for the Disabled. The first, located on the site of the former William Pullman Plant Evaluation Garden, inspired home gardeners to adopt landscape design ideas in their own properties. The Learning Garden for the Disabled, at 100 by 50 feet, included an adaptive tool display and demonstrated horticultural techniques for those with physical disabilities. It was closed in 1999 with its purpose better served by the Buehler Enabling Garden. These two gardens helped show the many design possibilities for the Chicago Botanic Garden.

Meanwhile, amid this busy start-up period, the Society continued to add detail to its master plan and approved an ambitious expansion for the next decade.

Gardens of the 1980s

Fourteen gardens were added to the Chicago Botanic Garden during the 1980s. Built in 1981, the Farwell Home Demonstration Garden (now the Farwell Landscape Garden) brought visitors to the main island to see the best plants for the Midwest used in imaginative but practical landscape treatments. Shortly thereaf-

ter, Rausch planned the Graham Bulb Garden and the Aquatic Garden (1983), to be followed the next year by a one-quarter-acre Naturalistic Garden (now the Native Plant Garden). This cluster of four gardens at the northwest lobe of the main island offered many ideas on how to use a wide diversity of landscape plants in small spaces.

The Regenstein Fruit & Vegetable Garden, a key destination connected to the northwest of the main island by a bridge, was dedicated in 1985. The garden encapsulated all of the Society's traditions of victory gardens, school gardens, and backyard growing gardens in a beautiful landscape. This demonstration of edible plants incorporated among ornamentals gave concrete examples to the growing body of popular literature on the topic.

During this flurry of activity on the main island, a quiet work of landscape art sculpted around the lakes rose as Sansho-En, the Garden of the Three Islands (today also known as the Elizabeth Hubert Malott

The Learning Garden for the Disabled demonstrated the Garden's deep commitment to the emerging field of horticultural therapy. Wide pathways and raised beds were early components of accessible gardens.

Courtesy Lenhardt Library of the Chicago Botanic Garden.

Japanese Garden). Dedicated in 1982 and designed by UCLA Professor Koichi Kawana, Ph.D., this traditional Japanese stroll garden was planned with exacting attention to authentic Japanese culture and design.

Garden director Roy Mecklenburg, Ph.D., articulated the obvious question during the garden's conception and construction phases: "Why are we developing a Japanese garden at the Chicago Botanic Garden? Wouldn't it be more appropriate to develop English, French or Spanish Gardens? There are many delightful styles of garden design but the design of Japanese gardens is unique, enticing the visitor to see nature in a fresh and exciting manner, the primary purpose of the Botanic Garden."[26]

Japanese gardens have enjoyed a popularity in American horticulture since their public debut at the 1876 Centennial Exposition in Philadelphia. World's fairs in the United States helped introduce many Americans to the unique beauty of Japanese gardens, including the garden on the Wooded Island at Chicago's World's Columbian Exposition of 1893.[27] That garden, today's Osaka Garden, had been renovated with structures from the Japanese garden at Chicago's 1933–34 Century of Progress World's Fair. Many other public gardens had created Japanese gardens, including Golden Gate Park (its Tea Garden was created in 1894), Huntington Botanic Garden (1911), and the Brooklyn Botanic Garden (1915). Missouri Botanical Garden in St. Louis dedicated its 14-acre Japanese Garden, Seiwa-En, in 1977. The Anderson Japanese Gardens in Rockford, Illinois, opened in 1978.

Despite other examples, with its series of islands surrounded by tranquil waters, perhaps no other public garden is as suited for a Japanese garden as the Chicago Botanic Garden. Dr. Kawana wrote of Japanese gardens, "Japan is a group of islands surrounded by oceans and seas. From ancient times the Japanese people had an affinity for the sea. Water as a design element in the garden is crucial. . . . A sea without islands is unthinkable and in the creation of such islands the Japanese owe much to the concepts imported from China. . . ." [28] Thus, John O. Simonds's initial inspiration of the Chinese Imperial Gardens melded brilliantly with the Society's vision for a Japanese Garden.

Koichi Kawana, Ph.D., designed the Sansho-En Japanese garden at the Chicago Botanic Garden, known today as the Elizabeth Hubert Malott Japanese Garden.

Courtesy Kris Jarantoski.

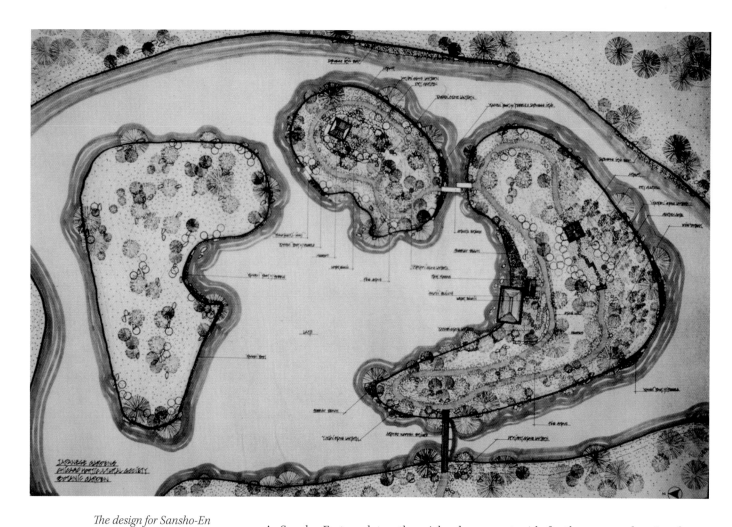

The design for Sansho-En features three islands, one of which is not reachable on foot.

Courtesy Lenhardt Library of the Chicago Botanic Garden.

As Sansho-En translates, three islands were set aside for the new garden. Sansho-En connected to the southeast side of the main island through an arched wooden bridge. Made of fragrant cedar and cypress, the bridge is the symbolic link between Earth and paradise. Keiunto (Island of the Auspicious Cloud) is the first and largest island of Sansho-En. A *shoin* building enhanced by a moss garden is furnished with traditional Japanese items. A zigzag granite slab bridge then leads to Seifuto (Island of Pure, Clear Breezes), from which can be seen—but not accessed—Horaijima (Island of Everlasting Happiness).

Kawana's design for Sansho-En includes all of the elements he deemed necessary for a true Japanese garden, including asymmetry, simplicity, and naturalness. An expert in Japanese culture as well as garden design, Kawana insisted on authenticity in all aspects. Writing to Dr. Mecklenburg, Kawana explained why the *shoin* house needed to be assembled in Japan despite the cost:

Today, even ordinary Japanese carpenters cannot build this kind of building. . . . Only a few Japanese carpenters called miyadaiku *who specialize in building traditional shrines and temples can construct this kind of structure. Due to the skill and details required many of these carpenters spend more than ten years as apprentices learning fundamental skills. After spending two years installing the Japanese garden with me you have realized that it is not merely a question of designing and drawing up the plan for the Japanese garden but, more important, it is the personal arrangement and installation of each element that makes the garden.*[29]

A light mist adds to the ethereal quality of Horaijima, the Island of Everlasting Happiness—one of three islands composing the Elizabeth Hubert Malott Japanese Garden, Sansho-en. Horaijima represents paradise and is intended to be viewed and contemplated from a distance.

Water mirrors the sculptured form of trees and hills in the Elizabeth Hubert Malott Japanese Garden.

The Arched Bridge connects the main island with Keiunto, the Island of the Auspicious Cloud. Note the various styles of Japanese lanterns.

The Zigzag Bridge, a granite slab, leads to Seifuto. Note the shoin *building in the background.*

Robert H. Malott oversaw the ribbon cutting for the Elizabeth Hubert Malott Japanese Garden, named after his wife and dedicated in 2006. Recipient of the 2012 Chicago Horticultural Society Medal, Malott has served as a Society Board member since 2000.

Even the smallest details on Sansho-En faithfully reference a traditional Japanese garden—from the many shapes of stone lanterns to the groomed dry gardens of gravel to the *ichimonji* tiled garden gate. Many plants hail from the Midwest, consistent with Kawana's philosophy that the plants in the Japanese garden should repeat those used in surrounding gardens and seen from the Japanese garden.

The meticulous design and construction of the Japanese garden served as a template for the design processes to follow. The 14 gardens of the 1980s remained true to the Chicago Botanic Garden's mission of the time: to "promote the enjoyment, understanding, and conservation of plants and the natural world." Many of the gardens reflected or presaged trends in the landscape design world, such as edible landscaping in the Regenstein Fruit & Vegetable Garden or the resurgence of popular interest in water gardening in the Aquatic Garden. The Learning Garden for the Disabled, revolutionary for its time, predated the 1990 Americans with Disabilities Act. The Prairie (1985) and the Naturalistic Garden (1984) brought burgeoning scientific movements such as the environmentalism of the late 1970s to the forefront.

Gardens of the 1990s and the New Millennium

In the 1990s, as the Chicago Horticultural Society celebrated its centennial, six new gardens emerged from the drawing board and ultimately onto the campus of the Chicago Botanic Garden. The decade opened with a nod to America's English garden heritage, with the dedication of the English Walled Garden in 1991. At the end of the decade, the Society recommitted to its roots in horticultural therapy by opening the Buehler Enabling Garden.

In 1995, Barbara Whitney Carr became president and CEO of the Garden. Formerly the president of the Lincoln Park Zoological Society, Carr spearheaded a multi-million-dollar long-range plan and fundraising campaign. The effort translated to several new or renovated gardens. Carr also dramatically enhanced the education program, forging relationships with Northwestern University, the University of Illinois, and the Illinois Institute of Technology. In choosing Carr as recipient of the Garden's 2007 Hutchinson medal, the award committee also recognized her success in laying the groundwork for the new Plant Science Center. During Carr's tenure, the following were created: McGinley Pavilion, Circle Garden, English Oak Meadow, Buehler Enabling Garden, Spider Island, the Crescent, and the Esplanade.

The latter three exemplify the many different design styles exhibited at the Garden. Spider Island, created by landscape architect Michael Van Valkenburgh, is the most diminutive of the Garden's nine islands, yet its naturalistic design offers a complete escape from the everyday world. Plantings along the shoreline blur the edges and make the island seem larger than it is. A curling perimeter path, slightly recessed into the ground, screens outside views and offers a sense of enclosure.

The Esplanade and Crescent are much more formal in design. The Esplanade presents a grand entrance to the Regenstein Center, with a majestic walkway of trees outlining a panel of lawn. The linear precision of the trees complements the modern lines of the building. The smooth arcs and brilliant colors of the nearby Crescent garden share the geometric design but provide a foreground to the sparkling fountain and lake beyond.

Sophia Shaw succeeded Carr as CEO and president of the Garden in 2007 and has further propelled the Garden into international prominence in the areas of science and new gardens. Shaw, previously the Garden's vice president of visitor operations, brought curatorial and museum management expertise from Chicago's Field Museum, the Art Institute of Chicago, and the Museum of Contemporary Art. New gardens are also planned under Shaw's leadership. An ambitious ten-year stragetic plan launched in early 2010 calls for new gardens from the Kris Jarantoski Campus on the south to the Regenstein Foundation Learning Campus on the north.

In 2008, the Dwarf Conifer Garden—featuring more than 150 varieties of the smallest members of the conifer family—was renovated. In 2009, the Green Roof Gar-

den (the collective name for the Josephine P. & John J. Louis Foundation Green Rood Garden North and the Ellis Goodman Family Foundation Green Roof Garden South) opened with both scientific and display gardens. Atop the Daniel F. and Ada L. Rice Plant Conservation Science Center, the Green Roof Garden demonstrates how plants can be used to reduce urban heat islands and insulate buildings from heat. Further assisting plant evaluations, in 2011, the Bernice E. Lavin Plant Evaluation Garden reopened following redesign. The Lavin Evaluation Garden provides the opportunity to evaluate plants in a sunny area; the William Pullman Evaluation Garden provided a shady site in which to evaluate plants until 2013, and similar evaluations will occur in a garden designed by Peter Wirtz for the Jarantoski Campus. The Trellis Bridge, completed in 2012,

Designed by Dan Kiley, the plan for the Esplanade offers a grand entrance to the front door of the Regenstein Center.

connects the Lavin Garden and Plant Science Center to Evening Island.

Evening Island (the centerpiece of the Gardens of the Great Basin, 2002) and Spider Island became the final two islands to complete today's nine islands of the Chicago Botanic Garden. Both new islands feature a naturalistic design. Evening Island, once designated and planted with evergreens, represents the New American Garden style pioneered by the Oehme, van Sweden landscape architecture firm. Integrating this island with the Garden's other islands required an extensive look at the water-shoreline-land interfaces and tapped into the Society's research on aquatic plantings. Fittingly, this prominent water garden of the new millennium addresses the Garden's heritage as a former marsh.

The firm of landscape architect Dan Kiley, pictured here, created the modern landscape to complement the Regenstein Center.

Courtesy Aaron Kiley.

The Native Plant Garden, formerly the Naturalistic Garden, features native plants arranged in landscape compositions.

The Sensory Garden includes plants with a variety of textures and fragrances.

The Waterfall Garden cascades from a man-made hilltop to a scenic path below.

The Circle Garden features an ever-changing landscape of annuals mixed with shrubs and perennials.

Chicago Botanic Garden Landscapes Over Time

1972

Turnbull Woods
(renamed McDonald Woods, 1994)

Formerly the Turnbull Woods, McDonald Woods is named in honor of Mary Mix McDonald, former Cook County Commissioner and Chicago Horticultural Society board member, who championed the cause to add this natural area to those under Chicago Botanic Garden management. The addition of the woods was also made possible through the support of the Cook County Forest Preserves Commissioners and former Forest Preserve Superintendent Joe Nevius.

Home Landscape Center
(renamed William Pullman Plant Evaluation Garden, 1982)

The William Pullman Plant Evaluation Garden was named in honor of William Allan Pinkerton Pullman to honor his interest in plant introductions and his pioneering work at the Chicago Botanic Garden. The garden was closed in 2014 to make room for future plant production greenhouses, and as a result the Pullman Room in the Regenstein Center was named to honor William A. P. Pullman. The original garden was designed by Environmental Planning & Design, and the redesign was done in-house.

1978

Greenhouses

The Greenhouses were dedicated in honor of former Woman's Board president Nancy Zimmerman Race and were designed by Edward Larrabee Barnes.

1981

Farwell Landscape Garden
(renovated 2001)

The Farwell Landscape Garden was named in 1984 in honor of Edith and Albert Farwell for their many contributions to the Society and the world of plants. In 2001, the Woman's Board of the Chicago Horticultural Society funded a revitalization of the garden. The Farwell Landscape Garden was designed by Environmental Design & Planning.

1982

Elizabeth Hubert Malott Japanese Garden
(rededicated 2006)

Designed by Koichi Kawana, Ph.D., the Japanese Garden was opened in 1982 as a result of the contributions of many thoughtful donors. In 2006 the garden was rededicated as the Elizabeth Hubert Malott Japanese Garden through an endowment gift from the Malott family.

1983

Graham Bulb Garden
(renovated 2001)

The Edna Kanaley Graham Bulb Garden was made possible through the support of William B. Graham, who named the garden in memory of his wife. Graham also provided an endowment to ensure that the Graham Bulb Garden will be enjoyed by future generations. The Graham Bulb Garden was designed by Environmental Planning & Design.

Aquatic Garden

The Aquatic Garden was made possible by the Kresge Foundation and was designed by Environmental Planning & Design.

1984

Heritage Garden

The Heritage Garden was made possible through the support of Gertrude B. Nielsen and was designed by Environmental Planning & Design.

Naturalistic Garden
(renamed Native Plant Garden, 2002)

The Ellen Thorne Smith Native Plant Garden, formerly the Ellen Thorne Smith Naturalistic Garden, was made possible by a gift from Ellen Thorne Smith's estate, her husband the late Hermon Dunlap "Dutch" Smith, and family and friends in 1984. In 2002, Chicago Wilderness provided additional support. The Native Plant Garden was designed by Environmental Planning & Design.

1985

Krasberg Rose Garden

The Krasberg Rose Garden was named in honor of rosarian Bruce Krasberg, Chicago Horticultural Society board member. He and his family created an endowment to help ensure that the Krasberg Rose Garden will be enjoyed by future generations. The Krasberg Rose Garden was designed by Environmental Planning & Design.

Regenstein Fruit & Vegetable Garden
(rededicated 1997)

The Regenstein Fruit & Vegetable Garden was made possible by the support of the Regenstein Foundation and was designed (and redesigned) by Environmental Planning & Design.

1987

Sensory Garden

The William T. Bacon Sensory Garden was made possible through the support of Martha Smith Bacon and the William T. Bacon family and friends, with additional support from the Dr. Scholl Foundation and Kraft, Inc., and in consultation with Hadley School for the Blind, which also provided financial support. The Sensory Garden was designed by Environmental Planning & Design and Scott Byron & Co.

1988

Dwarf Conifer Garden
(rededicated 2008)

The Dwarf Conifer Garden was made possible by a gift from the Woman's Board of the Chicago Horticultural Society in 1988 and then renovated in 2008 with a gift from Georgiana M. Taylor. Originally designed by the landscape design firm Marshall, Tyler, Rausch, the Dwarf Conifer Garden was redesigned by Douglas Hoerr Landscape Architecture.

Perennial Test Garden
(renamed Lavin Plant Evaluation Garden, 1998)

The Bernice E. Lavin Plant Evaluation Garden was made possible through the support of the Lavin Family Foundation. The original Perennial Test Garden was designed by Environmental Planning & Design; the redesigned Lavin Plant Evaluation Garden was designed by Oehme, van Sweden & Associates.

Waterfall Garden

The Waterfall Garden was made possible by a gift from the estate of James Brown IV with additional support from The Chicago Community Trust, The Field Foundation of Illinois, Inc., and the Chauncey and Marion Deering McCormick Foundation. The John W. Taylor Family has created an endowment to support an area of the Waterfall Garden for future generations. The Waterfall Garden was designed by Environmental Planning & Design.

1991

English Walled Garden

The English Walled Garden was made possible through the support of the Baird Foundation, Mr. and Mrs. John P. Bent, Mr. and Mrs. Kenneth A. Bro, The Catherine Galitzine Campbell Memorial Fund, the Mona and Neil Coleman Family, The Garden Guild of Winnetka, Mr. and Mrs. David W. Grainger, Mr. and Mrs. M. James Leider, Mrs. John J. Louis, The Honorable and Mrs. John J. Louis, Jr., Mr. Michael W. Louis, Geraldi Norton Memorial Corporation, Arch W. Shaw Foundation, Mr. and Mrs. Bruce Thorne, and the Woman's Board of the Chicago Horticultural Society. The English Walled Garden was designed by John Brookes.

1993

Dixon Prairie

The Dixon Prairie was created with the support of Sue and Wes Dixon, who also have provided an endowment through the Searle Family Trust to ensure that the prairie will be enjoyed by future generations. Early components of the prairie were completed through contributions from the John D. and Catherine T. MacArthur Foundation, the Dr. Scholl Foundation, and the Searle Family Trust. The Dixon Prairie was designed by Environmental Planning & Design.

1994

Skokie River Corridor

The Skokie River Corridor enhancement, begun in 1994, was made possible through the support of the U.S. and Illinois Environmental Protection Agencies.

1997

Circle Garden

The Circle Garden was made possible through the support of Anne and Morrison Waud, who also have provided an endowment to ensure that the garden will be enjoyed for future generations. The Circle Garden was designed by Environmental Planning & Design.

1999

Buehler Enabling Garden

The Buehler Enabling Garden was made possible through the support of the Buehler Family Foundation, which also has provided an endowment to ensure that the garden will serve future generations. The State of Illinois and the Public Museum Capital Grants Program, Illinois Department of Natural Resources, Illinois State Museum also contributed to the Enabling Garden. The Garden recognizes the Kenilworth Garden Club and the Garden Club of Barrington for their leadership in founding the original Learning Garden for the Disabled in 1974. The Buehler Enabling Garden was designed by the landscape design firm Marshall, Tyler, Rausch.

2001

Spider Island

Spider Island was made possible by a gift from Esther Grunsfeld Klatz and Ernest A. Grunsfeld III in memory of Sally Grunsfeld. Spider Island was designed by Michael Van Valkenburgh Associates.

English Oak Meadow

The English Oak Meadow was made possible through the support of the Dr. Scholl Foundation, as well as gifts from the Morrison Waud and Corwith Hamill Families in honor of Elizabeth Byron Brown, a former Woman's Board President. The English Oak Meadow was designed by Scott Byron & Co.

2002

Evening Island

Evening Island was made possible through a gift given by Pleasant T. Rowland in memory of her father, Edward M. Thiele. The Overlook was given by Mr. and Mrs. John H. Krehbiel, Jr., in memory of Connie Bates Lang. The State of Illinois and the Public Museum Capital Grants Program, Illinois Department of Natural Resources, Illinois State Museum also contributed to Evening Island, which was designed by Oehme, van Sweden & Associates.

Gardens of the Great Basin

The Gardens of the Great Basin, designed by Oehme, van Sweden & Associates, and including the Arch and Serpentine Bridges, were made possible by the generosity and vision of private donors and government agencies charged with maintaining the region's natural resources.

Lakeside Gardens

The Lakeside Gardens were made possible through a gift given by Pleasant T. Rowland in honor of her mother, Pleasant Williams Thiele, and were designed by Oehme, van Sweden & Associates.

Water Gardens

The Water Gardens were made possible through a gift from the Woman's Board of the Chicago Horticultural Society and from individual donors. The Water Gardens were designed by Oehme, van Sweden & Associates.

2005

The Crescent

The Crescent was developed with support from Neville F. Bryan and designed by Dan Kiley and Peter Morrow Meyer.

The Esplanade

The Esplanade was developed with support from Howard J. and Paula M. Trienens, the John Simms Family, Neville F. Bryan, Mr. and Mrs. James J. Glasser, Mr. and Mrs. Morrison Waud, and other donors. The State of Illinois and the Public Museum Capital Grants Program, Illinois Department of Natural Resources, Illinois State Museum also contributed to the Esplanade. The Esplanade was designed by Dan Kiley and Peter Morrow Meyer.

2009

Plant Science Center Gardens

Ellis Goodman Family Foundation Green Roof Garden South

Josephine P. & John. J. Louis Foundation Green Roof Garden North

The Green Roof Garden at the Daniel F. and Ada L. Rice Plant Conservation Science Center was made possible by the support of the Ellis Goodman Family Foundation and the Josephine P. & John J. Louis Foundation. The designer of the Green Roof Garden was Oehme, van Sweden & Associates.

Barbara Brown Nature Reserve

The Barbara Brown Nature Reserve was made possible by the support of Barbara and Roger Brown.

2011

Trellis Bridge

In 2011 the Trellis Bridge opened, designed by Oehme, van Sweden and connecting Evening Island with the Lavin Evaluation Garden and Plant Science Center. The Trellis Bridge was made possible by the support of Mr. and Mrs. William T. Hagenah.

2012

Garden Lakes/ Shoreline Restoration

The shoreline restoration project, completed in 2012, which restored 4.5 miles of shoreline surrounding a 60-acre system of lakes, was made possible by the U.S. Army Corps of Engineers' Chicago District; U.S. and Illinois Environmental Protection Agencies; John and Mary Helen Slater; the Illinois Department of Commerce and Economic Opportunity; the State of Illinois and the Public Museum Capital Grants Program, Illinois Department of Natural Resources, Illinois State Museum; and several other donors.

Grunsfeld Children's Growing Garden

The Grunsfeld Children's Growing Garden was made possible through the generosity of Esther Grunsfeld Klatz and Ernest A. Grunsfeld III; the Robert R. McCormick Foundation; the Woman's Board of the Chicago Horticultural Society; the Guild of the Chicago Botanic Garden; the support of the Public Museum Capital Grants Program, Illinois Department of Natural Resources, Illinois State Museum; Lorraine Ipsen-Stotler; The Hekman Gordon Family; Barbara and Richard Metzler; the Colonel Stanley R. McNeil Foundation; and Make It Better. The Grunsfeld Children's Growing Garden was designed by Scott Byron and Associates.

Kleinman Family Cove

The Kleinman Family Cove was made possible by the support of the Kleinman Family and designed by Oehme, van Sweden & Associates.

2014+

Keep Growing

Planning continues at the Chicago Botanic Garden, with many significant improvement projects under way or on the horizon. The "Keep Growing" ten-year (2010–20) strategic plan includes the Regenstein Foundation Learning Campus, with an Education Center planned as a Leadership in Energy & Environmental Design (LEED) certified project by the architecture firm of Booth Hansen, and a garden whose concept vision was provided by Mikyoung Kim. The Kris Jarantoski Campus—named to honor the executive vice president and director for his guiding vision— will feature an energy-efficient plant production facility that will alleviate the overtaxed existing greenhouses, some built in 1969 and others that were donated in 1981, and expand the nursery. Three other projects of the Keep Growing plan have been completed: a new addition to the North Branch Trail that connects the Garden's entrance to the Green Bay Trail, a renovated Garden View Café, and the Barbara Brown Nature Reserve. Improvements to the McDonald Woods will be imple- mented as a final part of the plan.

KEY:
1. Lake Cook Road Median
2. Lake Cook Road Entrance
3. Bike Path
4. McDonald Woods
5. Carr Administration Center
6. Entrance Garden & Parking Lot
7. Visitor Center
8. Education Center
9. Children's Growing Garden
10. Learning Campus Garden
11. The Cove
12. Bird Island
13. The Crescent
14. Heritage Garden
15. The Esplanade
16. Smith Fountain
17. Native Plant Garden
18. Regenstein Fruit & Vegetable Garden
19. Graham Bulb Garden
20. Aquatic Garden
21. Farwell Landscape Garden
22. Arbor Walk
23. Model Railroad Garden
24. Circle Garden
25. Spire Garden Overlook
26. Spider Island
27. Sensory Garden
28. Buehler Enabling Garden
29. Regenstein Center
30. Display Greenhouses
31. McGinley Pavilion
32. English Walled Garden
33. Krasberg Rose Garden
34. Dwarf Conifer Garden
35. English Oak Meadow
36. Waterfall Garden
37. Malott Japanese Garden
38. East Lakeside Gardens

39. West Lakeside Gardens
40. Great Basin
41. Evening Island
42. Butz Carillon
43. Festival Field
44. Aster Overlook
45. Winter Interest Garden
46. River Valley
47. Garden Wall
48. Spring Overlook
49. Oak Grove
50. Rose Cascade
51. Edens Sign
52. Rose Gallery
53. Great Lawn
54. Peony Walk
55. Amelanchier Collection
56. River Walk
57. Bird House Point
58. The Glen
59. Pine Grove
60. Dixon Prairie
61. Marsh Island
62. Lavin Plant Evaluation Garden
63. Rice Plant Conservation Science Center & Roof Gardens
64. Science Center Expansion Site
65. Storage Buildings
66. Nursery & Greenhouses
67. In-Ground Nursery
68. Heal-in Area
69. Native Plant Nursery
70. Storage Area
71. Leaf Mulch Area
72. Construction Building
73. Maintenance Building
74. Brown Nature Reserve
75. Dundee Road Entrance

CHICAGO BOTANIC GARDEN
MASTER SITE PLAN - OCTOBER 2012

The master planning process continues, designed by such firms as Oehme, van Sweden, with innovative landscapes complementing new buildings.

The diversity and innovation in the Chicago Botanic Garden's landscapes is evident in these two examples: Evening Island, which represents a uniquely American design style, and the English Walled Garden, which honors centuries of traditional English garden design.

CHICAGO BOTANIC GARDEN
The Lakeside & Water Gardens of the Great Basin

McGinley Pavilion

Buehler Enabling Garden

N

Puryer Point

Water Gardens

Lakeside Gardens

Lakeside Gardens

Great Basin

Water Gardens

Dudley Point

Evening Island

The centerpiece of the Gardens of the Great Basin, Evening Island was formerly called Evergreen Island.

Courtesy Lenhardt Library of the Chicago Botanic Garden.

The sun sets over the Great Basin, with the Arch Bridge in the background.

Judicious selection of aquatic plants helps prevent shoreline erosion and improve water quality.
Courtesy Robert Kirschner.

CHICAGO AND ITS BOTANIC GARDEN

Crabapple trees line a path on Evening Island leading to the Theodore C. Butz Memorial Carillon.

CHICAGO AND ITS BOTANIC GARDEN

Evening Island features hillside, woodland, and meadow gardens filled with broad sweeps of perennials and ornamental grasses.

The Lakeside Terrace of the Gardens of the Great Basin offers panoramic views from water level.

As the sun sets in summer, lights add drama to the beauty of Evening Island.

Designed by the influential landscape architecture firm Oehme, van Sweden of Washington, D.C., the Gardens of the Great Basin are an important example of the New American Garden style of landscape design. Pioneered by Wolfgang Oehme and James van Sweden, this style takes its inspiration from the American meadow and the midwestern prairie. The design is characterized by masses of perennials and ornamental grasses combined and layered to form dramatic tapestries of color, texture, and movement that change through the seasons.

The Gardens of the Great Basin—the Water Gardens, Lakeside Gardens, and Evening Island—encircle the Chicago Botanic Garden's central lake and extend into the water. They are linked by scenic pathways and distinctive bridges and graced with terraces, overlooks, and seating areas where one can linger and take in views of the lake and surrounding gardens.[30]

Evening Island and the Lakeside Gardens were given by Pleasant T. Rowland in memory of her father, Edward M. Thiele, and in honor of her mother, Pleasant Thiele. Here, Pleasant Rowland (right) is pictured with her sister, former Garden president and CEO Barbara Whitney Carr, who led the Garden from 1995 to 2007.

"We knew in approaching the site that the water was the true centerpiece of the garden, so we spent a great deal of time thinking about the way the water and the land would interface and how visitors would interact with the shoreline spaces," wrote James van Sweden of the design process.[31] During construction, the entire basin was drained of its 16 million gallons of water—van Sweden recounted the discovery of an old submerged car with a set of golf clubs in the trunk—to allow the work on the island. Oehme, van Sweden's founders lived to see the opening of the Gardens of the Great Basin but died not long after, Oehme in 2011 and van Sweden in 2013.

Lisa Delplace, the current CEO of Oehme, van Sweden, agrees that water is one of the key elements of the Chicago Botanic Garden. She carefully studied Evening Island's shoreline edges to determine the ideal plants and sculptural treatments for the new landscape. The plantings needed to withstand the rigors of wave action, winds, water temperature, and other microclimate factors. "There's so much science behind all of the gardens at the Chicago Botanic Garden," Delplace says, recalling numerous consultations with the Garden's scientists and tapping into the Garden's extensive research on aquatic plants.[32]

Evening Island and the other Great Basin gardens pay tribute to the heritage and natural history of the Chicago Botanic Garden. Delplace says the New American Garden style is rooted in "what the garden wants to be," that is, a site-specific design that does not impose on the natural features of the land. Delplace, who, like van Sweden, studied at the University of Michigan, is well versed in the prairie school of design. The council ring atop the knoll on Evening Island and the mix of native plantings with nonnative plants that were well adapted to the Midwest echo the early philosophy of Society member and landscape pioneer Jens Jensen.

Also Jensenesque are the more than 300 crabapple trees—one of Jensen's typically used plants—that encircle the Great Basin. But, while Jensen may have restricted himself to the native crabapple (*Malus ioensis*), five cultivars are used. Not only is this artistic blending of natives and cultivars a hallmark of the New American Garden style, but it is also important for the diversity of the Chicago Botanic Garden's plant collections and its education mission.

Although a self-contained island, Evening Island blends well with the Chicago Botanic Garden's other landscapes. Delplace calls Evening Island a "steppingstone" between the more manicured designs, such as the English Walled Garden, and the unbridled nature in the prairie.

Delplace says site-specific design is a restorative approach that helps rather than harms nature. The designers intended for visitors to see the beauty in seasonal changes and recognize that beauty and ecology are linked.

The English Walled Garden

Across the 120-foot Arch Bridge from Evening Island and through the Lakeside Gardens to the east, visitors can reach the English Walled Garden (also accessible past the Regenstein Center and Krasberg Rose Garden). Designed by noted English landscape designer and author John Brookes, the English Walled Garden includes six garden rooms surrounded by boundaries made of stone, brick, hedges, and trees: Vista Garden, Formal Daisy Garden, Courtyard Garden, Cottage Garden, Checkerboard Garden, and Pergola Garden. These rooms represent a variety of English gardening styles throughout history while featuring plants that are best for the Midwest.

"I was consciously peddling Englishness," wrote John Brookes of his design intent. "Being British I do it anyway, of course, but I was trying to define what Americans think is English. And of course it's their experience when travelling—Sissinghurst, Great Dixter and the like—all 19th century 'manor house' type gardens."[33]

The individual garden rooms were inspired by historical English gardens or writings. The Cottage Garden follows well-known English countryside scenes. The Checkerboard Garden draws from British landscape architect Russell Page's classics, as described in his book *The Education of a Gardener*. Brookes said, "The sunken garden is a bit of Great Dixter—the long border is Sissinghurst."[34] Christopher Lloyd (1921–2006) of Dixter, famed British garden designer and writer, popularized the English country garden style. Victoria Sackville West (1892–1962), poet and garden writer, directed the redesigned gardens at her estate, Sissinghurst.

British landscape designer John Brookes brought an English sensibility to the English Walled Garden. Brookes (right), is shown here with Kris Jarantoski, then vice president of horticulture and assistant director of the Garden (1986–93) and now executive vice president and director (left), and Janet Meakin Poor, who served as the Garden's Board chair from 1987 to 1993. Poor received the Chicago Horticultural Society Medal in 1985 and the Society's Hutchinson Medal in 1994. A landscape designer, author, and committed conservationist, she has received numerous awards, including those from the American Horticultural Society and Garden Club of America.
Courtesy Lenhardt Library of the Chicago Botanic Garden.

The English Walled Garden also features a welcoming mix of plants on the outside of its west wall. "There is something about the relaxed feel of an English garden which Americans like," Brookes noted.[35] At the Chicago Botanic Garden's English Walled Garden, there is something for everyone to like.

The English Walled Garden has a number of hardscape elements that add to its charm, including the bluntly named Male Grotesque Head on the back wall—one of two matching sculpture fountains on opposite sides of the sunken pool, both gifts to the Garden from the Art Institute in 1991.

167

A low balustrade forms the walls of this garden, with a brick folly anchoring the corner.

The Checkerboard Garden in the fall features clipped shrubs and multihued autumn trees.

Roses, the quintessential element of English gardens, drape an arbor over a brick path.

The wide walkways of the Buehler Enabling Garden show just one way that the Chicago Botanic Garden accommodates those with special needs. The Garden's horticultural therapy programs stem from its core values, including the belief that people—all people—live better, healthier, and more satisfying lives when they can create, care for, and enjoy gardens.

6

Education and Outreach

Bringing the Garden Home

The Chicago Horticultural Society came of age during the Progressive Era, when social and educational reformers such as Jane Addams and John Dewey shaped the course of Chicago's philanthropy. Addams brought social services directly to the doorsteps of those served near Hull House. Dewey espoused participatory and interactive learning and effecting social reform through education. Both of these philosophies influenced the Society's outreach efforts and hands-on learning.

A number of cultural institutions arose in Chicago throughout the 1890s. The University of Chicago opened in 1890. In 1891, the newly completed Auditorium Theatre housed the debut of the Chicago Symphony Orchestra. The World's Columbian Exposition of 1893 and subsequent Progressive Era ideals spurred further growth during the decade. The Columbian Museum (now Field Museum) launched in 1893, and the Art Institute of Chicago's first permanent facility opened the same year. The Chicago Public Library, created from the detritus of the Great Chicago Fire of 1871, opened its first permanent home in 1897, adorned with its exquisite Tiffany dome. The Newberry and John Crerar Libraries opened in 1893 and 1897, respectively.

All of these institutions enjoyed the privilege of a home: four walls and a roof to house both their curated treasures and their organizational meetings. While the edifices served to protect the valuable artifacts within, they also could be construed as a means to keep people out. Egalitarian access to Chicago's cultural treasures became a rallying cry during the Progressive Era. Inspired by the efforts of the University of Chicago and the Chicago Society for University Extension, other institutions sought ways to expand their resources to the public.[1] As cultural historian Helen Lefkowitz Horowitz notes, "The conception of extending the resources of an institution outside its walls had been developed by administrators in the 1890s. Its wide application at the University of Chicago, though initially resisted, captured the imagination of cultural philanthropists."[2] Thus, museums sought ways to loan exhibits off-site, and libraries expanded their lecture series to reach broader audiences.

The Chicago Horticultural Society, then unfettered by a permanent facility, knew no other option, no other mission, than to share its resources with the public. Even though the Society certainly longed for its own space in those formative years, the lack of facilities turned into an unexpected boon. Using satellite locations and sharing knowledge with the public became the Society's tradition. Community engagement and education underpinned the Society's mission before and after it ultimately built the Chicago Botanic Garden, and this approach, ingrained in the organizational mission, continues to the present day.

During its first two decades, the Society sought to inspire and educate people through flower shows. Lacking a permanent home, the Society made the most of the annual show to bring top-quality plant specimens and the foremost experts as presenters. Reinstated in 1945 at the end of World War II after a twenty-year hiatus, the Society sought to extend the sense of community wrought through victory gardens. Its members helped children and neighborhoods nurture the gardens long after the war ended. As the Society grew in the 1950s and early 1960s, it leveraged members' gardens, rental locations, schoolrooms, and the downtown Garden Center to offer exhibits and lectures. The dream of a new botanic garden was achieved

in 1972, but the wish for a proper education facility lingered. During the nation's bicentennial in 1976, this wish came true.

School Is Open: A New Education Building

Eleven years after the Society inked its agreement to lease the land with the Forest Preserve District of Cook County, the Education Center at the Chicago Botanic Garden was dedicated on June 26, 1976. Society president Louis B. Martin, Ph.D., wrote of the building: "It embodies all the potential for satisfying the objectives and goals set forth in the 1890 Constitution, [and] the Center rededicates the Society to the continuing use of all available resources to expand horticultural and botanical services for its many publics."[3] Martin noted that the Center marked the fulfillment of a promise contained in the 1965 agreement with the Forest Preserve District that the botanic garden was "for the horticultural education of residents of metropolitan Chicago and its environs."

The Education Center—now the Regenstein Center—was designed to fulfill a number of purposes and included seminar rooms, an auditorium, classrooms, a library, an exhibition hall, offices, and a cluster of greenhouses. Referencing the design challenge, architect Edward L. Barnes wrote, "Somehow all these spaces should be arranged so that they could operate independently of each other or as a unit. Flocks of schoolchildren, for example, should be able to tour the greenhouse without disturbing the people in their offices. A learned society should be able to meet in a quiet room at the same time that a garden club was preparing a show in the courtyard."[4] For nearly 40 years, the Regenstein Center has served its purpose well, and it will continue to be an integral part of the education programs at the Garden.

In the late 1990s and beginning of the new millennium, Barbara Whitney Carr launched an effort to transform the educational programming at the Garden into a comprehensive curriculum from prekindergarten through postgraduate science degrees. William Hagenah, then chairman of the Chicago Horticultural Society, noted, "Barbara was the guiding force behind the growth of the Garden as it developed into one of the premier botanic and scientific institutions in the world. She set the challenge for the Garden to become the nation's leading teaching garden."[5]

Today, the Joseph Regenstein, Jr. School of the Chicago Botanic Garden offers hundreds of adult classes, certificate programs, symposia, and conferences in horticulture, landscape design, botanic arts, photography, nature, and environmental science and serves nearly 5,000 adult lifelong learners, landscape professionals, and healthcare professionals. Certificate programs are offered in many disciplines, and through partnerships with Northwestern University, the Society offers innovative graduate school opportunities. Dan I. H. Linzer, provost of Northwestern University and member of the Garden's Board of Directors, and Barbara Carr together conceived of the joint graduate program in plant biology and conservation, created in 2005. In 2009 the program began training Ph.D. students in addition to the master's students, with the first doctoral students graduating in 2015.

Through the Garden's Science Career Continuum, a series of educational offerings that engages Chicago Public Schools students from diverse backgrounds and mentors them from middle school through college and beyond, the next generation of plant scientists is trained.

John H. Stroger, Jr., Cook County Forest Preserve president, and Peter Merlin, Chicago Horticultural Society Board chairman from 1972 to 1979 and again from 1993 to 1997, honor the partnership between the Cook County Forest Preserves and the Chicago Horticultural Society as they present a plan for the McGinley Pavilion, just south of the Regenstein Center, also designed by Edward L. Barnes. During the 1960s, as legal counsel for the Society, Merlin played an important role in developing the agreement with the Cook County Forest Preserves. He also led the capital campaign to build the Education Center, now the Regenstein Center. Merlin was awarded the Hutchinson Medal in 1980 and the Chicago Horticultural Society Medal in 1997.

Courtesy Lenhardt Library of the Chicago Botanic Garden.

Flanked by William Hagenah and Barbara Whitney Carr, Susan Regenstein wields the scissors and upholds her family's tradition of philanthropy and service to the Chicago Botanic Garden at the 2006 ribbon-cutting for the reopened Education Center, named the Regenstein Center for her father, Joseph Regenstein, Jr. Hagenah, who served as Chicago Horticultural Society Board chair from 2002 to 2009, helped expand education offerings to include graduate degrees and also created many partnerships with academic and cultural partners around the world for conservation and science issues. He was awarded the 2009 Chicago Horticultural Society Medal. Carr, president and CEO of the Garden from 1995 to 2007, led the redevelopment of the education programs into the comprehensive Joseph Regenstein, Jr. School of the Chicago Botanic Garden. Under her leadership, a ten-year master plan and successful $148 million fund-raising campaign resulted in many new gardens and a strong foundation for the Garden's global science achievements.

Nestled amid the natural features of the Chicago Botanic Garden, the former Education Center—now the Regenstein Center—offers a unified, modern structure that can accommodate a wide variety of uses.

Among the hundreds of classes offered to adults, family, and youth through the Joseph Regenstein, Jr. School of the Chicago Botanic Garden are nature appreciation classes such as this sunrise photography class.

Botanic art classes offered through the Regenstein School help students observe nature and express their creativity.

Container planting classes at the Regenstein Center give students hands-on instruction in horticulture and flower arranging.

At the Kleinman Family Cove on the Regenstein Foundation Learning Campus at the Chicago Botanic Garden, youngsters and their families learn about the importance of freshwater ecology.

Spreading the Word

The first *Garden Talks* issue, published in 1945, launched the printed version of horticultural information offered by the Society to members and the general public. The monthly periodical *Garden Talks*, which became *Garden Talk* in 1961 and evolved into today's member magazine, *Keep Growing*, contained how-to advice, expert opinions on new gardening technologies, plant evaluations, and trends to watch. Leveraging the latest media opportunities along with Chicago Horticultural Society director Fred Heuchling's publicity savvy, Society members appeared on television as early as 1950.[6] Radio program hosts often tapped Society leaders for advice. Today, experts from the Chicago Botanic Garden can often be seen on TV with tips on seasonal garden activities and other horticultural news.

Garden Talks and its successor magazines frequently included questions from readers with answers from experts, but often a more direct approach helped. A walk-in information service for gardeners began in the Society's old downtown Garden Center. Partnering with certified master gardeners[7] and other horticulture specialists, the Society established the Information Hotline (now the Plant Information Services) to answer questions ranging from insect identification to how to identify black spot.

The Plantmobile, a former pizza delivery truck converted into a sort of roving garden classroom staffed with volunteers, debuted in the early 1980s. The Plantmobile could be seen at scheduled stops throughout Cook County. Nancy Clifton, now a horticulture program specialist at the Garden, recalled the Plantmobile's early years: "We tried to bring a bit of the Garden to people who couldn't come to the Garden."[8] Clifton, who drove the Plantmobile herself, recounted how one year she personally conducted more than 300 visits to sites all over Cook County. Plantmobile programs were tailored for the audience: Clifton might have shown how tomatoes grow at a Society-sponsored Farmers' Market, demonstrated the difference between sweet and sour fruit to children with disabilities, or taught flower arranging at a senior center. The Plantmobile has since been retired, but its outreach mission continues through the Garden's many programs today.

Early outreach efforts included a lending library. Today's Lenhardt Library, housed at the Regenstein Center of the Chicago Botanic Garden, grew exponentially from its humble beginnings in 1950. In a cozy room furnished with rustic armchairs at the Society's Garden Center downtown location, Woman's Board members began clipping articles from stacks of magazines. These articles were pasted onto cardboard and filed for readers' perusal. The Woman's Board conducted house-to-house entreaties for book donations to increase the collection. Volunteers cataloged 600 books covering general gardening; specific flowers such as roses, daylilies, and dahlias; and magazine subscriptions to popular gardening magazines.

Beginning with examples of victory gardens, the periodical Garden Talks *debuted in 1945 and became an important source of horticultural information for the public.*

Courtesy Lenhardt Library of the Chicago Botanic Garden.

The Plantmobile visit became a highly anticipated event in many far-flung corners of Cook County.

Courtesy Chicago History Museum, ICHi-68454.

—in this issue   Page
Flowering Branches
   Needed 3
Garden Notes for
   February 7
Horticultural Society
   Library 2
Pruning Shrubs 5
Volunteer Workshop 4
FRONT COVER:–
View of Horticultural So-
ciety Library.

Comfortable chairs and botanic prints accented the downtown Garden Center.

Courtesy Lenhardt Library of the Chicago Botanic Garden.

As shown on this 1958 cover of Garden Talks, *the Chicago Horticultural Society's downtown Garden Center offered a library of member-loaned books and hand-pasted files of magazine articles.*

Courtesy Lenhardt Library of the Chicago Botanic Garden.

Lecture programs using the latest motion picture technology of the 1950s were hosted in the downtown Garden Center.

Exhibitions—of flowers and also community garden produce—were staged in the downtown Garden Center.

By the time that more permanent space was ready in the newly constructed Education Center at the Chicago Botanic Garden in 1976, the library collection had expanded tenfold to 6,000 books. By the late 1980s, the book collection approached 10,000. Today the Lenhardt Library, in the Regenstein Center, houses more than 125,000 volumes.

Library technologies have evolved greatly from the days of magazine clippings. In the late 1980s, the Woman's Board extolled the "recent innovation" of the library's videotape collection. In the Woman's Board's 1990 booklet *It's Fun to Remember*, writers recall the "most amazing modern concept of providing information," the "Dialogue Information Retrieval Service" comprising 320 databases.[9] Today, Lenhardt Library visitors have access to specialized databases leveraging the latest Internet technologies.

Yet not everything in the library is new—nor should it be; there is value in the old as well. The Lenhardt Library includes about 3,000 rare books and 2,000 historic periodical titles, including the important acquisition in 2002 of rare books and journals from the Massachusetts Horticultural Society of Boston. The oldest book in the collection, *Historia Plantarum* by Theophrastus, published in 1483, details the first known classifications of plants in the Western world. With support from the National Endowment for the Humanities, the rare book collection is cataloged, and conservation efforts are stabilizing the collection for generations to come. Today's digitization program provides access to these remarkable volumes through any Internet connection.

As in the past, library staff members also organize exhibitions each year, pulling from the extensive collections. Visitors can enjoy a curated display of beautiful botanical prints or other treasures from the vault. Library director Leora Siegel said, "Moving forward, the Lenhardt Library will continue to acquire rare books of botanical significance and will work to make these historic resources increasingly available to the public through ongoing exhibitions and digital sharing."[10] Siegel noted that the Library supports the Garden's conservation science programs by supplying a range of print and e-journals and other academic materials, and is a primary source of information to professional staff throughout the Garden. The Library's visitor programs include everything from rare book viewings for an adult audience to a weekly story time for toddlers.

In addition to ongoing adult and youth classes, the Garden's Woman's Board sponsored the Zimmerman Lecture Series from 1986 to 2005. Named for Elizabeth Zimmerman, former president of the Woman's Board and also a member of the Society's Board of Directors,

the lectures were open to the public for a nominal fee. Typically offered four times a year, the lectures focused on horticulture and landscape design. The 1986 roster is illustrative: "Growing Asian Plants for Midwest Landscapes," by Harrison Flint, Ph.D., Purdue professor of horticulture; "Hardy Plants Fact or Fiction," by John Sabuco, landscape architect and author of *The Best of the Hardiest*; "Plants of the Southeastern U.S. for the Northern Landscape," by Michael A. Dirr, Ph.D., University of Georgia professor of horticulture and author of *Manual of Woody Landscape Plants*; and "New Plants for the Chicago Landscape," by Janet Meakin Poor, editor of *Plants That Merit Attention*.

Horticulture for Health

The idea that flowers bring cheer to those in poor health has been tested by time. In the 1870s, Chicagoans, like citizens of other big cities in the United States, formed Flower Missions whose members contributed cut flowers from backyard gardens to distribute among hospitals and charitable institutions. The Chicago Flower Mission included early Chicago Horticultural Society members, or those whose progeny would become members.[11] In its 1890s incarnation, the Society's flower shows included bazaars for many hospitals or health charities.

In 1954, the Society's Woman's Board launched one of the earliest permanent gardens for sight-impaired persons. Partnering with the Lighthouse for the Blind (now the Chicago Lighthouse), the Woman's Board raised funds, consulted on the garden design, recruited other sponsors, and helped maintain the garden. Although there were a handful of other gardens for the blind in the United States, the Lighthouse for the Blind garden was said to be the first used for day-to-day therapy.[12]

Inspired by a similar garden in Exeter, England (probably the recently restored Belmont Sensory Garden in Exeter), Woman's Board chair LaVerne Hunter obtained the enthusiastic support of Edith Farwell, who promised her support and knowledge of scented plants. The Lighthouse for the Blind had just built its new training center at 1850 West Roosevelt Road in Chicago, where it still stands today. The Lighthouse Board dedicated 1½ acres—half the total property—toward the garden.

Thrilled with the possibilities, the Woman's Board visited the site but found it to be a wasteland: "It was a large area of demolished buildings, whose basements, ten feet deep were full of broken bottles, debris and trash, criss-crossed by many outdated and unused telephone and light poles."[13]

Chicago Horticultural Society president (1956–59) F. A. Cushing Smith, a prominent member of the American Society of Landscape Architects, drew a plan for the garden, as did member Harold Klopp, a landscape architect who would later design many exhibits at the Society's World Flower Shows. Klopp's budget-friendly design prevailed, and the fundraising drive

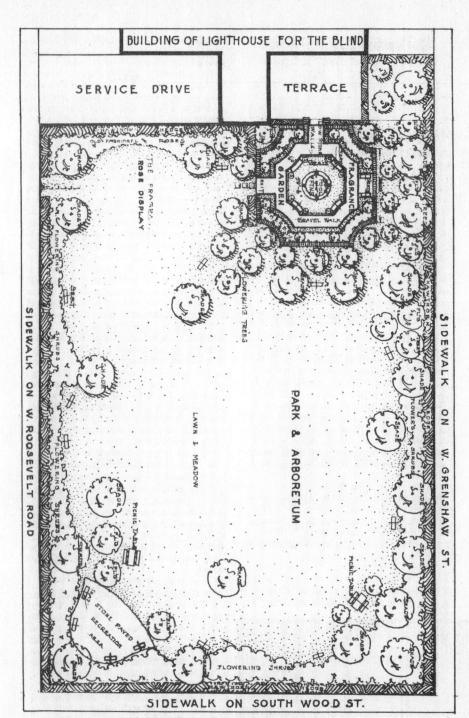

BUILDING OF LIGHTHOUSE FOR THE BLIND

SERVICE DRIVE

TERRACE

SIDEWALK ON W. ROOSEVELT ROAD

SIDEWALK ON W. GRENSHAW ST.

PARK & ARBORETUM

LAWN & MEADOW

SIDEWALK ON SOUTH WOOD ST.

Tentative Plan for Fragrance Garden and General Landscape Development.
Prepared for Woman's Board of Chicago Horticultural Society
By F. A. Cushing Smith & Associates, Landscape Architects & Engineers.
Page 3

*Architect F. Cushing Smith's plan for the Fragrant Garden
for the Blind was somewhat modified but retained elements
of discovery for sight-impaired individuals.*

Courtesy Lenhardt Library of the Chicago Botanic Garden.

was launched at a luncheon meeting at the Arts Club of Chicago. Hand-addressed solicitation letters, which each included an actual scented plant, spelled out the project goal: "If you were blind, would you enjoy a garden designed especially for you? One that would have fragrant flowers, shrubs and shade trees to attract the song birds; a garden in which could be heard the sounds of running water; a garden that would have raised flower beds, garden walks, plants labeled in Braille, and a terrace for recreational games?"[14]

Enthusiasm for the project spread, and donations of plants and building materials flowed in. The Illinois Road Builders Association offered trucks and workers, removing loads of rubble from the site. Trees, shrubs, and evergreens were donated by the Illinois State Nurserymen's Association, and the Ryerson Foundation donated iron edging for the pathways. Carson Pirie Scott & Co., in the midst of building the Edens Plaza, lent its contractor to install a patio for the garden, gratis. The retailer also permitted the dried plant creations made by the Woman's Board to be displayed and sold in the department stores' china and linen sections. Meanwhile, Woman's Board members grew pots of herbs from cuttings from Farwell's garden. Plant sales, featuring stock from members' gardens, raised more funds. The Cook County Forest Preserve donated picnic tables and benches, and the Oak Park and Garfield Park Conservatories propagated plants.

The dedication of the Garden for the Blind, or Fragrant Garden as it was sometimes called, occurred in July 1957. After hours, children from the neighborhood were allowed to skate or walk on the paths so that the garden became part of the community. Woman's Board volunteers continued to maintain the garden for several years. Although the garden is gone today, the Chicago Lighthouse continues to partner with the Chicago Horticultural Society in its horticultural therapy programs.

Always a mainstay in the Society's mission, horticultural therapy programs were formalized in the late 1950s. Society volunteers had been working with the Christopher School for Handicapped Children, as it was then called, since the turn of the twentieth century, and with other health facilities such as La Rabida Sanitarium (now La Rabida Children's Hospital). To broaden their outreach, Society members drew on the expertise of such pioneers in the emerging field of horticultural therapy as Alice W. Burlingame of Michigan, who helped launch the forerunner of today's American Horticultural Therapy Association.[15]

Chicago Horticultural Society president (1954–56) R. Milton Carleton, Ph.D., urged members and the public to participate in workshops sponsored by the Society and headlined by Burlingame in January 1958: "As the president of your Society, I am convinced that working with this program will be the most rewarding, heart-warming experience of your life." Recounting the moving scene of a young child with limited mobility making a corsage for his mother, Carleton continued, "The grim determination on [the child's] face as he worked, and the exultant look in his eyes as he went home with the corsage pinned to his shirt—these would have made us all resolve that this boy and the 2,000 other handicapped children in our new program must have an opportunity to know the pleasure and satisfaction that come from gardening."[16] Society members and the public registered for the classes that promoted on-site therapy for schoolchildren or in-home horticultural activities for bedridden or elderly family members. Throughout the Society's flower and garden shows in the 1960s and 1970s, hundreds of children with disabilities were invited from schools throughout the region as special guests to explore the displays.

Veterans with disabilities are another group to whom the Chicago Horticultural Society has reached out with horticultural therapy programs since the mid-twentieth century. Almost immediately upon its reinstatement following World War II, the Society renewed its philanthropy with hospitals. The war had resulted in an influx of wounded American soldiers. In 1944–45, Mrs. Joseph M. (Jean Morton) Cudahy, a Society Board member (and daughter of the Morton Arboretum founder Joy Morton), launched a project to landscape the grounds of the newly established Vaughan General Hospital (no known relation to J. C. Vaughan).[17] This military hospital served wounded veterans, and Cudahy, seeing a need to soften the bare grounds and give respite to the injured, partnered with the Red Cross, the Illinois Federation of Women's Clubs, and the Garden Club of Illinois. Erle O. Blair, also a Board member of the Chicago Horticultural Society, prepared the landscape design plan.[18] The team planted 75 barren acres with trees and shrubs. Donated elms from Daniel Rice's Wheaton Danada Farm, 1,200 hawthorns and crabapples, and about 1,600 vines formed the backbone of the design.[19] Now at the site of Edward Hines, Jr. Veterans Administration (VA) Hospital just west of Chicago in Hines, Illinois, some of the native hawthorns, crabapples, lilacs, and oaks may trace their lineage to this planting.

At the Chicago Horticultural Society's flower shows of the 1950s through 1970s, guests with disabilities were warmly welcomed and accomodated with easy access.

Chicago Botanic Garden programs throughout the region provide horticultural therapy for veterans and continue the early efforts of the Woman's Board of the Chicago Horticultural Society.

The Society has continued its relationship with Hines and also provides horticultural therapy to two other hospitals operated by the U.S. Department of Veterans Affairs in the Chicago area. So important was horticultural therapy to the Society that the Learning Garden for the Disabled became the second garden established at the new Chicago Botanic Garden in 1974. Said to be the first of its kind in the United States, this project evolved through the Woman's Board's interest in horticultural therapy.[20] Developed in conjunction with the Kenilworth and Barrington Garden Clubs, the project secured a Founders Fund Award from the Garden Club of America.

The Chicago Botanic Garden's Learning Garden for the Disabled included raised beds of concrete blocks, railroad ties, and treated boards. Wide concrete paths enabled safe passage for wheelchairs. Further grants permitted the construction of a greenhouse and tool house adapted to client needs. In the years before the Americans with Disabilities Act of 1990, this trailblazing garden brought cheer to many people. One mother of a 32-year-old man with disabilities, Ira, wrote to the *Chicago Tribune* of how a visit to the Garden gave her hope:

> *Attitudes [of society] are improving. I could see it at the Botanic [Garden] not only in the Learning Garden for the disabled, but in the people. A lady glanced over at Ira and smiled gently. During the tram tour when Ira made his sounds, nobody turned around to stare. Only once did a person say "Shhhhh"—and that was when us "normal" people talked during the tour guide's lecture.*
>
> *Ira enjoyed his trip to the Botanic Garden, and so did his family. What's more important, Ira was seen in the mainstream of life.[21]*

Garden trams serve many individuals. In addition to the regular trams that circumnavigate most of the Garden, a smaller tram ride is offered for those with special needs. Josephine P. Louis, Society Board of Directors member, recipient of the Garden's 2014 Hutchinson Medal, and wife of the late John J. Louis, Jr., spearheaded the Bright Encounters Tour Program at the Garden in 1996. This program offers Garden tours for persons of limited mobility aboard a small tram that circulates among some of the prominent Garden features.[22] Tram rides for individuals with disabilities and other accommodations for those with limitations are available today throughout the Garden.

The Learning Garden for the Disabled served visitors until 1999, when the Buehler Enabling Garden, in a more central location, replaced the earlier garden. Founder and director of the Garden's Horticultural Therapy Services Gene Rothert, former president of the American Horticultural Therapy Association (1992–1994), oversaw the development and management of the Buehler Enabling Garden.

Awarded the Chicago Horticultural Society Medal for 2010, Gene Rothert offered hands-on demonstrations in the Buehler Enabling Garden. "Because of Gene's unending dedication to horticultural therapy, the Garden is known and respected nationally for providing therapy and training therapists," said President and CEO Sophia Shaw. "Gene exemplifies the service, leadership, devotion, and courage the award recognizes."

Today, horticultural therapy is an integral service provided by trained Garden staff. With more than 40 years of programming experience, Horticultural Therapy Services plans and delivers seasonal therapeutic horticulture sessions at the Garden or at client sites. One of the country's biggest professional certificate programs in horticultural therapy is offered through the Regenstein School. Several publications have been authored by Garden staff, including *Garden for Life, Designing Your Home Enabling Garden, Horticultural Therapy: Helping People Grow, Vertical Gardening,* and *Barrier-Free Gardening in Containers.*

The Buehler Enabling Garden is a mecca for the fast-growing field of healthcare garden design and is used as a living laboratory for the Garden's Healthcare Garden Design Certificate program. Research focusing on the impact of horticultural therapy on human health and well-being is planned for the near future.[23]

Civic and Community Gardens

In the 1950s and 1960s, with its downtown location, the Chicago Horticultural Society cooperated with many local businesses to offer classes, hands-on advice, and volunteer work for their employees. The Society helped organize garden clubs, such as those for factory workers at Republic Flow Meters and at General American Transportation. The former enjoyed lectures such as that by a gladiolus expert at Gompers Park,[24] and the latter created a vegetable garden and displayed its harvest at a special exhibit at the Society's Garden Center.[25] Women employees of the Santa Fe, Carson Pirie Scott, and People's Gas companies were invited to an "herb luncheon" with Farwell as guest speaker.[26] Other neighborhood clubs received assistance from the Society, such as the Southwest Central Community Council in the 21st Ward, which cosponsored a home grounds improvement contest in 1951.[27]

The Society made civic beautification a priority in 1954 with a challenge to restore Chicago's honorific as the Garden City. A *Chicago Tribune* editorial on January 1 of that year explained, "The Chicago Horticultural Society has made its major project for 1954 an attempt to revive the gardening spirit and the natural beauty that once won the city its reputation."[28] The editorial argued that the most urgent need for beautification resided in individual yards—front and back—and in raising awareness in young people about the beauty of gardens.

The editorial mirrored the Society's plans, and a blitz of educational seminars and projects launched across the city and suburbs. Covering north, south, and west sides of the region in such venues as the Fair Store in Evergreen Park, Sears at Harlem and North Avenues, and the western suburb of LaGrange, the Society hosted a series of lectures. Landscape architect and Society president Smith presented "Beautifying Lawns," and the Garden Club of Morgan Park cohosted a talk on "Beautiful Home Grounds in Four Easy Steps." Jerrold Loebl, an architect known for incorporating green space into his designs, provided insight in his presentation on the value of nature in an urban environment. The Society worked with Chicago's Triangle area (Lincoln, Ogden, and North Avenues) to encourage gardening through printed circulars and hands-on help.[29]

In June 1954, the Woman's Board sponsored a 50-mile tour that explored the city's parks and boulevards to introduce more residents to Chicago's green spaces. The celebration of Chicago's natural assets continued for many years with subsequent tours of the parks, guided by Society volunteers. In 1963, the Society, after years of planning with the civic group Chicago Central Area Committee, helped create the legendary rose garden of Grant Park. Dedicated by Mayor Richard J. Daley on May 8, 1963, the formal garden north and south of Buckingham Fountain contained 8,000 roses of more than 120 varieties. According to the *Chicago Tribune*, the 8,000 plants were "donated by 11 firms through the efforts of Dr. R. Milton Carleton, research director of Vaughan's Seed Company [and former Society Board of Directors president]."[30] The Chicago Peace rose, new that year, composed one-eighth of the collection. The garden remains a city showpiece today, although in 2002, many of the varieties were replaced with newer, hardier plants.[31]

The Society continues to expand its programs that engage diverse communities in horticulture. Many programs have been offered through grant funding or collaboration with other kindred organizations. As noted in *Public Garden Management,* "The Chicago Botanic Garden has been engaged in community gardening for

The Grant Park Rose Garden, shown as it appears today, began with the help of the Chicago Horticultural Society.

Photograph by and courtesy of Leskra.

Windy City Harvest participants learn about the benefits of fresh food and how to grow it.

decades and developed programs to meet changing societal needs . . . This dynamic garden keeps its development department busy applying for grants . . . as well as state and local government agencies, foundations, corporations, and individuals, to match their programming with community needs and funding opportunities."[32] Since 1980, the Society—through the Chicago Botanic Garden—has been involved with more than 300 community gardens through programs such as Neighborhood Gardens, Green Chicago, and many more.[33]

During this revival of the Garden City, the Society also renewed its commitment to educating youth about gardens and horticulture—a robust program that has grown even more today.

Children's Gardens and Urban Agriculture

The role of nature in childhood development received considerable attention in the Progressive Era, with many historians citing the period from 1900 through 1920 as the heyday of children's gardens.[34] In Chicago, many initiatives converged to bring children in closer contact with the outdoors. Settlement houses sponsored or encouraged trips to outlying areas of the city where open space and forest glens could still be found. The Chicago Park District hired landscape designers such as Jens Jensen and the Olmsted brothers to create pocket playgrounds, or small neighborhood parks. Progressive education as found in the Avery Coonley School and its predecessors promoted curricula integrated with nature exploration.[35] Children's gardens also became a focus of the Chicago chapter of the American Park and Outdoor Art Association.[36]

Little wonder, then, that the Chicago Horticultural Society made children's gardens a focus. Consistent with the era's ideals of immersing children, particularly those living in urban conditions, in nature, the 1906 show featured a lecture by Susan B. Sipe, botany teacher in Washington, D.C., and author of *School Gardening and Nature*

Chicago Horticultural Society flower shows brought attention to the need for children to experience gardens.

Courtesy Special Collections of the Lenhardt Library of the Chicago Botanic Garden.

Study, in English Rural Schools, and in London.[37] The Society's 1907 Flower Show offered a "children's day" with a special ten-cent admission price. Children were also encouraged to participate in voting for flowers at the show—with a prize awarded to the school with the highest attendance.

Gardening helped Depression-era children reconnect with nature. During World War II, the Society worked with the Chicago Park District to help children create their own victory gardens. Gardens in Jackson, Douglas, Humboldt, and Garfield Parks received oversight from Society instructors.

But after World War II, the emphasis on the natural world in school curricula had declined. By 1953, *Garden Talks* reported, "The Society has long been concerned with the fact that Chicago and suburban school children pass through elementary grades—and in most cases graduate from high school—without having had any formal instruction dealing with nature's miracles that take place in the soil."[38] Working with Amling's Flowerland, the Society distributed kits containing instructions and a blossoming begonia or ageratum to participating classrooms. Teachers could follow the prepared lesson plans for making and rooting cuttings. From this simple start, the Society estimated that more than 100,000 students witnessed plant propagation and life cycles. In another project, the Society worked with the Association of Bulb Growers in Holland and distributed 10,000 hyacinth bulbs for classrooms to plant and record bloom cycles.[39]

Early school education programs undertaken by the Chicago Horticultural Society included the creation of terrariums or planting bulbs.

Courtesy Lenhardt Library of the Chicago Botanic Garden.

With the establishment in 1956 of the Laurance Armour Memorial Fund, the Society offered rewards for schools with the best gardening efforts. Society members reviewed applications, conducted site visits, and designated awards of plants and gardening supplies. In its first year, 14 elementary schools from all parts of the city received the award.[40] Students undertook a variety of projects: some built terrariums, others created herbaria or planted outdoors.

This collaboration with Chicago area schools would thrive through the present day. Later programs included the Environmental Education Awareness Program (1987–1996), the Collaborative Outreach Education Program (1988–1997), and the Chicago School Garden Initiative (1997–2003).[41] Many of these initiatives were conducted with corporate philanthropy and in cooperation with the City of Chicago, Chicago Park District, Chicago Public Schools, Chicago Public Library, and others. Today, more than 80,000 young people annually participate in Garden events and drop-in programs; 25,000 students and teachers take field trips to the Garden; 1,200 children are enrolled in the Garden's summer camp, Camp CBG; and 1,600 children and families enjoy specialized early childhood and special-needs programs at the Garden.

The Regenstein Foundation Learning Campus, a new location for the Regenstein School, continues to take shape on the north side of the Garden. This new campus greatly extends the range of educational programming offered for students and teachers. The campus includes the Education Center, designed by the Booth Hansen architecture firm, and display garden, whose concept vision was provided by Mikyoung Kim, along with the Kleinman Family Cove, Grunsfeld Children's Growing Garden, and Robert R. McCormick Foundation Plaza and entry drive.

One school project conducted by the Chicago Horticultural Society involved filming children for a garden education class, as shown on the cover of a special issue of Garden Talk *in 1963.*

Courtesy Lenhardt Library of the Chicago Botanic Garden.

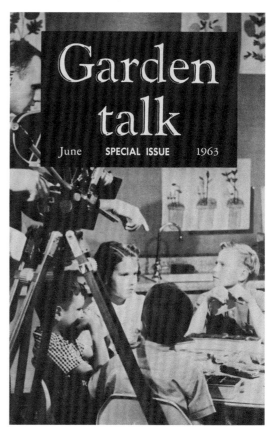

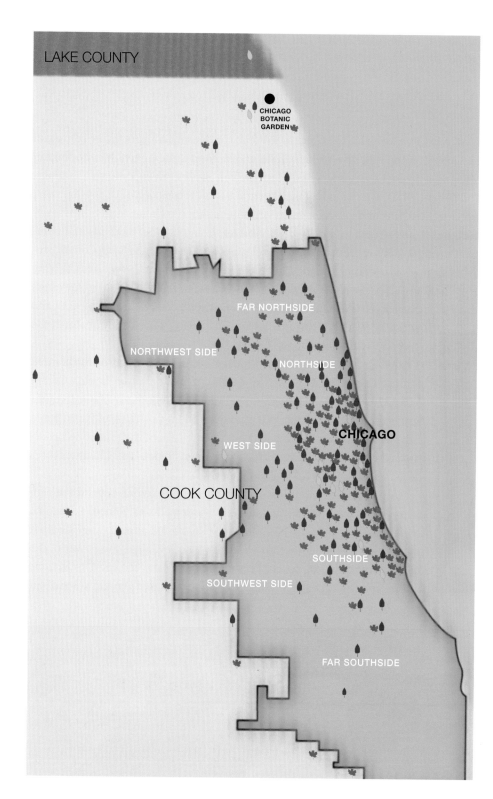

CHICAGO
BOTANIC
GARDEN

FAR NORTHSIDE

NORTHWEST SIDE

NORTHSIDE

WEST SIDE

CHICAGO

COOK COUNTY

SOUTHSIDE

SOUTHWEST SIDE

FAR SOUTHSIDE

This Chicago-area map shows where the Chicago Botanic Garden conducted programs throughout the Chicago region in education, urban agriculture, and horticultural therapy between 1986 and 2014.

 School and Community Gardens and Environmental Education

 Urban Agriculture Education and Training Programs/Windy City Harvest

 Horticultural Therapy Services

Brownies in the Girl Scouts of America work on a project conducted by the Chicago Horticultural Society. Today, the Chicago Botanic Garden works with a variety of youth groups.

Urban agriculture is an important group of programs that address a modern-day issue. Just as city-dwelling children at the turn of the twentieth century had limited access to nature due to industrialization, so do the youth at the turn of the twenty-first, but for different reasons. Some writers call this "nature deficit disorder,"[42] wherein millennial children are increasingly focused on electronic devices such as computers and phones or are limited to communities lacking green space. The Chicago Botanic Garden offers a range of programs, both off-site and on the campus, to bring gardening to young people for pleasure, and, in the case of teens, for potential job training.

Windy City Harvest is the Chicago Botanic Garden's urban agriculture education and jobs-training initiative to help build a local food system, healthier communities, and a greener economy. Windy City Harvest serves low-income youth, adults, and communities in a comprehensive program that focuses on youth development, workforce training and job placement, entrepreneurship training, farm business opportunities, and access to quality fresh produce. Using organic methods and operating on eight acres at a dozen locations throughout Chicago and Lake County, students annually grow approximately 100,000 pounds of fruits and vegetables, serving an estimated 143,00 people. The program has been nationally recognized for excellence by such groups as the Institute for Museum and Library Services (IMLS) and by the Pathways Project, an initiative of the Family Resiliency Center at the University of Illinois, Urbana-Champaign.[43]

Between 2009 and 2013, the Chicago Botanic Garden also collaborated with the Cook County Sheriff's Vocational Rehabilitation Impact Center to provide educational programs that served Cook County prison inmates during their incarceration and employed them postrelease. Participants in the program grew, maintained, and learned about the production of organic vegetables. Produce was sold to Women, Infants and Children (WIC) Centers and donated to local food pantries.

The Garden's commitment to youth gardens extends beyond the Chicago region. The first Chicago Botanic Garden Annual School Gardening Conference was held in 1998 and has been offered almost every summer since. The Chicago Horticultural Society also leverages the power of the Internet to expand its reach. In a partnership between the U.S. Botanic Garden and the Chicago Botanic Garden, the "School Garden Wizard" In-

At the Windy City Harvest Youth Farm Open House, a young participant displays a ripe tomato.

Participants cultivate the soil around plants at the North Chicago Windy City Harvest Youth Farm.

Windy City Harvest Youth Farm participants staff a Farmers' Market with produce grown through the program. The Junior Youth Farm for middle school students began in 2006.

ternet application offers a seed-to-harvest online tutorial for educators wishing to start a school garden.

Through the Garden's teacher and student programs, resource kits can be borrowed. The kits provide hands-on activities and lesson plans for topics ranging from Aquatic Illinois to fossils, insects, and spiders of Illinois. Even with its permanent home now assured in the living museum that is the Chicago Botanic Garden, staff and members continue to reach outside the garden walls to introduce more people to the benefits of horticulture.

The Garden's many education and science programs would not be possible without the significant contributions of its many volunteers. The tradition of volunteerism at the Garden traces back to the founding of the Chicago Horticultural Society. More than 1,300 volunteers today monitor butterflies, plant annuals, and help in the classrooms, the Garden View Café, and many other areas. They greet visitors, serve as tour guides, work in the library, enter plant data, or track rare plants. Specialized training is offered for some volunteer roles; for others, experience is necessary. Countless volunteer hours have helped the Garden achieve its mission throughout the years.[44]

One Windy City Harvest location sits atop the roof of McCormick Place—a fitting location given the many years that the Chicago Horticultural Society hosted World Flower Shows nearby.

The Grunsfeld Children's Growing Garden and Kleinman Family Cove on the Learning Campus help bring horticulture to youth and families—an experience that they can take home and continue to explore. The Buehler Enabling Garden, with its pioneering design and techniques, is a model for horticultural therapy. These gardens reflect the Society's long tradition of education and engagement.

The Grunsfeld Children's Growing Garden offers fun and education through hands-on experience.

Camp CBG sessions at the Children's Growing Garden help youth explore nature with experienced teachers.

Individual exploration within a safe garden setting is encouraged at the Children's Growing Garden.

Grunsfeld Children's Growing Garden

Budding gardeners and future scientists "learn by doing" in the Chicago Botanic Garden's Grunsfeld Children's Growing Garden. As they water, weed, and harvest plants, youth are guided by expert instructors in the sort of hands-on learning that makes a lasting impression. On weekends during the summer, families can enjoy drop-in activities there, growing closer together as they get closer to nature.

The Children's Growing Garden is designed to be kind to the environment. A water-harvesting system for the entire site plus an "adventure station" rain barrel help keep the plants growing; solar panels on the roof of the Tool and Potting Shed (actually an attractive support building) offset electrical needs and create a hot-water supply. The garden is surrounded by an open-weave fence covered with varieties of climbing plants, creating a safe, enclosed space for children. The Children's Growing Garden is divided into two outdoor garden classrooms: one featuring flowers with readily identifiable plant parts that is open to the general public for drop-in programs, and another that focuses on food plants and is designated for registered program participants. With a combined total of six raised beds, six in-ground demonstration beds, five display beds, and roll-under planting trays for students who use wheelchairs, the garden welcomes all children.

Kleinman Family Cove

Across the road from the Children's Growing Garden is the Kleinman Family Cove. Located on the Garden's North Lake along 800 feet of restored shoreline, the Family Cove teaches about the importance of water and its associated aquatic plants and animals.

Designed by the Oehme, van Sweden landscape architecture firm and featuring a boardwalk, an amphitheater, a protected wading area, and native plants, the Cove enables students, adult educators, and visitors to learn about the critical role freshwater systems play in the health of the natural world. With the nation's largest collection of aquatic plants and 81 acres of lakes and waterways, the Chicago Botanic Garden is uniquely positioned to teach about the importance of freshwater systems.

In the Cove, a canopied outdoor amphitheater overlooks a small bay. Here, students don waders and use nets to analyze aquatic animal life, assess water quality, and discover why water is important to human health. From a broad boardwalk, students can view aquatic plants at various depths, perform water tests, and sample water for aquatic creatures. A demonstration garden reveals the importance of shoreline management and aquatic plants.

The Cove serves the thousands of family members who take part in on-site programs, as well Chicago Public Schools students and students from other school districts on field trips. Teachers of youth from early childhood through high school visit the Cove annually through teacher development programs aimed at improving environmental education.

Buehler Enabling Garden

The Buehler Enabling Garden is a hands-on teaching garden that encourages gardening for people of all ages and abilities. This 11,000-square-foot garden demonstrates the latest strategies for easy lifelong gardening at home. The Buehler Enabling Garden is also a learning center for horticultural therapy programs.

Raised beds, dramatic container gardens, adaptive tool displays, and model exhibits illustrate gardening techniques that can be used to make gardening accessible. Water is used throughout the garden in shooting fountains, cascading sheets, and cooling pools. Vertical gardens, sensory plants, and smooth brick pathways are all key elements in accessible gardens. A level grade, a firm surface, good drainage, and color contrasts for visual discrimination contribute to improved mobility in the garden.

Raised garden beds show that by elevating the soil level, gardeners can care for a garden with minimal bending, stooping, or reaching. Baskets in this garden can be lowered to a gardener's working height and then raised for display. Similarly, raised water gardens bring plants within easy reach. For sensory enjoyment, the garden also has several fountains and uniquely designed water walls, which create 5-foot-wide sheets of water. Vertical wall gardens comprise special wood frames within easy reach on garden walls and make a striking display when filled with colorful annuals or vegetables.

Members of the Albert C. Buehler family are longtime friends of the Chicago Botanic Garden and ardent supporters of the benefits of therapeutic horticulture. They established an endowment for horticultural therapy services at the Garden in 1991 and worked to create a therapeutic garden. Pictured here in 1999 at the opening of the Buehler Enabling Garden are Albert C. Buehler, Jr. (left) with his sister Peppi Grosse and spouse Pat Buehler (right), along with then-Board chair Thomas A. Donahoe. The late Albert C. Buehler, Jr. followed in his father's footsteps in joining the Chicago Horticultural Society's Board of Directors and received the Chicago Horticultural Society Medal in 1998; his son, John Buehler, is a Board member today.

The 3,100 plants in the Enabling Garden were chosen largely for their beauty and appeal to multiple senses. In the tactile beds, plants of many textures are featured. A metal grid running across this garden bed provides a planting guide for people who garden by touch.

Located at the north end of the Enabling Garden, a canvas-covered outdoor teaching pavilion is the staging area for horticultural therapy workshops and classes. Discovery carts staffed by trained volunteers encourage visitors to use all their senses to experience plants and to sample tools that ease the practice of gardening. Similarly, the Tool Shed information center offers resources and tools that help visitors later try easy-does-it gardening techniques at home.

Designed by Environmental Planning & Design in consultation with horticultural therapy modern-day pioneer Gene Rothert, the Buehler Enabling Garden has won numerous awards, including the 2000 Accessibility Award from the American Association of Museums and the National Organization on Disability, the 2001 Therapeutic Garden Design Award from the American Horticultural Therapy Association, and the 2001 Excellence in Landscape Gold Award from the Illinois Landscape Contractors Association.

Container plantings in the Buehler Enabling Garden are easy to relocate and access.

CHICAGO AND ITS BOTANIC GARDEN

Raised plant beds accessible to visitors in wheelchairs are an important part of the Buehler Enabling Garden.

Sight-impaired individuals can enjoy their experience at the Buehler Enabling Garden by touching plants with a variety of textures.

Treasures from the Dixon Prairie at the Chicago Botanic Garden include seeds banked for future generations.

7

Plant Science

Save the Plants, Save the Planet

From the earliest flower shows to today's Chicago Botanic Garden, the Chicago Horticultural Society sought ways in which plants could improve the human condition. Sometimes this improvement could be the simple pleasure derived from an exquisite bouquet or a beautiful garden. More often, new plants or scientific discoveries about plants proved beneficial in healthcare or provided economic benefits. Today, the Chicago Botanic Garden is among the preeminent scientific research organizations in the country focused on plant biology and conservation.

The Chicago Horticultural Society of 1890 emerged in a time of exploding plant hybridization, promulgated by the stunning chromolithography in plant catalogs and general acclaim in flower shows. Plant wizard Luther Burbank of California, supported by Carnegie Institution grants between 1904 and 1909, introduced hundreds of new plants to popular acclaim if not scientific scrutiny. In the Chicago area, florists and nursery owners such as J. C. Vaughan, P. S. Peterson,

Willis N. Rudd, Peter Reinberg, and others raised hundreds of acres of plants for market. With national greenhouse builders such as the Moninger Company in Chicago, greenhouses sprang up all over the city. Illinois, and the Chicago area in particular, had more acres "under glass" than any state in the nation.[1]

Commercial uses of floriculture thrived, and academic interest in botany also grew. The University of Chicago, where Society members Charles Hutchinson and Martin Ryerson served on the board, appointed John Merle Coulter to head the Department of Botany. Coulter, a respected botanist, had previously served as president of Lake Forest College, where he would likely have been acquainted with many Society members. Under Coulter's later leadership at the University of Chicago from 1896 to 1935, the Department of Botany produced many influential scholars, including Henry C. Cowles and Herman S. Pepoon.

Cowles, sometimes called the father of North American ecology, led student field trips around the countryside to explore the native landscape. Among his frequent trips were excursions to the area around the present-day Chicago Botanic Garden. There, the dune bluffs, ravines, lagoons, and lakeshore served as an outdoor laboratory for his pioneering work in ecology. Property owners, many of them Society members, developed a strong sense of environmentalism, having witnessed firsthand Cowles's theories of plant succession on their own dunefront properties.

Society member Harriet Hammond McCormick, who studied botany under Coulter while at Lake Forest College, wrote of her and husband Cyrus's estate, Walden, in her monograph, *Landscape Art, Past Present and Future*.[2] Designed in the naturalistic style by landscape architect Warren Manning, Walden featured native plantings and espoused harmony with nature as suggested by its namesake described by Henry David Thoreau. When she read a draft of her book at a June 1900 meeting of the American Park and Outdoor Art Association held in Chicago, McCormick gave prominence to the area's natural features.[3]

Conservation was a national topic in the early 1900s, promoted not only by President Theodore Roosevelt but also by emerging conservation groups such as the Prairie Club, Friends of Our Native Landscape (both founded by Jens Jensen), the American Park and Outdoor Art Association (with O. C. Simonds among its leaders), and the Wildflower Preservation Society. Many of the early Chicago Horticultural Society members also espoused the aims of these conservation groups. Frances Kinsely Hutchinson (the wife of Charles Hutchinson) served as president of the Wildflower Preservation Society in 1919, sharing its leadership duties with other Chicago Horticultural Society members.[4] Mrs. Hutchinson also served as a director of the Chicago Outdoor Art League, along with fellow Chicago Horticultural Society members O. C. Simonds and Lena M. McCauley.[5]

Individual Chicago Horticultural Society members supported important local conservation movements of the day—those of creating the Cook County Forest

This image of the ravines near the county line in Glencoe was likely taken on one of the field trips sponsored by the University of Chicago.

University of Chicago Photographic Archive, AEP-ILN36, Special Collections Research Center, University of Chicago Library.

Saving the wildflowers became a rallying cry for those interested in conservation in the Cook County Forest Preserves, founded 1913–15.

Forest Preserve District of Cook County records, FPDCC_00_01_0012_002, University of Illinois at Chicago Library, Special Collections.

Frances Kinsely Hutchinson served as president of the local chapter of the Wildflower Preservation Society in 1919, which included many other Chicago Horticultural Society members.

Courtesy Chicago History Museum, ICHi-68241.

From her book on the Hutchinson country home, Wychwood, Frances Kinsely Hutchinson included a photo of the properly attired woman gardener.

The Wildflower Preservation Society sponsored numerous conservation activities—including children portraying precious wildflowers, as this hand-colored photograph, circa 1902, illustrates.

Courtesy Field Museum Library and Getty Images, T1619224_0007.

Preserves and saving the Indiana Dunes. A pageant, "The Dunes Under Four Flags," performed in May and June of 1917, involved a huge number of supporters and participants, including many Society members.[6] This massive extravaganza, performed at the current Indiana Dunes to an audience of about 25,000, brought together the most active conservationists of the era, including Jensen, Cowles, Dwight Perkins, Stephen T. Mather, Frank Dudley, Professor Graham Taylor, and Lorado Taft. Subscribing organizations, headed by Jensen's Prairie Club of Chicago, included the Municipal Art League, the Chicago Historical Society, the Chicago Woman's Outdoor-Art League, the Chicago Teachers' Federation, and a host of women's clubs. This pageant, and the many later lobbying and awareness campaigns, would lead to the successful formation of the state parks in the Indiana Dunes and eventually, in 1966, the establishment by the U.S. Congress of the Indiana Dunes National Lakeshore.

As a Society, the group resumed its focus on environmentalism shortly after its reinstatement in 1945. Even before Rachel Carson's seminal book *Silent Spring*, which appeared in 1962 as a warning bell against the indiscriminate use of DDT and other pesticides, a 1954 issue of the Chicago Horticultural Society publication *Garden Talks* offered a neutral view of the effectiveness of new products balanced against environmental concerns. Within the same issue, the article "What Is New in Pesticides?" listed new chemical products while "Practical Methods of Combating Insects and Pests" countered with a mix of homegrown solutions. Even the first article warned, "It may be that we have another miracle insecticide in Malathion. Or it may develop like in the case of DDT that the original promises were not completely fulfilled in the long run."[7]

Later that year, Chicago Horticultural Society Woman's Board president Edith Farwell wrote unsparingly about "The Danger of Spraying." Bucking the trend, she warned:

There is hardly a garden magazine or newspaper published, that is not full of various advertisements, telling us to spray for this, spray for that. Never a word of encouraging the birds, or of feeding our plants to make them strong, so that they have more of a chance to resist disease. Fifty years ago we had never heard of poisonous sprays. Farmers fertilized with manures, composted the soil and the trees and plants seemed to thrive.[8]

Midcentury *Garden Talks* also promoted other horticultural practices that, counter to the widespread fascination with new chemicals, offered time-tested natural solutions updated with scientific research. The newsletter frequently recommended mulching, particularly using organic material worked into the soil. The magazines cited university research on how the microscopic interactions of soil bacteria and organisms were relayed, "so it behooves every wise gardener to keep on adding organic matter to his soil along with his plant foods and to do everything possible to keep the soil porous."[9] The Society also promoted the use of rain barrels—considered old-fashioned in the 1950s but receiving renewed attention in the new millennium.[10] Presaging yet another trend, a 1959 article discussed "The Organic Method in Gardening and Farming."[11]

Mid-twentieth-century flower shows sponsored by the Chicago Horticultural Society included education exhibits, such as this one from 1966 hailing the importance of pollinators.

Courtesy Lenhardt Library of the Chicago Botanic Garden.

"Right plant, right place" is a gardener's mantra, and it is a fundamental precept in working with, not against, nature. A 1968 *Garden Talk* article explained the Chicago Botanic Garden's philosophy of choosing plants for the Garden: "Our first line of defense against winter damage should be in the selection of the plants to be grown."[12] Plants meeting the USDA Plant Hardiness Zone criteria, followed by a judicious local-sourcing policy, helped ensure that plants would survive the region's weather extremes. A 1971 *Garden Talk* article, "Cooperating with Nature," offered tips on how home gardeners could help. "Everybody is on the ecology kick," the article began, satirically describing "environmentalists [who] roar around in their huge automobiles."[13] Instead, for gardeners who wanted to do the "right thing," the article proposed practical organic methods of soil amendment with limited use of chemicals.

At the Garden—and Beyond

Across the nation and the world, environmentalism was growing. In 1970, the first national Earth Day was celebrated and the Environmental Protection Agency was formed. In 1972, a nationwide ban on DDT went into effect. The era of renewed commitment to the Earth informed all of the planning for the Chicago Horticultural Society's botanic garden, culminating in the opening of the Chicago Botanic Garden in 1972. The construction of the Garden itself aimed for an environmentally conscious blending into the Skokie Marsh watershed. According to early designs, "plans call for more than half the garden land to be devoted to native Illinois plants."[14] During the planning stages for the Garden, Society leaders carefully listened to environmental concerns and invited feedback from such conservation groups as the Izaak Walton League.[15]

The Society practiced what it preached in creating the Chicago Botanic Garden. All phases of the Garden's construction, from the 1960s through present day, have carefully considered ecological impacts. John Simonds's landscape plan of hills and lakes for the Garden stressed harmony with nature. In 1972, a section of

Turnbull Woods (now the McDonald Woods) west of Green Bay Road became the first area preserved in the Garden. During the first five years of the key garden development of the 1980s, the Prairie contributed to native plant study and research, and the William Pullman Plant Evaluation Garden helped identify plants that grew well in this environment.

These early years of the Garden were largely devoted to development of the display gardens and building infrastructures. Although a solid plant breeding and evaluation program was under way, the research emphasis of the Garden needed strengthening. Roy L. Taylor, Ph.D., the Garden's president and CEO (1985–1994), noted, "It [research] is an area that has received inadequate attention during the past decade of physical growth and development. Now is the appropriate time to redress this imbalance."[16]

Development of the Chicago Botanic Garden always considered the environment—note the number of "Wildlife Preserves" on this early plan.

Courtesy Lenhardt Library of the Chicago Botanic Garden.

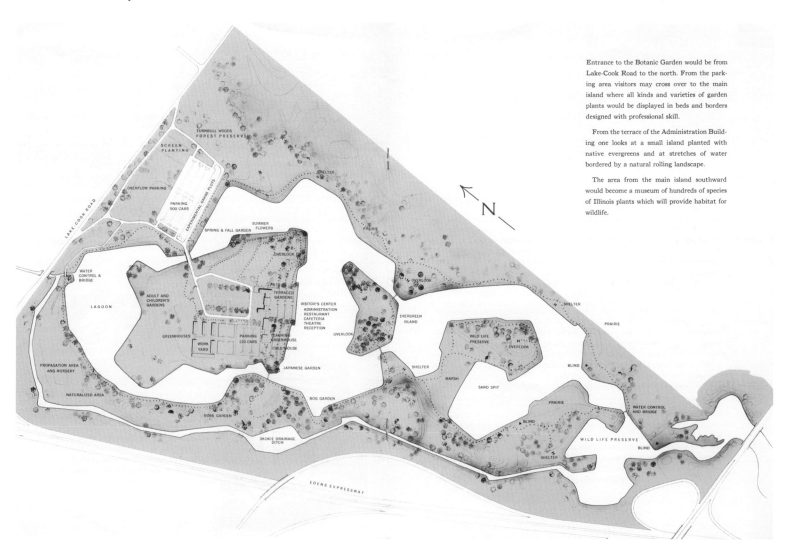

Entrance to the Botanic Garden would be from Lake-Cook Road to the north. From the parking area visitors may cross over to the main island where all kinds and varieties of garden plants would be displayed in beds and borders designed with professional skill.

From the terrace of the Administration Building one looks at a small island planted with native evergreens and at stretches of water bordered by a natural rolling landscape.

The area from the main island southward would become a museum of hundreds of species of Illinois plants which will provide habitat for wildlife.

Remnants of an old council ring—a reminder of landscape architect and conservationist Jens Jensen's influence in the Midwest landscape—were discovered in Turnbull Woods.

AERIAL VIEW RESEARCH GREENHOUSES

Research greenhouses were among the first buildings created at the Chicago Botanic Garden, pictured here in 1982.

Among the first initiatives to address the research gap was the Chicagoland Grows® program, created in 1986 by the Garden in partnership with the Morton Arboretum and the Ornamental Growers Association of Northern Illinois. Chicagoland Grows works with industry professionals throughout North America and abroad to develop, select, evaluate, produce, and market new and recommended plant cultivars. These selected plants offer fine ornamental attributes that are ecologically appropriate and dependable for both landscape professionals and home growers.

Taylor explained the significance of the Chicagoland Grows program: "Prior to 1985 no comprehensive plan for evaluation was in force. A Plant Selection Committee was established in 1986 to develop a program and determine 'target genera' and taxa for evaluation."[17] The Chicagoland Grows program was the beginning of a new era focusing on plant science at the Garden.

Janet Meakin Poor, the Chicago Horticultural Society's Board chair (1987–1993) spearheaded the reenergized foray into plant science. A landscape architect, author, and advisor for many national horticulture organizations, Poor was ideally suited to gather support for the Garden's revamped research capabilities. With her leadership, a $4 million capital campaign ensued to strengthen the Garden's science efforts.

Introduced in 2007, Starlite is a favorite among the new Prairieblues™ false indigos developed at the Chicago Botanic Garden for Chicagoland Grows.

Courtesy Jim Ault.

The Board examined how the Garden might best find its niche in plant science. The resultant focus was that of practical research in plant breeding and evaluation. Poor recalled how Arthur Nolan, Jr., then chairman of the Daniel F. and Ada L. Rice Foundation, was instrumental in the campaign.[18] Nolan and his wife, Patricia, relatives of the Rice family, were active with the Rice Foundation from the late 1960s until 2001 and 2003, respectively. (Daniel and Ada Rice had endowed the foundation since the 1940s to serve a variety of philanthropic causes, including plant conservation.) Arthur Nolan, a Korean War Purple Heart recipient, learned gardening techniques such as the use of stone and gravel while recuperating from war injuries in Japan. "He has gardened for as long as I have known him as a form of release, of relaxing after a busy day," said son Peter Nolan, president of the Rice Foundation since 1997. "He loved to put together different types of plants in areas very difficult for plants, shaded areas."[19]

One of the many tangible results of the campaign was the dedication of the Rice Foundation Plant Resource Center in 1995. With this new facility came research workspace for scientists, and recognition that science would increasingly play a larger role at the Garden.

State Street® Miyabe Maple

Through Chicagoland Grows, new, adaptable plants are introduced to the region, such as the State Street® Miyabe Maple pictured on this brochure and introduced in 2001.

Courtesy Lenhardt Library of the Chicago Botanic Garden.

The newest Chicagoland Grows selection, Pink Profusion phlox is a large-flowered, vibrantly colored hybrid that was introduced in 2015.

Courtesy Jim Ault.

Introduced in 2004, Orange Meadowbrite™ coneflower was developed through controlled crossbreeding for Chicagoland Grows at the Chicago Botanic Garden.

Courtesy Jim Ault.

Perennial plant breeding and evaluation have been a part of the Chicago Botanic Garden's research program since the 1980s, and they remain vital components of the Garden's science program today.

Plant Breeding and Evaluation at the Garden

Breeding begins with cross-pollinating two plants, moving pollen by hand from the flowers of one plant to the flowers of another plant with different traits. The two related plants—which ideally will produce exceptional offspring—are selected for breeding based on various noteworthy attributes, such as flower color and quantity, drought tolerance, ability to resist diseases or pests, and their overall growth habit, while eliminating less desirable characteristics.

Thousands of seeds are collected and germinated in the Garden's plant production facility, and from them, the best are selected for breeding and evaluation. The best plants from these are further bred and evaluated, until a generation of plants is produced that features the most desirable traits from the original parents. The most promising new plants are propagated by cuttings or tissue culture, then meticulously assessed through the Plant Evaluation Program. Over a period of years, they are compared to existing cultivars and species to ensure they are unique and worthy of introduction to the public.

The Chicago Botanic Garden's Plant Evaluation Program began in 1982, when the William Pullman Plant Evaluation Garden opened. The first evaluation projects were relatively casual, used for internal information during the development of the earliest display gardens. In 1985 targeted genera trials began, with a five-year effort to evaluate the performance of, among other plants, a select group of rhododendrons. In 1991 the results were published in the first issue of *Plant Evaluation Notes*, and the Garden began sharing its findings with the world in journal form. Today the Chicago Botanic Garden's Plant Evaluation Program is one of the largest and most diverse in the nation, with more than 1,200 taxa (about 55,000 plants) in a recent year.[20] It is also one of the few evaluation programs that formally evaluates perennials. In 2008,

At the base of the Trellis Bridge crossing from Evening Island to the Plant Science Campus is the Bernice E. Lavin Plant Evaluation Garden, where the Chicago Botanic Garden's Plant Evaluation Program assesses plants in a sunny area.

the Plant Evaluation Program received the Award for Program Excellence from the American Public Garden Association.[21] From asters to rhododendrons, scientists conduct and report on the trials at the Garden, with *Plant Evaluation Notes* now published online and also available through podcasts.

Plants from the breeding program that complete the evaluation process with strong performances ultimately are introduced to consumers through the Chicago-land Grows® partnership among the Garden, the Morton Arboretum, and the Ornamental Growers Association of Illinois. Some of the more coveted perennials in recent years, including the Prairieblues™ series of *Baptisia* (false indigo), were the result of the Garden's remarkable plant breeding program.

Science in the New Millennium: Understanding and Conserving Plants in Peril

In the new millennium, science continues to be a priority of the Chicago Botanic Garden as the issues faced by the planet and its plants intensify. More than a quarter of the world's approximately 400,000 plant species now face extinction, and their habitats are also threatened. At the same time, the number of trained botanists is diminishing, and fewer and fewer universities offer an expertise in plant biology or plant conservation. During the first decade of the new millennium, the Garden embarked upon an array of programs to address these issues, including Plants of Concern (2000); the Conservation Land Management Internship (2001); Seeds of Success (2003); a graduate program with Northwestern University in plant biology and conservation (2005); and Project BudBurst (2007).

The Daniel F. and Ada L. Rice Plant Conservation Science Center is at the forefront of plant science.

Summing Up Success

Plants of Concern

In 2001 Plants of Concern, a rare-plant monitoring program, was co-launched by the Chicago Botanic Garden and Audubon–Chicago Region, with Chicago Wilderness funding. Since then, the Garden has taken on sole management of the program. More than 600 participants in several states have helped locate and count rare, endangered, and threatened plants, and recorded threats, including invasive plants that affect these precious species. Plants of Concern brings together a diverse constituency of trained volunteers—from college students to retirees—public and private land managers, and scientists to monitor 237 rare plant species at 308 sites, including regional forest preserves, the Midewin National Tallgrass Prairie, and privately owned land parcels.

Among plants monitored in Plants of Concern is marsh speedwell (Veronica scutellata).

Seeds of Success

Seeds of Success, the national native seed collection program led by the U.S. Department of the Interior Bureau of Land Management, began in 2001 as the U.S. collecting partner of the Millennium Seed Bank Project, coordinated by the Royal Botanic Gardens, Kew. In 2003 the Chicago Botanic Garden became a collecting partner along with federal agencies and nonfederal organizations. The Garden agreed to collect seeds from 1,200 native species across the Midwest, with an emphasis on tallgrass prairie species. Today, Seeds of Success collects wildland native seed for long-term germplasm conservation and for use in seed research, development of native plant materials, and ecosystem restoration. Garden staff and volunteers continue to collect and preserve germplasm of native plant species from the Upper Midwest for the Garden's Dixon National Tallgrass Prairie Seed Bank and Seeds of Success. The Garden currently holds 3,325 accessions of 2,473 species. Over the years, Seeds of Success collectors have made more than 16,500 native seed collections.

Seeds of tallgrass prairie plants are collected and preserved through the Seeds of Success program.

"Working with our partners in the Seeds of Success consortium, the Garden's Dixon National Tallgrass Prairie Seed Bank is the only seed bank in the world that focuses conservation efforts on the native species of the United States tallgrass prairie, one of the most endangered habitats on the planet."
—Kay Havens-Young, Medard and Elizabeth Welch Director, Plant Science and Conservation, Chicago Botanic Garden

Project BudBurst

In 2007, the Garden became a cofounder of Project BudBurst, a nationwide initiative currently hosted by the National Ecological Observatory Network, which uses "citizen scientist" observers to track climate change by recording the leafing and flowering of flora across the United States. Participants have included school groups, backyard naturalists, gardeners, retirees, scout groups, college professors and their students, hikers, professional botanists and ecologists, visitors to botanic gardens and wildlife refuges, and others interested in contributing to a better understanding of plants and climate change.

A young citizen scientist helps record data for Project BudBurst.

213

Garden scientist Krissa Skogen, Ph.D. (right), awaits the arrival of hawkmoths at Alamogordo, New Mexico, as part of her research into the geographic diversification of interacting organisms.

Garden scientist Nyree Zyega, Ph.D. (center right), travels to Southeast Asia as part of her research on the evolutionary history of Artocarpus *and the genetic diversity of two important tropical crop plants in the genus.*

To support its expanded work in plant research, conservation, and education, the Garden launched the Science Initiative in 2006, which included plans for a new plant research facility. Once again the Rice Foundation responded, becoming the single largest contributer to the Garden's science program since its inception.

In 2009, the 38,000-square-foot, Gold LEED-certified Daniel F. and Ada L. Rice Plant Conservation Science Center opened, designed by the Booth Hansen architectural firm. Today, within the Plant Science Center and at sites throughout the United States and other countries, more than 200 Chicago Botanic Garden scientists, graduate students, and interns uncover new information about habitat fragmentation and restoration, plant and pollinator interaction, the impact of invasive species, and much more. The Plant Science Center houses nine laboratories (see separate section), each with windows that open to an airy concourse where visitors can watch the scientists at work. In 2008 the Negaunee Foundation provided the Chicago Botanic Garden an endowed fund for research on invasive species, and in 2013 the Foundation named the chief scientist position the Negaunee Foundation Vice President of Science.

Garden scientists conduct plant-based research in the Chicago area and the Midwest, elsewhere within the United States, and throughout the world. Research sites are located within 37 states—including Alaska and Hawaii—and 29 countries, from Argentina to the Yucatan in Mexico. In Malaysia, for example, Garden scientists are researching underutilized crop plants. In China, researchers are documenting the effects of pollution on the ecology and diversity of beneficial fungi symbiotic with forest trees. These and other research projects will help the global scientific community save the plants and save the planet.

The Garden's plant science research and training programs thrive through collaborations with government, academic, corporate, and private partners. The Conservation Land Management (CLM) Internship program is a case in point. Since 2001, the Bureau of Land Management in the U.S. Department of the Interior has worked with the Garden to offer college graduates plant conservation internships throughout the United States. Since the Conservation and Land Management

Internship program began, the Garden has selected, trained, and placed more than 850 interns in paid internships at federal agencies to assist biologists and other professionals, increasing botanical capacity in federal land-managing agencies.

Another Garden collaboration is with Northwestern University, which has partnered with the Garden since 2005 to offer a graduate degree in plant conservation and biology. Students take courses at both the Chicago Botanic Garden and Northwestern University and interact with outstanding researchers and faculty from both institutions.

In 2009 the joint program began training doctoral as well as master's students, and in 2012 a combined bachelor's–master's degree was introduced to allow Northwestern undergraduates the opportunity to simultaneously work toward both degrees. In 2014, the Garden and Northwestern began offering a nonthesis M.S. program focusing on coursework and a mentored internship. Through 2014 the program had graduated 50 master's candidates, with the first Ph.D. students graduating in 2015.

Garden scientist Jeremie Fant, Ph.D., collects seed of buckwheat (Eriogonum) *on Bureau of Land Management (BLM) land in Idaho for post–fire restoration work.*

"The importance of partnerships between academic and scientific institutions is vital as we strive to understand, from a molecular level to ecological levels, how the world works. The role of the Chicago Botanic Garden goes far beyond creating horticultural masterpieces. All of the botanic splendor and knowledge on these 385 acres is deeply rooted in the scientific research that is part of the Garden's mission. Our missions complement each other, and we are proud to be a partner with the Chicago Botanic Garden in research and education."
—Daniel I. H. Linzer, Ph.D., Garden Board member and provost, Northwestern University

Garden scientist Shannon Still, Ph.D., photographs a specimen. He is studying the distribution of more than 500 plant species, mostly in the western United States, calculating future migration due to climate change, and creating species distribution models.

In 2010 the Chicago Botanic Garden joined forces with the utility company ComEd in a public-private partnership to reestablish native species in overgrown utility corridors.

The graduate program has benefitted from the support of people like Robert Hevey and Constance Filling, and from entities like the Harris Family Foundation, which is guided today by Society Board members Pam Szokol and Caryn Harris, both members of the Harris family.

Alumni of the graduate program are working in fields of environmental policy, science writing, education, research, and land management for institutions such as the Illinois Department of Natural Resources, the Chicago Park District, the Field Museum, the Morton Arboretum, the U.S. Department of Energy, and the U.S. Environmental Protection Agency, among others.

Conservation-based partnerships between the Garden and companies in the private sector are also proving to be mutually beneficial. In 2010, the Chicago-area utility ComEd invited the Garden to help review research design options and determine best practices for converting overgrown corridors under power transmission lines into sustainable native landscapes. The Garden was able to assist ComEd and, at the same time, benefit from a tremendous restoration research opportunity. By the program's third year, plant life

"The lasting impact of the partnership between the Garden and ComEd will reintroduce, protect, and enhance native ecosystem locations. . . . We are hopeful that lessons learned from this collaboration can one day serve as a road map on how a groundbreaking public-private partnership can protect natural habitats beyond northern Illinois."
—Greg Mueller, chief scientist and Negaunee Foundation Vice President of Science at the Garden

Doctoral student Kelly Ksiazek conducts research atop the Chicago City Hall's 20,000-square-foot green roof.

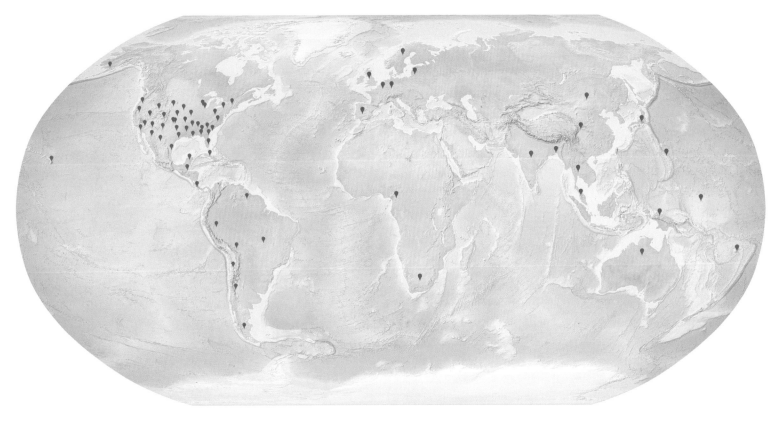

Chicago Botanic Garden scientists conduct research in sites throughout the country and around the globe.

abundant nearly 200 years ago had reemerged in these areas. The goal is that this pilot project will develop a cost-effective and ecologically sound approach to ComEd's ongoing maintenance of 3,000 corridor right-of-way miles and 5,300 miles of power lines throughout Illinois.

The role of science at the Chicago Botanic Garden has received national and international acclaim. Between 2004 and 2012, the dollar amount of grants awarded to Garden scientists nearly tripled.[22] In 2007, recognizing the Garden's leading role in plant conservation, the Botanic Gardens Conservation International (BGCI) moved its U.S. headquarters to the Garden. BGCI's global plant conservation network includes 600 botanic gardens in 120 countries. The Chicago Botanic Garden has participated in the network since 1995, and as its U.S. headquarters, it is helping to expand BGCI's resources globally. The Garden also

is a leader in the Plant Conservation Alliance, an alliance of more than 300 federal and nonfederal organizations committed to conserving native plants and their habitats in the United States. Internationally, Garden scientists are active in the International Union for the Conservation of Nature (IUCN). The IUCN is the largest conservation organization globally, and the Chicago Botanic Garden is one of only a few botanic gardens among its members.

Equipped for Research and Education

The Daniel F. and Ada L. Rice Plant Conservation Science Center provides sophisticated laboratories for research in a wide array of plant science disciplines, and teaching facilities critical to the Garden's efforts to train the next generation of plant scientists. Vital discoveries about plant biology, associated pollinators and fungal symbionts, the impact of habitat destruction, and methods for restoring native habitats are being made within these nine specialized laboratories and the building's green roof garden, which includes the Ellis Goodman Family Foundation Green Roof Garden South and the Josephine P. & John J. Louis Foundation Green Roof Garden North.

Abbott Ecology Laboratory

From investigating the insects and other microfauna associated in leaf litter to assessing the success of restoration in the Garden's natural areas to documenting how wetlands help filter and detoxify polluted water, research in the Abbott Ecology Laboratory focuses on understanding the diversity and ecosystem functions of natural areas. Garden scientists and students are aided in their work by the lab's specialized microscopes and an automated chemical analyzer. The combined space for the Ecology Laboratory and Population Biology Laboratory is 2,400 square feet.

Astellas Economic Botany Laboratory and Harris Family Foundation Plant Genetics Laboratory

DNA analyses are essential tools in plant biology and conservation research. Such studies enable scientists and students to investigate the genetic diversity remaining in small fragmented plant populations, identify wild crop relatives of underutilized food crops for potential use in breeding studies, understand how management of natural areas and cultivation of crop plants affects the ability of plants to thrive under changing conditions, and reveal evolutionary relationships among species. Together, the Astellas Economic Botany Laboratory and the Harris Family Foundation Plant Genetics Laboratory are 2,000 square feet and contain the equipment needed to extract and sequence DNA.

ITW Plant Systematics Laboratory and Nancy Poole Rich Herbarium

Plant systematics is the basis for fields as diverse as restoration, medicinal research, and climate research. Supporting this work is the preparation, mounting, and accessioning of new herbarium specimens. A herbarium is a collection of curated preserved plants; it provides a historical record documenting which plants grew where and when. The herbarium has the capacity to house approximately 70,000 specimens and currently holds more than 14,000 accessioned specimens.

Rebecca Tonietto, Ph.D.—one of the first two graduates to receive their doctoral degrees through the Garden–Northwestern graduate program in plant biology and conservation, in May 2015—sorts bees in the Abbott Ecology Laboratory.

Population Biology Laboratory

For plants to persist in their natural habitat and avoid extinction, they must survive and reproduce. In this laboratory scientists, students, volunteers, and interns measure growth and survival of plants in two walk-in environmental chambers that simulate growing conditions, such as a mild spring, a summer drought, or an atmosphere with high concentrations of carbon dioxide. They measure reproduction of plants by analyzing computer images of flowers, fruits, and seeds taken with digital scanners or an X-ray machine. Each year, citizen scientists in this lab count more than 500,000 individual fruits from thousands of purple coneflower plants growing in experimental plots in prairie habitat. This information helps scientists learn how human activities influence the persistence or extinction of plants in vanishing prairie habitat.

Reproductive Biology Laboratory

Under what conditions do seeds germinate? How long can they be stored and remain viable? The 700-square foot Reproductive Biology Laboratory is where scientists and graduate students discover the answers to these questions. In addition to learning more about the reproductive process, they assess the viability of seed before it is stored in the adjacent Dixon National Tallgrass Prairie Seed Bank.

Soil and Soil Preparation Laboratory

Research in this laboratory (technically, two labs, one for soil research and one for soil processing and other dirty work) focuses on the ecological links between the above- and below-ground biota, and in particular how mycorrhizal fungi are fundamental to the well-being of all above-ground communities and ecosystems. Mycorrhizal fungi form relationships with plant roots and grow fine root-like hyphae into the soil, where they acquire and transfer resources (water, phosphorus, and nitrogen) to the plant in return for sugars to sustain growth. Two primary questions are being addressed: how these plant-fungal interactions affect community and ecosystem processes, and what the consequences are of alterations in climate, land-use, and species invasions on this relationship. The two labs of the Soil and Soil Preparation Laboratory together cover 1,200 square feet. They provide a closed environment for soil research and contain equipment for soil analyses, including microscopes (light, dissecting, and Fourier-transformed infra-red spectrometer [FTIR]), plate readers, balances, centrifuges, gels, rigs, and a carbon-nitrogen determinator.

Within the Daniel F. and Ada L. Rice Plant Conservation Science Center, the open and airy Grainger Gallery features large interior windows that enable visitors to watch scientists at work in the nine laboratories.

The Dixon National Tallgrass Prairie Seed Bank and National Tallgrass Prairie Preparation Laboratory

The tallgrass prairie is one of the earth's most endangered habitats, having lost 96 percent of its land to agricultural and other human activities. To preserve the species found in the region, the Dixon National Tallgrass Prairie Seed Bank is focused on increasing collections from species that are integral to the tallgrass prairie biome of the midwestern United States. This includes flora of the tallgrass prairie and connected ecosystems such as forests and wetlands, plus species of importance to the conservation and restoration of the tallgrass prairie habitat. Scientists and collaborators are collecting multiple samples of more than 500 species selected for their importance for habitat restoration and their ability to survive in cold storage. Seeds are stored in the Dixon National Tallgrass Prairie Seed Bank at -20 degrees Celsius for long-term preservation.

Seeds are stored in the Dixon National Tallgrass Prairie Seed Bank at -20 degrees Celsius.

Josephine P. & John J. Louis Foundation Microscopy Laboratory

Research in the Josephine P. & John J. Louis Foundation Microscopy Laboratory includes studying plant fossils, documenting morphological features of extant plants and fungi, and interpreting spatial data revealing trends in plant distributions. The laboratory contains microscopes fitted with digital image capture and analysis systems, a fluorescent microscope, and Geographic Information System (GIS) equipment (the latter of which was made possible by a grant from the National Science Foundation). The GIS section of the laboratory is dedicated to becoming a regional center for spatial analysis and cartographic production promoting collaboration with regional partners in spatial analysis, research, teaching, and training in support of plant conservation and restoration ecology.

Senior scientist Patrick Herendeen, Ph.D., studies a herbarium specimen of a plant collection from Southeast Asia, using a Leica dissecting microscope in the Josephine P. & John J. Louis Foundation Microscopy Laboratory.

Some of the Garden's landscapes are particularly important in the research work at the Daniel F. and Ada L. Rice Plant Conservation Science Center. The Green Roof Garden—which includes the Josephine P. & John J. Louis Foundation Green Roof Garden North and the Ellis Goodman Family Foundation Green Roof Garden South—is part of the Plant Science Center itself and offers ideas for mitigating urban heat islands.

Green roofs are becoming increasingly popular, but little research has been done to determine which plants are best suited for this extreme environment. The Chicago Botanic Garden's evaluation of plants atop the Daniel F. and Ada L. Rice Plant Conservation Science Center is one of the largest, most encompassing such trials in the United States.[23] Approximately 40,000 plants representing 200 distinct species and cultivars are currently under evaluation within three soil levels (4, 6, and 8 inches deep) on the 16,000-square-foot green roof, divided into the Josephine P. & John J. Louis Foundation Green Roof Garden North and the Ellis Goodman Family Foundation Green Roof Garden South. The plants in the back half of each garden are scientifically evaluated for effectiveness in the semi-intensive roof garden environment, while the front half is for display.

This living laboratory is outfitted with equipment to monitor soil moisture, wind and light levels, and temperatures in the various layers of the plants. Scientists evaluate plant health, aesthetics, and survivorship of plants, ultimately recommending plants that are low-maintenance, absorb water and nutrients from rainfall (lessening runoff into storm sewers), and cool the building below (lessening energy use), while providing an aesthetic retreat.

Plants' performances in 30 characteristics are tracked for a minimum of four years before staff members assess their suitability. Results are shared through the Garden's *Plant Evaluation Notes*, a publication distributed broadly to gardeners and horticultural professionals and through horticulture and gardening magazines and educational classes and symposia. Successful plants are promoted to the green roof industry, both locally and nationally, to ensure that the most appropriate and sustainable plants are used for this unique environment.

An aerial view shows the Josephine P. & John J. Louis Foundation Green Roof Garden North (left) and the Ellis Goodman Family Foundation Green Roof Garden South (right), part of the Daniel F. and Ada L. Rice Plant Conservation Science Center.

The Josephine P. & John J. Louis Foundation Green Roof Garden North features a mix of tried-and-true green roof plants from around the world that Garden staff believe will do well in this environment. The garden is half display and half plant evaluation, with display plants closest to the observation deck and evaluation plants in the back half, where they are trialed for rooftop conditions.

The Ellis Goodman Family Foundation Green Roof Garden South is limited to plants native to America, many of which are not currently used as rooftop plants. Both green roof gardens include a display section, showing a beautiful roof garden (per the standards of other Chicago Botanic Garden display gardens) and an evaluation section where plants are tested for inclusion in the display section.

The four natural areas at the Chicago Botanic Garden—McDonald Woods, Dixon Prairie, Skokie River Corridor, and Garden Lakes—serve as living laboratories for plant conservation, habitat restoration, and student training.

The Natural Areas

The natural areas are managed to enhance habitat quality and increase biodiversity. These natural areas are also beautiful and welcoming places for visitors to enjoy. Recently, four distinguished groups honored the Garden for multiyear projects that have beautified the Garden and enhanced fragile natural habitats. Chicago Wilderness, the North American Lake Management Society, the Landscape Architecture Foundation, and the Illinois Landscape Contractors Association recognized the Garden for its dedicated efforts and impressive results along the shorelines of the Garden Lakes as well as in the McDonald Woods.

In addition to these four areas, in 2011, through the support of Roger and Barbara Brown, a 12-acre area including a small lake on the Garden's southeast side, near Dundee Road, was restored. Previously infested with nonnative invasive plants, these beautiful woodland, wetland, and lake habitats now compose the Barbara Brown Nature Reserve, which has become a favorite spot for bird-watchers.

McDonald Woods

Formerly part of Turnbull Woods, the McDonald Woods is a 100-acre piece of a larger oak woodland that thrived in this region just a century ago. The site was added to the Garden through the efforts of namesake Mary Mix McDonald, former Cook County Commissioner and head of the Cook County Forest Preserve's Botanic Garden Committee. While oak woodlands once dotted northeastern Illinois, today only small remnants such as this treasured tract remain.

The plants in the McDonald Woods, a native woodland system, include more than 400 species of native plants, including several rare and threatened species, 20 species

of mammals, and 118 species of birds. Hundreds of species of mushrooms and thousands of insect varieties call the Woods their home.

In 1989, the Garden initiated a program to restore the biological diversity, integrity, and sustainability of McDonald Woods. Staff and volunteers cut and pull invasive plants such as buckthorn and garlic mustard, and ecologists conduct carefully controlled burns in selected areas of the Woods to keep these unwanted invaders at bay. They also collect and plant seeds of native grasses, sedges, and wildflowers.

Research in the McDonald Woods has shown that a restored woodland is more than aesthetically pleasing. Garden scientists documented that with six to 14 years of active management, restored woodland areas provide substantially more carbon storage than unrestored areas dominated by buckthorn.[24] It is the setting for environmental education and conservation research and has been designated a demonstration site for oak woodland restoration in the Chicago area.

Dappled sunlight filters into McDonald Woods, where the restored woodland shows a healthy, open ecosystem—in contrast to areas once choked by buckthorn and other invasive plant species.
Courtesy Jim Steffen.

Dixon Prairie

During the 1980s, the Garden embarked on construction of a complex prairie habitat featuring portions of prairie landscape once common in northeastern Illinois. Dedicated in 1993, the 15-acre Dixon Prairie is composed of six prairie ecosystems: tallgrass, sand, gravel hill, wet prairie, bur oak savanna, and fen. Each type of prairie has its own topography, hydrology, soil conditions, and native plant species.

The tallgrass prairie—representative of the tallgrass prairies that once covered 60 percent of Illinois—features classic tallgrass prairie grasses and wildflowers, some of which are more than 8 feet tall. The sand prairie is a re-creation of the type of prairie found naturally at the southwestern end of Lake Michigan, where the shoreline encompasses low dunes with a marshy habitat sited between them. The plant varieties found there reflect the dual nature of the environment. The steeply sloped gravel hill prairie is a dry, exceptionally well-drained area with slightly sandy or gravelly soil. Plants found there are lower to the ground and flower earlier than those of the tallgrass prairie. The wet prairie is located in a low area where the soil stays moist during the growing season, in a habitat historically hydrated through groundwater. The bur oak savanna is an open grassland prairie that incorporates scattered native bur oak trees with partial-sun-loving grasses and wildflowers. The fen is an unusual wetland where the water contains a high degree of mineral salts leached from underground limestone.

Birds, butterflies, bees, and other buzzing insects are drawn to the rich diversity of the Dixon Prairie, with its 260 native plant species. Late summer and early fall are the seasons of peak prairie growth, with wildflowers and grasses reaching their mature height. In every season, the Dixon Prairie offers visitors a rich mosaic of prairies to enjoy.

Dixon Prairie namesake Suzanne Dixon shares a laugh at the Chicago Botanic Garden during the on-site filming of an episode of the Discovery Channel series Dirty Jobs *in 2011. An avid outdoorswoman and recipient of the 2013 Chicago Horticultural Society Medal, Dixon has long been a hands-on friend of the Garden, serving as a President's Circle member since 1971 and on the Board since 1997. She and her husband, Wes Dixon, named their own home Prairie Dock for the native plant that grows abundantly on the 5-acre prairie parcel.*

The John D. and Catherine T. MacArthur Foundation contributed to the Dixon Prairie and supported a multiyear marketing and branding campaign. The Foundation also provides significant annual general operating support that reaches all aspects of Garden operations.

Late-afternoon sunlight casts a mellow glow on this fall view from the Dixon Prairie to Evening Island.

Skokie River Corridor

The mile-long Skokie River Corridor, which meanders along the western edge of the Chicago Botanic Garden, is a demonstration site featuring natural methods to enhance urban waterways, with plantings of sedges, grasses, and forbs (wildflowers) of varied textures, shapes, and hues—and, most important, biodiversity.

The beautiful valley is a continuing experiment in how to use low-impact, natural methods to improve the water quality of urban waterways, restore floodplains, and increase the variety of native plant, insect, animal, and bird life. This living laboratory demonstrates river enhancement techniques and the establishment of floodplain wetlands, upland prairie, and oak savanna-woodland along a 22-acre, human-built riparian corridor. Today, approximately 200 species of native herbaceous plants are thriving within the Skokie River Corridor, including fast-growing trees that form a backdrop on the Garden's western edge as slow-growing oaks—primarily bur oak (*Quercus macrocarpa*)—reach maturity.

Today, approximately 200 species of native plants thrive within the Skokie River Corridor. Among other things, the beautiful valley is a continuing experiment in how to use low-impact, natural methods to improve the water quality of urban waterways.

In June the native iris (*Iris virginica* var. *shrevei*) blooms in abundance here, much as it did in the Great Skokie Marsh that preceded the Chicago Botanic Garden. Toward the end of July, reds and purples steal the show—swamp milkweed (*Asclepias incarnata*), ironweed (*Vernonia fasciculata*) and spotted Joe-Pye-weed (*Eupatorium maculatum*). Into September and October, goldenrods (*Solidago graminifolia, S. ohioensis, S. riddellii*) and New England aster (*Aster novae-angliae*) present a last burst of color before the fall freeze. In winter, the dried plants present a more austere beauty of muted browns, tans, and grays.

Though no longer the original stream channel that was part of a much larger marsh habitat before being converted to a drainage ditch in the early 1900s, the restored Skokie River Corridor is a valuable natural resource and source of enjoyment to the many Garden visitors who walk along it each year.

Garden Lakes

The Chicago Botanic Garden's lakes took form when the nine islands of the Garden were sculpted during its construction. Of the Garden's 385 acres, nearly one-quarter (81 acres) are covered in water. The 60-acre system of Garden Lakes winds throughout the Garden, encircled by 5.7 miles of shoreline. The lakes have evolved into a thriving ecosystem through skilled ecological management, providing living laboratories for Garden conservation scientists and their colleagues studying urban water resources. The Garden's programs to reduce soil erosion and nutrient runoff improve water quality in the downstream Skokie Lagoons, Chicago River, and beyond.

In 1998, a study of shoreline conditions revealed that 80 percent of the Chicago Botanic Garden's lakeshores were experiencing moderate to severe erosion. In June

Nearly one-quarter of the Chicago Botanic Garden's acreage is covered in water, as shown in this 1982 photograph.

Courtesy Lenhardt Library of the Chicago Botanic Garden.

Before the North Lake Shoreline Restoration Project, erosion had worn away much of the shoreline.

After completion of the project in 2012, the shoreline extended much farther and was anchored by more than 120,000 water-loving plants.

2000, the Garden began to restore its most critically eroding shorelines. Since the shoreline enhancement program began, more than 4½ miles of the Garden's shoreline has been restored. The North Lake Shoreline Restoration Project, encompassing 1¼ miles of shoreline around the 20-acre North Lake, was completed in 2012 as part of the U.S. Army Corps of Engineers' Ecosystem Restoration Program.

The result: wetland habitats along the lakeshores, previously measured in inches, now expand out from the lake edge by 30 feet or more. Innovative bioengineering approaches for creating stable, shallow-water "shelves" along the shoreline allow water-loving plants to flourish and anchor shoreline soils. More than a half-million native plants and shrubs were added to stabilize shoreline soils. Representing 240 native taxa, these plants, some with roots more than 6 feet deep, anchor eroding shoreline soils while withstanding the environmental stresses inherent to urban waterways, such as flooding. They provide form and function, while filtering excess nutrients and enhancing habitat for frogs, turtles, fish, mussels, aquatic insects, and birds.

The rejuvenated Garden shorelines not only are beautiful and functional but also provide practical examples of ways to restore, protect, and manage the shorelines along urban lakes and detention ponds.

As part of the shoreline restoration program, the entire perimeter of the Regenstein Fruit & Vegetable Garden was restored, including a beautiful and functional vegetable-garden terrace welcoming visitors into the garden (shown here before and after construction).

Top: Courtesy Robert Kirschner.

With a team of experienced scientists, horticulturists, educators, interns, volunteers, and supporters, the Chicago Botanic Garden today brings to Chicago and the world all that horticulture promises—and even more than the early Chicago Horticultural Society envisioned.

Acknowledgments

Many individuals over the past 125 years put the "garden" in Chicago, the Garden City. The men and women of the Chicago Horticultural Society carried the torch for decades and brought the beauty of nature to the city and beyond.

Sophia Shaw, president and CEO of the Chicago Botanic Garden, championed this book from the outset. I am also indebted to the many Chicago Botanic Garden staff members who provided invaluable contributions: Leora Siegel, the Garden's Lenhardt Library director, and the library staff and volunteers including Dorren Gertsen-Briand. Carol Abbate, the Garden's director of design and production; Robin Carlson, Garden photographer; and Garden editorial director Amy Spungen provided design and editing assistance. Leigh Armstrong, of Armstrong-Johnston, obtained and organized the many images in this book.

Early reviewers of the manuscript caught many of my errors. I wish to thank Kris Jarantoski, executive vice president and director; Jim Boudreau, vice president, Marketing and Development; Patsy Benveniste, vice president, Education and Community Programs; and Gregory Mueller, chief scientist and Negaunee Foundation Vice President of Science. Any remaining errors are mine.

The staff at Northwestern University Press provided excellent counsel and design and editing expertise, especially director Jane Frances Bunker, managing editor Anne Gendler, and art director Marianne Jankowski.

As always, I am greatly indebted to GMG, GVG, Mike, Tom, and the family.

Cathy Jean Maloney

Appendixes

Board Leadership, Chicago Horticultural Society

Horticultural Society of Chicago 1890–1945

1890–1891	George Schneider	President, Board of Trustees
1891–1904	William H. Chadwick	President, Board of Trustees
1904–1908	Edward G. Uihlein	President, Board of Trustees
1908–1909	William E. Kelley	President, Board of Trustees
1910–1912	Charles L. Hutchinson	President, Board of Trustees
1913–1916	Willis N. Rudd	President, Board of Trustees
1943–1945	Carl Croop, Sr.	President, Board of Trustees

Chicago Horticultural Society and Garden Center 1945–1954

1945–1949	Laurance Armour	Chairman, Board of Trustees
1945–1949	C. Eugene Pfister	President, Board of Governors
1949–1951	Paul Battey	President, Board of Governors
1950–1954	Albert C. Buehler	Chairman, Board of Trustees
1951–1953	Elmer Claar	President, Board of Governors

Chicago Horticultural Society 1954–Present

1954–1956	F. A. Cushing Smith	President, Board of Trustees
1956–1959	Dr. R. Milton Carleton	President, Board of Trustees
1959–1968	William A. P. Pullman	President, Board of Trustees
1968–1972	Dr. George Beadle	President, Board of Trustees

1970–1972	Eric Oldberg	Chairman, Board of Trustees
1972–1979	Peter H. Merlin	Chairman, Board of Directors
1979–1986	Ralph A. Bard	Chairman, Board of Directors
1986–1987	Nancy Race (Mrs. Charles O.)	Chairman, Board of Directors
1987–1993	Janet Meakin Poor (Mrs. Edward King Poor III)	Chairman, Board of Directors
1993–1997	Peter H. Merlin	Chairman, Board of Directors
1997–2002	Thomas A. Donahoe	Chairman, Board of Directors
2002–2009	William Hagenah	Chairman, Board of Directors
2009–2012	Susan A. Willetts	Chairman, Board of Directors
2012–present	Robert F. Finke	Chairman, Board of Directors

Executive Leadership, Chicago Horticultural Society

1961–1971	Robert P. Wintz	Executive Director
1972–1977	Louis B. Martin, Ph.D.	President and CEO
1977–1985	Roy Mecklenburg, Ph.D.	President, CEO, and Director
1985–1994	Roy Taylor, Ph.D.	President, CEO, and Director
1995–2007	Barbara Whitney Carr	President and CEO
2007–present	Sophia Shaw	President and CEO

Woman's Board Presidents, Chicago Horticultural Society

1951–1954	Mrs. E. Eugene Pfister (Alice)
1954–1957	Mrs. C. Kenneth Hunter (LaVerne)
1957–1969	Mrs. Albert D. Farwell (Edith)
1969–1971	Mrs. Stewart Owen (Gary)
1971–1972	Mrs. Charles O. Race (Nancy)
1973–1975	Mrs. Bruce Thorne (Marianne)
1975–1977	Mrs. Paul W. Oliver (Caroline)
1977–1981	Mrs. Austin M. Zimmerman (Sodie)
1981–1983	Mrs. Gardner Brown (Betty)
1983–1985	Mrs. Joseph E. Rich (Nancy)
1985–1986	Mrs. Thomas E. Noyes (Ginny)
1986–1987	Mrs. John V. Farwell (Liz)
1987–1989	Mrs. John S. Dean III (Betty)
1989–1991	Mrs. Robert W. Anderson (Taimi)
1991–1993	Mrs. Thomas D. Heath (Marilyn)
1993–1995	Mrs. J .W. William Volckens (Susie)
1995–1997	Mrs. Theodore L. Horne (Penny)
1997–1999	Mrs. Frank A. Priebe, Jr. (Julie)
1999–2003	Mrs. Robert W. Crowe (Liz)
2003–2005	Mrs. Charles E. Schroeder (Beth)
2005–2007	Mrs. Carl H. Boyer (Mary)
2007–2009	Mrs. O. Renard Goltra (Alice)
2009–2011	Mrs. Melville C. Hill, Jr. (Mary)
2011–2013	Mrs. William J. Kirby (Catherine)
2013–2015	Mrs. Richard Metzler (Barbara)

Guild Presidents, Chicago Botanic Garden

1998–2001	Susan K. Canrnann
	John D. Fornengo
2001–2003	Brooke D. Kuehnle
	John P. McEnaney
2003–2005	Jennifer Kasten
	Stephanie A. Madigan
2005–2007	Michael J. Busch
	Anne S. Loucks
2007–2009	Susanna R. Block
	Jay L. Owen, Jr.
2009–2010	Jay L. Owen, Jr.
	Joseph M. Brickman
2010–2011	Joseph M. Brickman
	Gloria S. Masterson
2011–2012	Gloria S. Masterson
	Riley S. O'Neil
2012–2013	Riley S. O'Neil
	Lindsey C. Axel
2013–2014	Lindsey C. Axel
	Brayton B. Alley
2014–2015	Brayton B. Alley
	Kimberly J. Burt

President's Circle Co-chairs, Chicago Botanic Garden

1999–2006	Mary L. McCormack
	Josephine P. Louis
2008–2009	Susan Stone
	Michael Busch
2009–2010	Michael Busch
	Jane O'Neil
2010–2011	Jane O'Neil
	Susan Canmann
2011–2012	Jane O'Neil
	Benjamin Lenhardt
2012–2013	Benjamin Lenhardt
	Betsy Hough
2013–2015	Dorothy Gardner
	James DeYoung

Hutchinson Medal

1911	Edwin A. Kanst
1951	Edith Foster Farwell
1952	Joseph M. Cudahy
1953	Oakley Morgan
1955	David Francis Hall
1956	Fred Heuchling
1957	Nels J. Johnson
1958	John Ott, Jr.
1959	R. Milton Carleton, Ph.D.
1960	Garden Club of America
1963	Hubert A. Fischer
1967	Clarence E. Godshalk
	Charles (Cap) G. Sauers
1968	William A. P. Pullman
1969	Virginia Carlson
1971	John Lundgren
1972	May Thielgaard Watts
1974	Eric Oldberg, M.D.
1975	Art Kozelka
1976	Richard J. Daley
1977	Franz Lipp
	Anthony Tyznik
1978	James Brown IV
	Bruce Krasberg
1979	Edward Larrabee Barnes
	John O. Simonds
1980	Arthur L. Janura
	Peter H. Merlin
1981	Garden Clubs of Illinois
	Rose Vasumpaur
1982	Donald R. Egolf, Ph.D.

1983	Herbert C. Swim
1984	Robert Carlson, Ph.D.
	Joseph Vandemark, Ph.D.
1985	William T. Stearn, D.Sc.
1986	Peter H. Raven, Ph.D.
1987	John L. Creech, Ph.D.
1988	Mildred E. Mathias, Ph.D.
1989	Vernon H. Heywood
1990	Marion T. Hall, Ph.D.
1991	Elizabeth Scholtz
1992	Robert H. Mohlenbrock, Ph.D.
1993	Allen P. Paterson
1994	Janet Meakin Poor
1995	Ardath H. Rodale
1996	Elvin McDonald
1997	George Ware, Ph.D.
1998	Darrel G. Morrison
1999	John Brookes
2000	Francis H. Cabot
2001	Peter R. Crane, FRS
2002	Susumu Nakamura
2004	Edward O. Wilson, Ph.D.
2007	Barbara Whitney Carr
2008	James Gustave Speth
2010	Chicago Wilderness
2011	George B. Rabb, Ph.D.
2012	Gerald W. Adelmann
	August A. De Hertogh, Ph.D.
2013	Forest Preserves of Cook County
	Elwin R. Orton, Ph.D.
2014	Allan M. Armitage, Ph.D.
2015	William J. Radler

Chicago Horticultural Society Medal

1981	Francis de Vos, Ph.D.
1982	William A. P. Pullman
	Elizabeth T. Zimmerman
1983	Nancy M. Race
1984	George W. Dunne
1985	Ralph A. Bard, Jr.
	Janet Meakin Poor
1986	Mrs. Charles H. Hodges III
	Ralph Synnestvedt, Jr.
1987	Mary M. McDonald
1988	Bruce Krasberg
1991	Gertrude B. Nielsen
	William B. Graham
	Joseph Regenstein, Jr.
1993	Neil McKay
1994	Richard J. Phelan
	Roy L. Taylor, Ph.D.
1995	Taimi T. Anderson
	J. Melfort Campbell
	E. Norman Staub
1996	John H. Stroger, Jr.
1997	Peter H. Merlin
1998	Albert C. Buehler, Jr.
1999	Elizabeth Coulson
	Lauren Beth Gash
	Kathleen K. Parker
	Jeffrey M. Schoenberg
2001	The Woman's Board of the Chicago Horticultural Society
2002	Senator Richard Durbin
	Thomas A. Donahoe
2003	Linda W. Doede

2004	Gaylord and Dorothy Donnelley Foundation
	Daniel F. and Ada L. Rice Foundation
	John G. and Frances C. Searle Family
2005	Pleasant T. Rowland
2008	Geoffrey L. Rausch
2009	William J. Hagenah
2010	Posy Krehbiel
	Eugene A. Rothert
2011	Oehme, van Sweden & Associates, Inc.
	Charlene and Robert Shaw
2012	Robert H. Malott
	Richard L. Thomas
2013	Suzanne S. Dixon
2014	Josephine P. Louis
2015	Gary G. Brown
	Thomas B. Hunter III
	Howard J. Trienens

Notes

Chapter 1

1. The Society's name has changed over the years. Originally chartered as the Horticultural Society of Chicago, it was reinstated in 1945 as the Chicago Horticultural Society and Garden Center. In 1954 it changed to its current name, the Chicago Horticultural Society. For clarity, the Society will be referred to in this book as either the Society or the Chicago Horticultural Society. Additionally, references to the Garden, post-1972, refer to the leadership of the Chicago Botanic Garden who perform the day-to-day management activities of the Garden.

2. Minutes of the Chicago Horticultural Society, October 14, 1890. Horticultural Society of Chicago. Miscellaneous records of the Horticultural Society of Chicago, 1890–1904. Lenhardt Library Collections, Chicago Botanic Garden, Glencoe, Illinois (hereafter cited as Horticultural Society records).

3. Cathy Jean Maloney. *Chicago Gardens: The Early History* (Chicago: University of Chicago Press, 2008), chapters 2 and 3.

4. *Puck*, July 23, 1884.

5. World's Columbian Exposition. Report of the President to the Board of Directors of the World's Columbian Exposition (Chicago: 1892–93), 8.

6. "Daddies of the Fair," *Chicago Daily Tribune*, October 11, 1890, 9, accessed June 15, 2013, ProQuest.

7. "Visited the Proposed Sites," *Chicago Daily Tribune*, August 29, 1890, 9, accessed June 22, 2013, ProQuest. The Columbian Horticultural Association was sometimes called the Columbian Horticultural Society. Its membership appears to have folded into various departments and interest groups associated with the World's Columbian Exposition.

8. Horticultural Society records. This formative group appears to have had other names, such as the Agricultural and Horticultural Society of Chicago and Cook County, and also met on August 21, 1890, according to "The Chicago Horticultural Society," *Chicago Daily Tribune*, August 17, 1890, and "For Flowers and Fruit Growers," *Chicago Daily Tribune*, August 22, 1890, 3, accessed June 22, 2013, ProQuest.

9. "Display Ad 1—no Title," *Chicago Daily Tribune*, September 2, 1890, 3, accessed June 22, 2013, ProQuest.

10. Among the members who belonged to predecessor groups were, from the Columbian Horticultural Society: J. C. Vaughan (American Seed Trade Association), James D. Raynolds (Society of American Florists), Andrew Dunning (Northern Horticultural Society), G. L. Grant (Chicago Floral Club), Edgar Sanders (Cook County Horticultural Society); from the Agricultural and Horticultural Society of Chicago and Cook County: Edgar Sanders, Andrew McNally, and Jonathan Periam. Bailey, L. H. *Annals of Horticulture in North America for the Year 1890: A Witness of Passing Events and a Record of Progress* (New York: Rural Pub. Co, 1891). Internet resource.

11. Minutes of October 3, 1891, meeting, 27, Horticultural Society records. Among the charter members of that first year were Bertha (Mrs. Potter) Palmer, W. H. Rand, and Frederick Kanst. Although Thorpe hailed from New York, during the Columbian Exposition he listed his address in the Rand McNally Building upon acceptance as a Chicago Horticultural Society member in January 1892. Minutes of January 9, 1892, meeting, 37, Horticultural Society records.

12. Frederick Law Olmsted, Jr., to Frederick Law Olmsted, Sr., July 1, 1891, in Frederick L. Olmsted, *The Papers of Frederick Law Olmsted* (Washington, D.C.: Library of Congress Photoduplication Service, 1975), print from the Olmsted Collection, Riverside, Illinois Public Library (hereafter cited as FLO papers).

13. Frederick Law Olmsted, Jr., to Frederick Law Olmsted, Sr., July 2, 1891, FLO papers.

14. Frederick Law Olmsted, Sr., to Harry S. Codman, April 20, 1892, FLO papers.

15. James W. Ellsworth to Frederick Law Olmsted, July 26, 1890, FLO papers.

16. L. H. Bailey, *Annals of Horticulture in North America for the Year 1893: A Witness of Passing Events and a Record of Progress* (New York: Orange Judd, 1894), 27.

17. Minutes of January 13, 1894, meeting, 82–83, Horticultural Society papers.

18. Minutes of January 9, 1897, and April 10, 1897, meeting, 162, Horticultural Society papers.

19. Jens Jensen, "Insects Destroying Our Ornamental and Shade Trees," *Gardening* 197, 147. Also see "Will Show Rare Blooms," *Chicago Daily Tribune*, November 5, 1899, 5, accessed June 24, 2013, ProQuest.

20. Horticultural Society of Chicago Constitution and By-Laws, 1908, 7. Chicago History Museum Collection. F38MA H7C 1908. Horticultural Society of Chicago Constitution, Bylaws, Officers and Members.

21. Carl Smith, *The Plan of Chicago: Daniel Burnham and the Remaking of the American City* (Chicago: University of Chicago Press, 2006), 19.

22. "Outer Belt of Forest Preserves and Parkways for Chicago and Cook County." 1904. Biodiversity Heritage Library, accessed March 30, 2014, http://www.biodiversitylibrary.org/title/62518.

23. The newly formed district faced legal challenges, and it wasn't until 1916 that the Illinois Supreme Court declared the Forest Preserve Act constitutional. See Forest Preserve District of Cook County website, http://fpdcc.com/about/history.

24. Cook County (Ill.), *The Forest Preserves of Cook County Owned by the Forest Preserve District of Cook County in the State of Illinois* (Chicago: Clohesey, 1918), 40–42. Digitized Books from the University of Illinois at Urbana–Champaign and the Open Content Alliance, accessed March 30, 2014, http://hdl.handle.net/10111/UIUCOCA:forestpreserveso00cook.

25. "Notice of Agreement between Daniel H. Burnham and Merchant's Club of Chicago, 1906," Encyclopedia of Chicago, accessed March 30, 2014, http://www.encyclopedia.chicagohistory.org/pages/10845.html.

26. C. L. Hutchinson to Charles H. Wacker, 21 May 1909, in Art Institute of Chicago, "Without Bounds of Limits: An Online Exhibition of the *Plan of Chicago*," accessed June 15, 2013, http://digital-libraries.saic.edu/cdm/ref/collection/mqc/id/4386.

27. "The Tribune's Prize Garden Contest," *Chicago Daily Tribune*, March 30, 1908, 7, accessed June 25, 2013, ProQuest.

28. "The Tribune's Prize Garden Contest," *Chicago Daily Tribune*, April 25, 1908, 6, accessed June 25, 2013, ProQuest.

29. "Finest Gardens Win Many Prizes," *Chicago Daily Tribune*, August 19, 1908, 1, accessed May 7, 2013, ProQuest.

30. See Maloney, *Chicago Gardens*, 62–73.

31. "Enlist Rich Men in Floriculture," *Chicago Daily Tribune*, May 27, 1912, 10, accessed June 25, 2013, ProQuest.

32. "Women Will Rescue City Flower Society," *Chicago Examiner* 13, no. 31, 1913.

33. Gertrude Gallagher, interview by Cathy Jean Maloney, June 26, 2013.

34. Fred G. Heuchling, "In Defense of OCD," *Chicago Daily Tribune*, October 18, 1943, 14, accessed June 26, 2013, ProQuest.

35. Nancy M'inerny, "North Shore Shows Gardens Today," *Chicago Daily Tribune*, August 2, 1942, 1, accessed June 26, 2013, ProQuest.

36. June Reedy, *It's Fun to Remember*, (Chicago: Chicago Horticultural Society, 1974), 2 vols., 2:4.

37. Chicago Horticultural Society and Garden Center memo, January 29, 1945. From CHS archives, Box 1, Box 3001A, Folder 13.

38. Reedy, *It's Fun to Remember*, 1:6.

39. Ibid., 1:8.

40. C. Eugene Pfister in opening remarks at First Annual Spring Garden Meeting, April 7, 1945, as quoted in *Garden Talks* 1, no. 1 (April–May 1945): 6.

41. Reedy, *It's Fun to Remember*, 1:19.

42. *Garden Talks* 8, no. 8 (August 1960): 3, 6–7.

43. Initially, the Garden was called the Botanic Garden of the Chicago Horticultural Society. Its current name, the Chicago Botanic Garden, became official in 1980.

44. "Vital Statistics," Chicago Botanic Garden, accessed March 30, 2014, http://www.chicagobotanic.org/info/statistics/.

45. "Regenstein Sets Standard for Edible Gardening," *Garden Talk* 12, no. 5 (May 1997): 4.

Chapter 2

1. H. S. Pepoon, *Flora of the Chicago Region* (Chicago: Lakeside Press, 1927), 26–27.

2. "The Skokie Lagoons," *Nature Bulletin*, no. 646, September 9, 1961, by Forest Preserve District of Cook County on Newton website, http://www.newton.dep.anl.gov/natbltn/600–699/nb646.htm, accessed May 16, 2014.

3. "Big Blaze in Skokie Marsh," *Chicago Daily Tribune*, December 5, 1898, 9, accessed August 1, 2013, ProQuest.

4. "Brief History of the U.S. Botanic Garden." United States Botanic Garden, accessed August 1, 2013, http://www.usbg.gov/brief-history-us-botanic-garden.

5. Maloney, *Chicago Gardens*, 30–31.

6. Minutes of the Chicago Horticultural Society, April 27, 1895, 123, Horticultural Society papers.

7. For a discussion of Jensen's career in the West Side parks, and the graft that was "rampant in the system," see Robert E. Grese, *Jens Jensen, Maker of Natural Parks and Gardens* (Baltimore: Johns Hopkins University Press, 1992), 62–63.

8. President's Address 1897, 145, Horticultural Society papers.

9. "Talk of Permanent Home for the Big Flower Shows." *Chicago Daily Tribune*, November 20, 1904, 6, accessed October 24, 2013, ProQuest.

10. Dwight D. Perkins, *Report of the Special Park Commission to the City of Chicago on the Subject of a Municipal Park System* (Chicago: W. J. Hartman, 1905), 87, 96.

11. According to the *Chicago Tribune*, the Special Park Commission and Civic Federation of Chicago opposed the proposed legislation for forest preserves in 1905. The *Tribune* cited Jens Jensen and settlement leader Graham Taylor as the only advocates of the legislation, along with members of the Chicago Woman's Club. "Outer Park Act Gets Hard Jolts," *Chicago Daily Tribune*, October 26, 1905, 4, accessed August 6, 2013, ProQuest.

12. "The Early History of the Forest Preserve District of Cook County, 1869–1922," Forest Preserve District of Cook County, accessed April 10, 2014, http://fpdcc.com/about/history.

13. "Trees to Teach," *Chicago Daily Tribune*, April 15, 1919, 17, accessed August 6, 2013, ProQuest.

14. "Chicago to Have World's Finest Flower Garden," *Chicago Daily Tribune*, June 28, 1919, 5, accessed August 6, 2013, ProQuest.

15. Forest Preserve District of Cook County, Illinois (Ill.). 1921. *The forest preserves of Cook County owned by the Forest Preserve District of Cook County in the state of Illinois*. Chicago: Clohesey & Co. [printers].

16. The zoo was modeled after the Tierpark Hagenbeck in Hamburg, Germany. For more on the Brookfield Zoo landscape, see Maloney, *Chicago Gardens*, 278–83.

17. "Artist's Work Boosts Skokie Marsh Purchase." *Chicago Daily Tribune*, February 19, 1920, 3, accessed August 7, 2013, ProQuest.

18. FPDCC Advisory Board to the President and Members of the Board of Forest Preserve, January 9, 1935. FPDCC Collection, Box LA-AC 4, FBDCC Advisory Committee Minutes 1931–35. UIC Library FPDCC Collections.

19. "Find Caretaker of Ickes Home a Boss of CCC," *Chicago Daily Tribune*, October 12, 1940, 5, accessed August 12, 2013, ProQuest.

20. Thomas Buck, "Plan to Spend 20 Million on Forest Preserves," *Chicago Daily Tribune*, March 18, 1957, accessed August 12, 2013, ProQuest.

21. "CHS Report of Survey Committee," March 23, 1956, 4–5, Chicago Horticultural Society archives, Box 3001A, folder 4.

22. Ibid.

23. William A. Pullman, Report of the President, July 29, 1965, 1. Chicago Horticultural Society archives, Box 4001A, folder 3.

24. Chicago Horticultural Society biographical information for Fairchild portrait. Horticultural Society papers.

25. "Movers and Shakers," *Forbes*, February 9, 2001, http://www.forbes.com/2001/02/09/0209movers.html.

26. Reedy, *It's Fun to Remember*, 1:72.

27. "Horticulture Society Backs Grant Pk. Plan." *Chicago Daily Tribune*, April 12, 1961, accessed August 24, 2013, ProQuest.

28. William A. Pullman, Report of the President, July 29, 1965. 1. Chicago Horticultural Society archives, Box 4001A, folder 3.

29. William A. Pullman to the President and Board of Commissioners of the Forest Preserve District of Cook County, September 1962. Date is based on earlier draft of letter as follows: "Chicago Needs a Botanic Garden—Draft," 4–5. UIC Collections. In this earlier draft, some Society members believed that the newly opened Old Orchard and Edens Plaza shopping malls might draw Chicago area residents on a day trip to the Skokie Marsh area. During the 1950s and 1960s, freestanding suburban shopping malls became popular destinations, and their novelty might have inspired land use planners to assume that the malls would consistently draw visitors. A location near the North Shore suburbs was also mentioned as a benefit in donor recruitment.

30. Roland F. Eisenbeis to Charles G. Sauers, June 12, 1962; Noel B. Wysong to Sauers, June 12, 1962; Glenn K. Wiedemann to Sauers, July 10, 1962; all in UIC Library FPDCC Collections.

31. Pullman to the President and Board.

32. Pullman, Report of the President, July 29, 1965, 1.

33. Charles G. Sauers to Seymour Simon, December 31, 1963, 2, UIC Library FPDCC Collections, Box C, Folder 222.

34. Thompson, John H. "Chicago Against Air Raids," *Chicago Daily Tribune*, May 8, 1955, 2, accessed August 12, 2013, ProQuest.

35. Pullman, Report of the President, July 29, 1965, 2.

36. Bauer had had previous experience in a similar Forest Preserve project, and his expertise in hydraulics later solidified his role as a key designer of Chicago's Deep Tunnel project.

37. Pullman, Report of the President, July 29, 1965, 2.

38. John O. Simonds, "From Scrabble and Ooze, Chicago's New Botanic Garden," in *Landscape Architecture*, March 1978, as reprinted from *Earthscape: A Manual of Environmental Planning* (New York: McGraw-Hill, 1978).

39. Ibid.

40. Geoffrey Rausch, interview by Cathy Jean Maloney, October 23, 2013.

41. Francis de Vos, "The Chicago Botanic Garden—A Progress Report," June 20, 1969. Chicago Horticultural Society archives, Box 4001A, folder 4.

42. Art Kozelka, "Notes for Gardeners," *Chicago Tribune* [1963–Current file], October 2, 1971, 1, accessed September 2, 2013, ProQuest.

43. Named for Garden Board member and former Cook County Forest Preserve Commissioner Mary McDonald.

44. Perkins, *Report of Special Park Commission*, 106.

45. William A. Pullman, Report of the President, July 21, 1966, 2. Chicago Horticultural Society archives, Box 4001A, folder 3.

Chapter 3

1. For a discussion of Chicago's overall role in flower shows, see "Fairs and Flowers: Chicago Hosts a World of Fairs," in Maloney, *Chicago Gardens*, 287–317.

2. "Elevation of our business," reprinted in *American Florist*, September 15, 1889, 57.

3. In 1889, Buffalo; Boston; Chicago; Indianapolis; Philadelphia; Cincinnati; Orange, New Jersey; and Worcester, Massachusetts each held fall flower shows, as evidenced by *American Florist* postings throughout the year.

4. John Thorpe, "Cut Flowers for Exhibition," *American Florist*, November 1, 1889, 136.

5. Among them, the Cook County Agricultural and Horticultural Society (CCAH) which also hosted a floral show at the Exposition Building September 16 through September 24, 1891 ("Display Ad 2—No Title," *Chicago Daily Tribune*, September 13, 1891, 6, accessed April 29, 2013, ProQuest). The CCAH was established in 1890 with such prominent nurserymen as Johnathan Periam and John Ure as well as business leaders George Lill and former governor John Beveridge ("Wolf's Period Comet Is Due," *Chicago Daily Tribune*, September 4, 1891, 3, accessed April 29, 2013, ProQuest). The venerable Northern Illinois Horticulture Society dated to the 1850s, with an impressive membership of professional horticulturists.

6. "For the World's Fair," *Chicago Daily Tribune, (1872-1922)*: 8. August 28, 1890, accessed May 16, 2014, *ProQuest*.

7. Among the Columbian Exposition Board of Directors were Chicago Horticultural Society early members Charles L. Hutchinson, V. F. Lawson, Andrew McNally, George Schneider, and Charles Wacker. Harlow N. Higinbotham served as president of the exposition.

8. Program of the Horticultural Society of Chicago Annual Autumn Exhibition 1892, 9. Chicago Horticultural Society papers.

9. "No Other Like It," *Chicago Daily Tribune*, November 3, 1895, 29, accessed December 10, 2013, ProQuest.

10. *The Chautauquan; A Weekly Newsmagazine* (Meadville, Penn.: Chautauqua Press, 1892), 180.

11. "Classified Ad 6—No Title." *Chicago Daily Tribune*, November 9, 1892, 7, accessed May 2, 2013, ProQuest.

12. "The Horticultural Society of Chicago Annual Autumn Exhibition, 1892," CHM collection: Chicago Horticultural Society records 1901–1916, Folder F38MAH7 (hereafter cited as CHM collection).

13. Horticultural Society records, 82–83.

14. Ibid., 143–47.

15. "Program and Premium List of the Chrysanthemum Show and Annual Exhibition of the Horticultural Society of Chicago, 1898," 10–12, CHM collection.

16. Ibid., 18.

17. "Flower Show at an End," *Chicago Daily Tribune*, November 12, 1899, 8, accessed May 6, 2013, ProQuest.

18. "Plan Big Flower Show," *Chicago Daily Tribune*, October 15, 1905, 2, May 30, 2013, ProQuest.

19. Whitnall is credited with a civic planning approach that emphasizes preservation of natural resources (http://images.library.wisc.edu/EcoNatRes/EFacs/NAPC/NAPC05/reference/econatres.napc05.dreed.pdf), and Routzahn would go on to publish several seminal articles on public health and policy.

20. "Turn Coliseum into 'Park' for Horticultural Show," *Chicago Daily Tribune*, October 13, 1907, 6, accessed May 30, 2013, ProQuest.

21. Grese, *Jens Jensen*, 137.

22. "Mrs. J. Pierpont Morgan and Rose That Bears Her Name," *Chicago Examiner* 6, no. 264 (October 24, 1908): 3.

23. "Flowers Coming in Private Cars," *Chicago Daily Tribune*, November 4, 1908, 15, accessed May 31, 2013, ProQuest.

24. "Seventeenth Annual Exhibition, Horticultural Society of Chicago," 7. CHM collection.

25. "Wonderful Display at Flower Show This Week 15,000 Blooms of All Tints to Be Exhibited," *Chicago Examiner* 10, no. 18 (October 31, 1909): 28.

26. "Seventeenth Annual Exhibition, Horticultural Society of Chicago," 5; "Eighteenth Annual Exhibition, Horticultural Society of Chicago," 9; CHM collection.

27. "Flower Show to be Held in Spring," *Chicago Examiner* 9, no. 177 (July 15, 1911), 5.

28. "Enlist Rich Men in Floriculture: Horticultural Society Officials Send Out Pledges to Prominent Chicagoans," *Chicago Daily Tribune*, May 27, 1912, accessed June 3, 2013, ProQuest.

29. "Crowd Sings at Naming of 'Mum,'" *Chicago Daily Tribune*, November 10, 1915, 17, accessed June 3, 2013, ProQuest.

30. "Plans Completed for Flower Festival," *Chicago Examiner* 12, no. 33 (February 18, 1912): 12. http://digital.chipublib.org/u?/CNP1912,1276.

31. "Plans for Chrysanthemums," *Chicago Daily Tribune*, October 29, 1899, 8, accessed December 10, 2013, ProQuest.

32. "Posters Ready for the Flower Show," *Chicago Daily Tribune*, October 20, 1906, 5, accessed May 7, 2013, ProQuest.

33. Eleanor Page, "Two Flower Shows Loaded with Thorns," *Chicago Daily Tribune* [1923–1963], March 6, 1959, 1, accessed June 5, 2013, ProQuest.

34. Originally named the National Council of State Garden Clubs, Inc., the National Garden Club headquarters moved in 1959 from New York City to St. Louis, Missouri. *The Fiftieth Year: The Garden Club of Illinois 1927–1977* (Chicago: Garden Club of Illinois, 1977), 4.

35. "Official Guide Book: Chicago World Flower & Garden Show 1961," 37, author's collection.

36. Ibid., 39.

37. Ibid., 13.

38. From welcome letter cosigned by William Pullman, Chicago Horticultural Society president, and Dr. R. Milton Carelton, general chairman of the Flower Show Committee, quoting longtime gardening author and editor Richardson Wright. "Official Guide Book," 1.

39. Art Kozelka, "City Flower Show to Be Discontinued," *Chicago Tribune* [1963–Current], May 1, 1979, 3, accessed June 14, 2013, ProQuest.

40. Art Kozelka, "The Biggest Garden Show of Them All," *Chicago Tribune* [1963–Current], August 19, 1979, 2, accessed June 14, 2013, ProQuest.

41. "Flower Show Is to Start Today," *Chicago Daily Tribune*, November 7, 1905, 7, accessed November 26, 2013, ProQuest.

42. Susumu Nakamura, Ivan Watters, Terry Ann R. Neff, and Tim Priest, *Bonsai: A Patient Art: The Bonsai Collection of the Chicago Botanic Garden* (Glencoe, Illinois: Chicago Botanic Garden, 2012), 15–16; "Bonsai Collection," Chicago Botanic Garden, accessed February 8, 2015, http://www.chicagobotanic.org/explore/bonsai.php.

43. "A Walk Through the Bonsai Courtyards," Chicago Botanic Garden, accessed April 15, 2014, http://www.chicagobotanic.org/walk/bonsai.

44. Stephanie Lindemann, interview by Cathy Jean Maloney, June 17, 2013.

Chapter 4

1. Walter T. Punch and William Howard Adams, *Keeping Eden: A History of Gardening in America* (Boston: Bulfinch Press, 1992), 22.

2. "Fine Flowers on View: Annual Exhibit of the Chicago Horticultural Society," *Chicago Daily Tribune*, November 11, 1891, 1, accessed May 16, 2014, ProQuest.

3. "How Chicago Millionaires Spend Fortunes Cultivating Rare Plants, *Chicago Daily Tribune*, November 1, 1908, 1, accessed October 24, 2013, ProQuest.

4. "Chrysanthemum Display at Chicago Garden Center," *Chicago Daily Tribune*, October 15, 1950, 1, accessed October 21, 2013, ProQuest.

5. "Talk on Chrysanthemums to be Given in Library," *Chicago Daily Tribune*, September 17, 1945, 15, accessed October 21, 2013, ProQuest. Voth had studied under the late Ezra Kraus, who developed the so-called Chicago strain of frost-resistant chrysanthemum. "Hardy Chrysanthemums Subject of Conference," *Chicago Daily Tribune*, February 8, 1953, 1, accessed October 21, 2013, ProQuest.

6. "The Chrysanthemum," *Garden Talk*, September 1980, 1.

7. "A Beautiful Flower Will Be City's Own," *Chicago Tribune*, November 17, 1966, F2.

8. "Chrysanthemums Come on Strong," *Garden Talk*, April 1972, 28.

9. President Chadwick's address, January 12, 1895, 110. Horticultural Society records.

10. "Chicago's 1912 Flower Show to Be the Biggest in History," *Chicago Daily Tribune*, March 10, 1912, 11, accessed May 18, 2014, ProQuest.

11. Mrs. C. Eugene Pfister, "The 'First Years' of the Woman's Board," in Reedy, *It's Fun to Remember*, 1:19.

12. Bruce Krasberg, "Roses: The Best All-Around Flowers," *Garden Talk*, October 1973, 6.

13. Kris Jarantoski, interview by Cathy Jean Maloney, October 1, 2013.

14. William H. Chadwick, "Exotic Orchids," paper read before the Chicago Horticultural Society on October 3, 1891. Horticultural Society records, 33.

15. Andreas Simon, *Chicago the Garden City* (Franz Gindele, 1894), 203–4.

16. "Mrs. Selfridge's 2000 Varieties," *Chicago Daily Tribune*, May 10, 1903, 1, accessed October 24, 2013, ProQuest.

17. Herma Clark, "When Chicago Was Young," *Chicago Daily Tribune*, November 9, 1952, 1, accessed October 21, 2013, ProQuest.

18. "Orchids Are Not Houseplants," *Garden Talks*, May 1961, 7.

19. "Guidelines for Planting at the Botanic Garden," Planning Committee Meeting agenda, January 6, 1970, CHS archives Box 17A, No. 2.

20. Geoffrey Rausch, Lecture at the Chicago Botanic Garden, "History of CBG," September 25, 1985, CHS archives Box 3006.

21. Donald Andrew Rakow and Sharon A. Lee, *Public Garden Management* (Hoboken, N.J.: John Wiley & Sons, 2011).

22. Kris Jarantoski, "Chicago Horticultural Society Living Collections White Paper," July 2012, 1.

23. Ibid., 2.

24. Ibid., 7.

25. "Specialized Collections," Chicago Botanic Garden, accessed April 19, 2014, http://www.chicagobotanic.org/collections/specialized.

26. "Rose Garden, "Chicago Botanic Garden, accessed April 19, 2014, http://www.chicagobotanic.org/downloads/gardenguides/RoseGuide.pdf.

27. Geoffrey Rausch, interview by Cathy Jean Maloney, October 25, 2013.

28. "Dwarf Conifer Garden," Chicago Botanic Garden, accessed April 19, 2014, http://www.chicagobotanic.org/downloads/gardenguides/DwarfConiferGuide.pdf.

Chapter 5

1. Ann Leighton, *Early American Gardens: "For Meate or Medicine"; American Gardens in the Eighteenth Century: "For Use or for Delight"; American Gardens of the Nineteenth Century: "For Comfort and Affluence"* (Amherst: University of Massachusetts Press, 1970, 1976, 1986).

2. J. A. Pettigrew, "The Flower Garden," Horticultural Society records, 22.

3. William C. Egan, "The Flower Basket at Egandale," *Gardening*, October 1, 1895, 20. Egan is likely referring to Charles Eliot, although the spelling of his name makes this unclear.

4. Egan quoted in L. H. Bailey, *How to Make a Flower Garden: A Manual of Practical Information and Suggestions* (New York: Doubleday, Page, 1914), 327.

5. "The Chicago Flower Show a Unique Exhibit," *Park and Cemetery* 27, no. 9 (November 1907): 225.

6. "Chicago's Fall Flower Show," *Park and Cemetery* 20, no. 7 (November 1910): 402.

7. Irene Powers, "'Romance of the Rose' Pageant to be Given at Horticultural Society Institute," *Chicago Daily Tribune*, June 15, 1952, 1, accessed April 3, 2013, ProQuest.

8. *Garden Talks* 7, no 4 (April 1959): 8.

9. Bruce Krasberg, "Front Yard Gardening," *Garden Talks* 2, no. 11 (November 1954): 3.

10. Christopher Grampp, *From Yard to Garden: The Domestication of America's Home Grounds* (Chicago: Center for American Places at Columbia College, 2008), 131.

11. As evidenced by the flurry in publication of such books as: Mary Riley Smith, *The Front Garden: New Approaches to Landscape Design* (Boston: Houghton Mifflin, 1991); S. Daniels, *The Wild Lawn Handbook: Alternatives to the Traditional Front Lawn* (New York: Macmillan, 1995); Jeni

Webber, *Taunton's Front Yard Idea Book* (Newtown, Conn.: Taunton Press, 2002); Liz Primeau, *Front Yard Gardens: Growing More Than Grass* (Toronto: Firefly Books, 2003); Sandra S. Soria, *New Front Yard Idea Book* (Newtown, Conn.: Taunton Press, 2011).

12. "'Keep Chicago the City of Gardens'—1954 Theme." *Garden Talks* 2, no. 1 (January 1954): 4.

13. "Neighborhood Beautification Project." *Garden Talks* 2, no. 12 (December 1954): 2.

14. Mr. & Mrs. Kurt Melzer, "City Kitchen Gardens Go Formal," *Garden Talk* 5, no. 7 (May 1962): 4–5.

15. Harold O. Klopp, "Improving the Old Garden," *Garden Talks* 4, no. 1 (January 1956): 3.

16. Harold O. Klopp, "The Landscape Architect of the Show," Chicago's World Flower and Garden Show 1959 program, 38, author's collection.

17. Francis De Vos, "The Chicago Botanic Garden: A Progress Report," June 20, 1969. CHS Archives, Box B4001A, Folder 4.

18. Kris Jarantoski, interview by Cathy Jean Maloney, October 1, 2013.

19. "About Haystack: Campus Architecture," Haystack Mountain School of Crafts, accessed April 20, 2014, http://www.haystack-mtn.org/campus.php.

20. Franz Schulze, "Ed Barnes' crisply patrician Botanic Garden," *Inland Architect*, January 1979, 9.

21. Chicago Horticultural Society Education Center Dedication program, June 26, 1976, CHS archives, Box 17A, folder 2.

22. "John Ormsbee Simonds," Cultural Landscape Foundation, accessed April 20, 2014, http://tclf.org/pioneer/john-simonds.

23. Bill Brown, "Garden Design Process at the Chicago Botanic Garden," October 1996. CHS archives, Box 4002D, Folder 9.

24. Ibid.

25. Rausch interview, October 23, 2013.

26. Roy A. Mecklenburg, "Why a Japanese Garden?" CHS archives, Box 4002C, Folder 1.

27. Cathy Jean Maloney, *World's Fair Gardens* (Charlottesville: University of Virginia Press, 2012).

28. Koichi Kawana, "Symbolism and Esthetics in the Traditional Japanese garden," *AABGA Bulletin*, April 1977, 33–34.

29. Koichi Kawana to Roy Mecklenburg, February 10, 1980, CHS archives Box 4002C, Folder 6. "The Edna Kanaley Graham Bulb Garden: A Beautiful Remembrance," 85.

30. Chicago Botanic Garden, accessed May 18, 2014, http://www.chicagobotanic.org/explore/great_basin.php.

31. James van Sweden, "A New American Garden," *WaterShapes*, March 2005, 56.

32. Lisa Delplace, interview by Cathy Jean Maloney, October 23, 2013.

33. John Brookes, e-mail message to author, October 25, 2013.

34. Ibid.

35. Ibid.

Chapter 6

1. The Chicago Society for University Extension was founded November 28, 1891, with the following officers: Mr. Franklin H. Head was elected president, Mrs. Charles Henrotin, vice president; Mr. Franklin MacVeagh, treasurer; and Mr. Charles Zeublin, secretary. Schools represented included Northwestern, Chicago, Lake Forest, Indiana, Wisconsin, and Illinois Universities, and Beloit and Wabash Colleges. "The proceedings of the first annual meeting of the National conference on university extension, held in Philadelphia, December 29–31, 1891, under the auspices of the American society for the extension of university teaching," 1892. Internet Archive, accessed May 2, 2014, http://www.archive.org/stream/universityextension00natirich/universityextension00natirich_djvu.txt.

2. Helen Lefkowitz Horowitz, *Culture and the City: Cultural Philanthropy in Chicago from the 1880's to 1917* (Lexington: University Press of Kentucky, 1976), 209.

3. Dr. Louis B. Martin, Education Center Dedication program, June 26, 1976, CHS archives, Box 17A, folder 2.

4. Edward L. Barnes, ibid.

5. *Garden Talk*, Summer 2007.

6. Reedy, *It's Fun to Remember*, 2:51.

7. Master Gardeners have earned a certificate in horticulture through classes offered at the Garden in partnership with the University of Illinois Extension Service.

8. Nancy Clifton, interview by Cathy Jean Maloney, January 15, 2013.

9. Reedy, *It's Fun to Remember*, 2:52–53.

10. Leora Siegel to Cathy Jean Maloney via email, November 22, 2013.

11. Nurserymen and florists of the Chicago Flower Mission included J. C. Vaughan, Edgar Sanders, and P. S. Peterson; other members included Mrs. J. V. Farwell, Mrs. E. Buckingham, and the Teachers and Young Ladies of Ferry Hall. *Fourth Annual Report of the Chicago Flower Mission for 1877* (Chicago: Knight & Leonard Printers, 1878), 10.

12. Mrs. C. Kenneth Hunter, "The Fragrant Garden for the Blind," in Reedy, *It's Fun to Remember*, 1:51.

13. Ibid., 1:52.

14. Ibid.

15. Previously known as the National Council for Therapy and Rehabilitation through Horticulture, founded in 1973.

16. "Gardening for the Handicapped Children," *Garden Talks*, December 1957, 3–4.

17. "Hospital Lawn at Vaughan to be Landscaped," *Chicago Daily Tribune* November 12, 1944,1, accessed November 24, 2013, ProQuest. (Vaughan Hospital namesake is not a known relation to nurseryman J. C. Vaughan).

18. Beautification of Vaughan General Hospital Grounds," *Garden Talks* 1, no. 3 (August–September 1945): 4. UIC Library Forest Preserve District of Cook County collections, Box 3, Folder 376.

19. Ibid.

20. Reedy, *It's Fun to Remember*, 2:60.

21. M. S. B. "A Trip to the Botanic Garden Shows Hope for a New Understanding," *Chicago Tribune* [1963–Current], February 7, 1986, accessed November 25, 2013, ProQuest.

22. "New Tram at Botanic Garden Provides Close Up Viewing," *Pioneer Press*, August 1, 1996.

23. "Strategic Plan Overview," Chicago Botanic Garden, accessed May 2, 2014, http://strategicplan.chicagobotanic.org/strategic-plan-overview.

24. "Garden Club of Factory to Meet in Gompers Park." *Chicago Daily Tribune*, April 17, 1952, 1, accessed November 29, 2013, ProQuest.

25. "Flower Show Scheduled by Loop Workers," *Chicago Daily Tribune*, August 16 1953, 1, accessed November 30, 2013, ProQuest.

26. Thalia, "Musical College Friends Open Drive Tomorrow," *Chicago Daily Tribune*, March 25, 1951, 2, accessed November 30, 2013, ProQuest.

27. "Civic Council to Hold Annual Housing Exhibit," *Chicago Daily Tribune*, May 20, 1951, 1, accessed November 30, 2013, ProQuest.

28. "The City and its Gardens," *Chicago Daily Tribune* January 1, 1954, 16, accessed November 30, 2013, ProQuest.

29. "Gardening Bug to Get Boost in Triangle Area," *Chicago Daily Tribune*, March 7, 1954, accessed November 30, 2013, ProQuest.

30. Art Kozelka, "8,000 Roses to be Planted in Grant Park," *Chicago Tribune*, May 1, 1963, accessed December 4, 2013, ProQuest.

31. Liam Ford, "Grant Park Wakes, Smells Rose Problem." *Chicago Tribune*, July 1, 2002, accessed May 18, 2014, ProQuest.

32. Susan Lacerte, "Public Gardens and Their Communities: The Value of Outreach," in *Public Garden Management*, by Donald Andrew Rakow and Sharon A. Lee (Hoboken, N.J.: John Wiley & Sons, 2011), 183.

33. "Neighborhood Gardens," Chicago Botanic Garden, accessed May 2, 2014, http://www.chicagobotanic.org/community/neighborhood.

34. See, for example, "School Gardens with Constance Carter," Library of Congress, accessed May 2, 2014, http://loc.gov/rr/program/journey/schoolgardens.html; Sally Gregory Kohlstedt, "'A Better Crop of Boys and Girls': The School Gardening Movement, 1890–1920," *History of Education Quarterly* 28, no. 1 (February 2008); "Francis Griscom Parsons and New York's Children's Garden Movement," Cultural Landscape Foundation, May 9, 2011, accessed May 2, 2014, http://tclf.org/news/features/frances-griscom-parsons-and-new-yorks-childrens-garden-movement.

35. Queene Ferry Coonley, for example, began her experimental cottage school in Riverside, Illinois, in 1907, and helped expand the Progressive education to include kindergartens around the Chicago area, including the Avery Coonley School of Downers Grove.

36. "Want to Clean Whole County," *Chicago Daily Tribune*, March 22, 1904, 3, accessed November 26, 2013, ProQuest.

37. "Rose Day at Flower Show," *Chicago Daily Tribune*, November 8, 1906, 3, accessed November 26, 2013, ProQuest.

38. "Gardening Enters Chicagoland Schools," *Garden Talks* 1, no. 5 (May 1953): 2.

39. Tina Vicini, "Plant Desire for Gardens in Youths' Minds," *Chicago Daily Tribune*, January 6, 1957, accessed November 29, 2013, ProQuest.

40. "Laurance Armour Memorial Fund Award Winners," *Garden Talks* 4, no. 9 (September 1956): 2. Winning Chicago schools included Byrne, Dawes, Farren, Fiske, Forestville, Gage Park, McCosh, Parker, and Penn from the South Side; Mayfair and Sauganash from the North Side; and

Bryant, Jackson, and Pulaski from the West Side. Suburban winning schools included Evanston High School, Thacker Elementary School of Des Plaines, and the Riley Elementary school of Northlake.

41. The Chicago School Garden Initiative was a City of Chicago program administered through the Chicago Park District with the Chicago Botanic Garden as lead agency in partnership with the Garfield Park Conservatory and Openlands. The Garden's Woman's Board was a prominent donor toward this initiative.

42. As proposed by Richard Louv's hypothesis in his book *Last Child in the Woods* (Chapel Hill, N.C.: Algonquin Books of Chapel Hill, 2005).

43. "College First," Chicago Botanic Garden, accessed May 2, 2014, http://www.chicagobotanic.org/ctl/cf_highlights.

44. "The Learning Campus," Chicago Botanic Garden, accessed May 2, 2014, http://www.chicagobotanic.org/learningcampus.

Chapter 7

1. Maloney, *Chicago Gardens*, 48.

2. Arthur Miller, "Lake Forest Country Places XVII and XVIII: Cyrus and Harriet Hammond McCormick's 'Walden' and the Estate's Endangered Bridge," Lake Forest College, May 15, 1996, accessed May 2, 2014, http://www.lakeforest.edu/library/archives/lf-country-places/walden.php.

3. Warren Manning, "Walden, A Plant Life Community," 12. Lake Forest College archives.

4. Including Mrs. Martin A. Ryerson and Mrs. Cyrus M. McCormick. "Society and Entertainments," *Chicago Daily Tribune*, January 11, 1919, 11, ProQuest.

5. Chicago Outdoor Art League 1933–1934 membership book, author's collection.

6. For example, among the Society Dunes Pageant supporters listed in a 40-page book published for the pageant were Charles Hutchinson, treasurer; Caroline McIlvaine, trustee; Mrs. Walter Brewster and Mrs. Tiffany Blake, reception; and Lena MacCauley, book committee; subscribers included (in addition to those previously listed) Cyrus McCormick, Mrs. George M. Pullman, Edward G. Uihlein, G. F. Swift, Jr., and other Swift family members, and Martin A. Ryerson and other Ryerson family members. "Book of the Historical Pageant of the Dunes," InGenWeb Project, accessed May 2, 2014, http://www.inportercounty.org/Data/Misc/PageantOfTheDunes-1917.pdf.

7. "What Is New in Pesticides?" *Garden Talks* 7, no. 4 (June 1954): 3.

8. Mrs. Albert D. Farwell, "The Danger of Spraying," *Garden Talks* 8, no. 10 (October 1954): 3.

9. *Garden Talks* 6, no. 3 (March 1958): 8.

10. "Rain Water in the Garden," *Garden Talks* 1, no. 7 (July 1953): 7.

11. Oscar H., "The Organic Method in Gardening and Farming," *Garden Talks* 7, no. 12 (December 1959): 5.

12. "Selecting Plants for the Botanic Garden," *Garden Talk* 11, no. 2 (February–March 1968): 11–12.

13. "Cooperating with Nature," *Garden Talk* 11, no. 25 (October–November 1971): 4.

14. "Plan Detailed for Skokie Lagoon," *Chicago Sun-Times*, June 10, 1964.

15. "Walton League to Hear Talk on Botanic Garden," *Wilmette Life*, November 28, 1963, 10. Lenhardt Library Collections, Box 3004, Folder 2.

16. Roy L. Taylor, "Director's Message," *Garden Talk*, January 1989, 2.

17. Ibid.

18. Janet Meakin Poor, interview with Cathy Jean Maloney, July 1, 2014.

19. Ana Mendieta, *Chicago Sun-Times*, July 18, 2001, 78.

20. As quoted in "Understanding and Conserving Plants in Peril," *We cultivate the power of plants to sustain and enrich life*, publication of the Chicago Botanic Garden.

21. Chicago Botanic Garden, 2013 Science Program Highlights from 2013 Annual Report.

22. Chicago Botanic Garden website, Annual Science Report for 2012, http://www.chicagobotanic.org/downloads/research/Annual_Science_Report_2012.pdf.

23. "Green Roof Garden," Chicago Botanic Garden, http://www.chicagobotanic.org/research/building/green_roof.php, accessed Feb. 24, 2015.

24. "Garden Research: Restoring and Managing Our Woods," *Keep Growing*, Fall 2011, 22.

Image Credits

Unless otherwise indicated in the photo captions or below, all images were taken by Chicago Botanic Garden photographer Robin Carlson.

William Biderbost, pages 87, 88, 150 (timeline 1983, bottom)

Bill Bishoff, pages 109 (image at center, right), 123 (bottom), 141, 143, 154 (timeline, top right), 176, image on jacket flap

Commonwealth Edison, photograph copyright © ComEd, page 216 (top)

Tom Harris copyright © Hedrich Blessing, pages 26, 55, 86, 212

Index

References to illustrations appear in *italic*.

Addams, Jane, 12, 171
Allerton, Samuel, 8
American Alliance of Museums, 110
American Association of Nurserymen, Florists, and Seedsmen, 63
American Florist, 62
American Horticultural Therapy Association, 183, 185
American Park and Outdoor Art Association, 189, 202
American Public Garden Association, 211
American Rhododendron Society, 84
Americans with Disabilities Act, 137, 145, 185
Amlings Flowerland, 132, 189
Annals of Horticulture of 1893, 10
arboretums, 35–36; Arnold Arboretum (Harvard), 32, 133; Morton Arboretum, 36, 110, 208, 216
Armour, Laurance, 18
Arnold Arboretum (Harvard), 32, 133
Art Institute of Chicago, 7, 15, 67, *72*, *73*, 101, 171
Arturo Velasquez Institute (Daley College), 27–28, *29*
asters, *117*, 211
Atwell, Charles, 35
Auditorium Building, 68, 171
Audubon–Chicago Region, 213
Avery, George, Jr., 42
Avery Coonley School, 189

Babcock, Henry H., 32
Bacon, Marth Smith, 151
Bacon, William T., 151
Bailey, L. H., 10
Baird Foundation, 151
Baldridge, Cyrus Leroy, 75
Balthis, Frank, 18
Barnes, Edward L., 133–34, *135*, 150, 172, 173
Bauer, William, 48
bees, *218*
Bent, John P. (Mr. and Mrs.), 151

Better Gardening Association, 132
Blair, Erle O., 183
bonsai collections, 81, *81–83*
Booth, Laurence, 134
Booth Hansen, 154, 190
botanic garden: definitions, 32; early examples, 32–35, *33*
Botanic Gardens Conservation International (BGCI), 217
Brewster, Kate, 128
Brewster, Walter S., Mrs., 18
Bro, Kenneth A. (Mr. and Mrs.), 151
Bromeliad Society of Greater Chicago, 84
Brookes, John, 151, 166, *166*
Brookfield Zoo, 36
Brown, Barbara, 153
Brown, Elizabeth Byron, 152
Brown, James, IV, 151
Brown, Lancelot "Capability," 125
Brown, Roger, 153
Bryan, Neville F., 153
Bryan, Thomas B., 9, 61, 63–64
Buckingham, Clarence, 12
buckwheat, *215*
Buehler, Albert C. (family), *197*
Buehler, John, 197
Buehler, Pat, *197*
Buehler Family Foundation, 152. *See also* Chicago Botanic Garden: Buehler Enabling Garden
Burbank, Luther, 69, 201
Burdett, James, 17, 18
Bureau of Land Management (Department of Interior), 213
Burger Nursery and Garden Center, 132
Burlinggame, Alice W., 183
Burnham, Daniel H., 13
Byrd's Nest (Elmhurst estate), 63
Byron, Scott, 154

Cactus and Succulent Society of Greater Chicago, 84
Calvary Cemetery, 126
Campbell Memorial Fund, 151

Carleton, R. Milton, 18, 42, 183, 186
Carr, Barbara Whitney, 145, *164*, 172, *173*
Carson, Rachel, 204
Carson Pirie Scott, 132, 182
cemeteries, 126; Calvary Cemetery, 126; Graceland Cemetery, 63, 126; Mount Greenwood Cemetery, 126; Rosehill Cemetery, 126
Centennial Exposition in Philadelphia (1876), 139
Central States Dahlia Society, 84
Century of Progress Exposition of 1933–1934 (Chicago), 16, *16*, 139
Chadwick, William, 33, 64, 67, 99, 108
Chauncey and Marion Deering McCormick Foundation. *See* McCormick Foundation
Chautauquan, 64
Chicago Academy of Fine Arts, 7
Chicago Academy of Science, 97
Chicago and Cook County Horticultural Society, 9
Chicago Botanic Garden, *30*, *46*, *52–53*, *96*, *117*, *234*
administration: "Keep Growing" ten-year strategic plan, 154, *155*; membership, 21, 42; mission, 137; public-private partnership, vii, *216*; sales, 84, *94*
buildings: carillon, *159*, *162–63*; Education Center, 172–73; greenhouses, 150, *207*; McGinley Pavilion, 145; modern buildings, 133–35, *134–35*; Regenstein Center, *82*, *86*, 109, 113, 134, *135*, 145, *146*, 172–73, *174–75*, 190; Rice Plant Conservation Science Center, 146, 153, 208, *212*, 214, 218–19, *219*, 221, *221*; shoin building, 140, *144*
campuses: Kris Jarantoski campus, ix, 146; Regenstein Foundation Learning Campus, ix, 146, 190
education, 113, 137; of children, 190–95, *191*; Conservation Land Management internship program, 214–15; Garden Chef series, *90*; graduate program, 173, 215; Healthcare Garden Design Certificate program, 186; Joseph Regenstein, Jr. School of the Chicago Botanic Garden, 173, *176–77*; prisoners, 192; Regen-

stein Center, 172–73, *174–75*, 190; Roadside Flower Sale workshops, 84; School Gardening Conference, 192–93; School Garden Wizard (Internet), 192–93; Science Career Continuum, 173

environmentalism: harmony with nature, 206; native plants, *113*, 133, 138, *147*, 151, 152, *200*, 206, *226–29*; natural areas, 224–30, *224–30*; wildlife preserves, *206*

exhibits: Antiques, Garden, and Design Show, 84, *88*; Big Bugs, 84, *87*; Chapungu, 84, *87*; flower shows, 80, 84, *84–86*; hanging displays, *105*; Ikebana International Show, 84, *92*; Illinois Mycological Association Show & Sale, 84; music performance, *93*; North Shore Iris and Daylily show, 84, *92*; orchid show, 84, *86*; Show of Summer, 84; Three Friends of Winter bonsai silhouette show, *95*

gardens: Aquatic Garden, 138, 145, 150; Barbara Brown Nature Reserve, 153; Betty Brown Meadow, 137; Buehler Enabling Garden, 138, 145, 152, *170*, 185–86, 196–97, *197–99*; Butterflies and Blooms, *89*; Circle Garden, *104*, 137, 145, *149*, 152; Crescent, *102–3*, 145, 153; Dixon Prairie, 133, 152, *200*, *226–29*; Dwarf Conifer Garden, *111*, 122, *122–23*, 146, 151; English Oak Meadow, 145, 152; English Walled Garden, 21, 145, 151, 165, *166–67*; Esplanade, 145, *146*, 153; Farwell Landscape Garden, 56, *56*, *57–58*, *59*, 138, 150; Gardens of the Great Basin, 153, *156*, *157*, *162*, 164; Graham Bulb Garden, 138, 150; Green Roof Garden, 146, 153, 221, *221*; Grunsfeld Children's Garden, 154, 190, *194*, 195, *195*; Heritage Garden, *2*, 21, 54, *54–55*, 133, 151; Home Landscape Center, *137*; Kleinman Family Cove, 154, *177*, 190, 196, *196*; Krasberg Rose Garden, 106, 118, *118*, *119*, *120*, *121*, 133, 151; Lakeside Gardens, 153, 164; Lavin Plant Evaluation Garden (Perennial Test Garden), 137, 146, 151, *211*; Learning Garden for the Disabled, 138, *138*, 145, 185; Model Railroad Garden, *91*; Native Plant Garden, *113*, 138, *147*, 151; Naturalistic Garden, 145, 151; Prairie, 145; Pullman Evaluation Garden, 146, 150, 206, 210; Regenstein Fruit and Vegetable Garden, 22, *22–25*, 133, 138, 145, 151; Sansho-En Garden of the Three Islands (Elizabeth Malott Japanese Garden), 138–45, *139*, *140–44*, 150; Sensory Garden, *148*, 151; Waterfall Garden, *113*, *148*, 151; Water Gardens, 153, 164; Wonderland Express, *90*

history: first plantings, 50, *51*, 110; groundbreaking, 3, 20, *48*, 48–51; House Bill 1487, 20, 44; opening, 48–51, 110, *110*; reasons for Skokie location, 42–44; timeline, 150–54

islands, 48, *49*; Arch Bridge, *117*, 153, *157*, 165; Evening Island, *114*, 147, 153, *156*, *159–63*, 164; Evergreen Island, *156*; Sansho-En Garden of the Three Islands (Elizabeth Malott Japanese Garden), 138–45, *139*, *140–44*; Serpentine Bridge, 153; Spider Island, *115*, 145, 147, 152; Trellis Bridge, 146–47, 153

lakes, *vi*, *116*, 231–32, *231–33*; Arch Bridge, *117*, 153, *157*, 165; Great Basin, *117*, *156*; Serpentine Bridge, 153; shoreline restoration, 153, 231–32, *231–33*; Trellis Bridge, 146–47, 153

landscape design, 21, 118, *124*, 133–69; Americans with Disabilities Act, 137, 145; harmony with nature, 206; modern buildings, 133–35, *134–35*; New American Garden style, 164; Regenstein Center, *82*, *86*, 109, 113, 134, *135*

outreach programs, *ix*; Bright Encounters Tour Program, 185; children, 190–95, *191*; community gardens, 189; health issues, 181–86; horticultural therapy, 186; Lenhardt Library, 178, 180; Plantmobile, 178, *179*; prisoners, 192; tram rides, 185; veterans with disabilities, *184*, 185; Windy City Harvest, 22, *26*, *27–29*, 27–30, *188*, 192, *192*, *193*; Zimmerman Lecture series, 180–81

plant collections, 110–16, *112*; aquatic, *113*, *158*; arborvitae (*Thuja plicata*), 116; bonsai collection, 81, *81–83*, *95*; buckeye (*Aesculus*), 116; crabapple trees, *159*, 164; dogwood (*Cornus*), 116; geraniums (*Geranium*), 116; ginkgo (*Ginkgo*), 116; hardy kiwi (*Actinidia*), 116; number of acres, 133; number of plants, 133; number of taxa, 112; oak (*Quercus*), 116; perennials, 210–11; rose (*Rosa*), 116; serviceberry (*Amelanchier*), 116; spirea (*Spiraea*), 116; willow (*Salix*), 116; woodland plants, *113*; woody plants, *111*, 112

research, 98, 112–13, *217*; Abbott Ecology Laboratory, 218; Astellas Economic Botany Laboratory, 218; Chicagoland Grows Program, 208, *208*, *209*; Dixon National Tallgrass Seed Bank, 220, *220*; grants, 217; green roof gardens, 221, *221–23*; Harris Family Foundation Plant Genetics Laboratory, 218; invasive species, 214; ITW Plant Systematics Laboratory, 218; Josephine P. and John J. Louis Foundation Microscopy Laboratory, 220, *220*; Nancy Poole Rich Herbarium, 218; National Tallgrass Prairie Preparation Laboratory, 220; native species in utility corridors, *216*, 217; partnerships, 217; plant breeding, 208, *209*, 210–11; plant evaluation, 208, *209*, 210–11; Plant Selection Committee, 208; plants in peril, 212–13; Plants of Concern program, 213, *213*; Population Biology Laboratory, 219; Project Budburst, 213, *213*; Reproductive Biology Laboratory, 219; Seeds of Success program, 213, *213*; Soil and Soil Preparation Laboratory, 219

sculptures: Chapungu, 84, *87*; Linnaeus statue, *2*; *Naughty Faun*, *59*; Sansho-En landscape art, 130

water, 48, 147, 164, *231* (*see also* Chicago Botanic Garden: lakes); Aquatic Garden, 138, 145, 150; aquatic plants, *158*; fountains, *104*; Skokie River corridor, 230, *230*; Skokie River Corridor enhancement, 152; Waterfall Garden, *113*, *148*, 151; Water Gardens, 153

woods: council rings, *207*; McDonald Woods, 51, 150, *150*, 224–25, *225*; Turnbull Woods, 51, 150, *150*, *207*

Chicago City Hall: green roof, 216

Chicago Community Trust, 151

Chicago Edison Company, 67

Chicago Examiner, 15, 71

Chicago Exchange for Woman's Work, 67

Chicago Florists' Club, 9, 63–64, 72

Chicago Gardeners Society (1858), 5

Chicago history, 4–5, 97, 171–72; architecture after fire, 7; cemeteries, 126; conventions, 63; early botanic gardens, 32–35, *33*, 41–42; early fairs, 61 (*see also* flower shows); East coast opinions of Chicago, 8; Great Chicago Fire (1871), *6–7*, 7, 171; park district formation, 7, 126 (*see also* Chicago park system)

Chicago Horticultural Society
  administration: membership, 41; mission, 12; partnerships, 74, 76, 79; patrons, 71; public-private partnerships, 5; survey, 41
  educational work, 4, 17, 74, 109, 130, 171–99; in schools, 189–90, *190*
  flower shows, 4, *4*, 10, 11, *11*, 16, 20, 41, *60*, 61–95, 106, 127, 132, *132*, 172, *183* (*see also* flower shows)
  garden tours, 4, 20, 98, 128, *128–29*, 186
  history: founding, 3–5; hiatus until 1945, 15–16; incorporation, 9; role of women, 15–16; victory gardens, 16–17, *17*, 19; Women's Board, 19–20, 76, 106, 128, 151, 153, 154, 181, 182,

186; World's Columbian Exposition, 9–10 (*see also* World's Columbian Exposition (1893))

landscape architecture, *124*, 125–69

medals: Chicago Horticultural Society medal, 165, 226, 245; Hutchinson Medal, 135, 145, 165, 185, 243

outreach programs, 171–99 (*see also Garden Talks*); children's gardens, 189–95, *189–95*; civic gardens, 186–89; community gardens, 186–89; downtown garden center, 178, *179, 180*; health issues, 181–86; Information Hotline, 178; media, 178, *180*; publications, 178; veterans with disabilities, 183–85, *184*

philanthropic work, 4, 19, 67, 74, 76; Fragrant Garden for the Blind, 20, *20*, 181–82, *182*

plant science, 97–123, 201–34; environmentalism, 204; organic gardening, 204; pesticides, 204, 205; pollinators, *205*; selecting plants, *205*

Chicago Horticultural Society and Garden Center, 18–20; Board of Governors, 18; Board of Trustees, 18; democratization, 18; publications, 19; Woman's Board, 19–20. *See also* Chicago Horticultural Society

Chicago International Amphitheater, 76

Chicagoland Grows Program, 208, *208, 209*

Chicago Outdoor Art League, 202

Chicago park system, 101, 216; flowers, 108; flower shows, 64; Grant Park, 34, 41–42, 186, *187*; lakefront, 34; landscape architecture, 126; Lincoln Park, 33, 64, 108; park district formation, 7, 32; politics of, 10–11; South Side parks, 32, 126; superintendent, 10–11; Union Park, 33; Washington Park, 108; West Side parks, 33, 70, 108, 126

Chicago Public Library, 7, 171

Chicago Symphony Orchestra, 7, 171

Chicago the Garden City (Simon), 108

Chicago Tribune, 15, 32, 37, 42, 50–51, 69–70, 72, 76–77, 80, 99, 185, 186; citywide garden contest, 15

Chicago Woman's Club, 7

Chinese Garden of Perfect Brightness, 50, *50*

Choyo, Professor, 99

Christopher School for Handicapped Children, 182

chrysanthemums, 72–73, *98, 99*, 99–101, *100, 102–3*; arrangements, 99, *100*; chrysanthemum show, 10, *11*, 61, *62*, 64, *67*; Chrysanthemum Society of America, 72; history of, 99; named in honor of Chicago women, *70*; National Chrysanthemum Society, 10, 64;

posters, *67–68, 70*; varieties, 61, *62*

City Beautiful Movement, vii, 11–16, 69, 71, 74, 101; yards, 69–70

Civilian Conservation Corps (CCC), *36*, 37–38, *37–38*, 50

Claar, Elmer A., 128, *129*

Clauss, Otto, 18

Clay, John Cecil, 69

Cleveland, H. W. S., 32, 126

Clifton, Nancy, 178

Codman, Harry, 9

Coleman family, 151

Coliseum, The, 70, 72

Columbian Horticultural Association, 9, 63

Columbian Museum (Field Museum), 171

ComEd, *216*, 217

Commercial Club, 13

compass plant, 110

conifers, 122, *122–23*

Cook County Agricultural and Horticultural Society (1856), 5

Cook County Board, 12

Cook County Sheriff's Vocational Rehabilitation Impact Center, 192

Coulter, John Merle, 202

Cowles, Henry C., 35, 202, 204

cranberry bush viburnum (*Viburnum opulus*), 113

Cregier, De Witt, 8

Crerar Library, 171

Cudahy, Joseph M., Mrs., 18, 183

Daley, Richard J., 42, *44*, 186

Delplace, Lisa, 164–65

de Vos, Francis, 50, 110, 133, 137

Dewey, John, 171

Dirr, Michael A., 181

Dixon, Sue and Wes, 152, *226*

Dixon National Tallgrass Prairie Seed Bank, 213, 220, *220*

Donahoe, Thomas A., *197*

Dorsey, M. J., Dr., 18

Douglas Hoerr Landscape Architecture, 151

Dr. Scholl Foundation, 151, 152

Dudley, Frank, 204

dwarf conifers, 122, *122–23*

Earth Day, 205

edible gardens, 130, *130*

Education of a Gardener, The (Brooks), 165

Egan, W. C., 64, 98, 126–27; estate, *127*

Egan, William B., 5, 32; garden, *5*

Egan garden, *5*, 32

Ellis Goodman Family Foundation. *See* Goodman Family Foundation

Ellsworth, James W., 10

environmentalism, 127, 134, 136, 146, 154, 204, *206*; conservation groups, 202; pesticides, 204

Environmental Planning and Design, 136, 150, 151, 152, 197

Environmental Protection Agency, 152, 154, 205, 216

Fant, Jeremie, *215*

Farwell, Albert D., 18, 150

Farwell, Edith, 17, 18, 150, 181, 204; estate, *129*

Farwell, John V., Jr., 13

Farwell garden tour, 20

Field, Marshall, Mrs., 101

Field Foundation of Illinois, 151

Field Museum, 171, 216

Filling, Constance, 216

Fine Arts Building, 7

Finke, Robert, ix

Fischer, Hubert A.: Fischer daylily institute, 128; garden, *129*

Flint, Harrison, 181

Flower Missions, 181

flower shows, *60*, 61–95, *69*; art nouveau images, *69, 75*; arts and crafts images, *76*; attendance, 69, 71, 72; at Chicago Botanic Garden, 84, *84–86*; Chicago Flower and Garden Show, 4, 16; chrysanthemum show, 10, *11*, 61, *62*, 64, *67, 67–68*, 99, *100*; criteria for judging exhibits, 63; daylily show, 128; Fall Flower Show (1891), 61; Fall Flower Show (1911), 72; with fashion shows, *79*; female judges, 63; flower show of 1899, 11, *75*; flower show of 1905, 70; flower show of 1906, 70, *71*; flower show of 1907, 70, 71, *75*; flower show of 1908, 71; flower show of 1909, 71; flower show of 1910, *76*, 128; flower show of 1912, 101; flower show of 1913, 72; flower show of 1915, 72, *73*, 74; flower show of 1966, 132, *132*; with formal table settings, *79*; Hanging Gardens of Babylon, 70, *71*; landscape design, 127; outreach to business community, 72; post–World War II shows, 76–79; pre–Civil War flower shows, 4; preparation for shows, 62; Progressive Era, 69–74; Rose Festival (1951), 106; Spring Flower Show (1912), 72; water gardens, 79; World Flower and Garden Shows, vii, 20, *21*, *44*, 62, *65*, 76, *77, 78, 80*; World's Columbian Exposition (1893), 63–69

Forest Preserve District of Cook County, vii, ix, 12, 35–37, 136, 172, 173, 182, 202, *203*, 204; Palos area, 35; purchase of Skokie Marsh, 37
Forest Preserve Plan Commission, 12, *12*, 37
Fragrant Garden for the Blind, 20, *20*, 181–82, *182*
Friends of Our Native Landscape, 12, 127, 202

Gallagher, Gertrude, 16
Garden Club of America, 77, 84, 128
Garden Club of Berrington, 152
Garden Club of Illinois, 16, 76–77, 84
Gardeners of the North Shore, 84
Garden Guild of Winnetka, 151
Garden Talks (also *Garden Talk*), 19, 101, 106, 108, 109, *129*, 130, 131, 178, *179*, 189, *190*, 204–5. *See also Keep Growing*
Garfield Conservatory, 84, 110, 182
General American Transportation, 186
Geraldi Norton Memorial Corporation, 151
geraniums, 116, *116*
Gilded Age, 3–11
Girl Scouts, 78
Glasser family, 153
Glessner, John, 9
Glessner, John J., Mrs., 67
Godshalk, Clarence, 48
Gompers Park, 186
Goodman Family Foundation, 153, 221, *221*
Goodnow, Charles, 35
Graceland Cemetery, 63, 126
Graham, Edna Kanaley, 150
Graham, William B., 150
Grainger, David W. (Mr. and Mrs.), 151
Grampp, Christopher, 130
Grant, G. L., 63, 64
Grant Park, 34, 41–42, 186, *187*
Great Chicago Fire (1871), *6–7*, 7, 171
Great Depression, The, 16, 189
greenhouses, 150, 202, *207*. *See also* nurseries
green roofs, *146*, *153*, 216, 221, *221–23*
Grosse, Peppi, *197*
Grunsfeld, Ernest A., 152, 154
Grunsfeld, Sally, 152
Guild of the Chicago Botanic Garden, 154

Hadley School for the Blind, 151
Hagenah, William, 172, *173*
Hamill, Corwith family, 152
Hamill, Ernest A., Mrs., 17
Hanging Gardens of Babylon, 70, *71*
Hardy, Alpheus, Mrs., 61; chrysanthemum, *62*
Harris, Bette, 216

Harris, Caryn, 216
Harris, King, 216
Harris, Neison, 216
Harris Family Foundation, 216, 218
Haystack Mountain School of Crafts, 134
health issues, 181–86
Hekman Gordon family, 154
Herendeen, Patrick, *220*
Heuchling, Fred, 17, 18
Hevey, Robert, 216
Highland Park, 17
Higinbotham, Harlow, 8, 64
Hines Veterans Administration Hospital, 19, 183, 185
Home Insurance Building, 7
Horowitz, Helen Lefkowitz, 172
horticulture as art, 75, 76
Horticultural Palace, 10, 64, *66*
Hull House, 7, 12, 171
Hunter, LaVerne, 181
Hutchinson, Charles, 8, 9, 12, 13, *13*, 15, 33, 36, 64, 67, 72, 202
Hutchinson, Frances Kinsely, 202, *203*

Ickes, Harold, 38
Ikebana International Show, 84
Ikenobo Ikebana Society, 84
Illinois Department of Natural Resources, 216
Illinois Gourd Society, 84
Illinois Institute of Technology, 145
Illinois Mycological Association, 84
Illinois Natural Survey, 97
Illinois Orchid Society, 84
Illinois Roads Builders Association, 182
Illinois State Horticultural Society, 63
Illinois State Museum, 152, 153, 154
Illinois State Nurserymen's Association, 76, 182
Indiana Dunes: "The Dunes under Four Flags," 204
Inland Architect, 134
In Love's Garden (Clay), 69
Institute for Museum and Library Services (IMLS), 192
International Photo Company, 67
International Union for the Conservation of Nature (IUCN), 217
Inter-State Exposition Building, 9, 71
Ipsen-Stotler, Lorraine, 154
Izaak Walton League, 206

Japanese barberry (*Berberis thunbergii*), 113
Japanese gardens, 139, 140. *See also* Chicago Botanic Garden

Jarantoski, Kris, 106, 110, 133, *166*
Jefferson, Thomas, 32
Jenney, William LeBaron, 7, 64, 126
Jensen, Jens, 11, *11*, 12, 37, 70, 98, 126, 127, 128, 164, 189, 204; council rings, *207*
John Crerar Library, 171
Judson, Sylvia Shaw, 59
Jungle, The (Sinclair), 11

Kanst, Edwin A., 15, 17, 18, 64
Kawana, Koichi, 139, *139*, 140
Keep Growing, 19, 178
Keller, Anna P., 18
Kenilworth Garden Club, 152
Kennicott, John A., 5, 32
Kennicott, Ransom, 37
Kesner, Jacob, 17
Kiley, Dan, 135, 146, *147*, 153
Kill, Leonard, 17
Kim, Mikyoung, 190
Kinzie, John H., 5, 77
Klatz, Esther Grunsfeld, 152, 154
Kleinman family, 154
Klopp, Harold O., 77, 131–32, 181–82
Koch, August, 18
Kozelka, Art, 50, 80
Kraft, Inc., 151
Krasberg, Bruce, *44*, 79, 106, 130, 151
Kraus, Ezra, 99
Krehbiel, John H., Jr. (Mr. and Mrs.), 153
Kresge Foundation, 150
Kropp, Carl, 17
Ksiazek, Kelly, *216*

Lake Forest College, 202
Lake Forest Garden Club, 15, 17
landscape architecture, 9, 70, 77–78, *124*, 124–69; approaches to arrangements, 133; Chicago Botanic Garden, 133–69; historical overview, 125–26; naturalistic style, 126–27; New American Garden style, 164; Vaughan General Hospital, 183; yards, 69–70, 130, 131, *131* (*see also* yards)
Lang, Connie Bates, 153
La Rabida Children's Hospital, 182
Laurance Armour Memorial Fund, 190
Lavin, Bernice F., 151
Lawson, Victor, 8, *12*, 13, 37
LEED ceritfication, 154, 214
Leesley, Clyde, 17
Leider family, 151
Leighton, Ann, 126

Le Nôtre, André, 125
Lighthouse for the Blind, 20, 181, 182
Lincoln Park Conservatory, 108, 110
Lindemann, Stephanie, 80
Linnaeus, Carolus, *2*, *3*
Linzer, Dan I. H., 173
Lloyd, Christopher, 165
Loebl, Jerrold, 186
London Kew Gardens, 125
Louis, John J., Jr., 151, 153, 185. *See also* Chicago
    Botanic Garden: green roof gardens
Louis, Josephine P., 151, 153, 185
Louis, Michael W., 151
lumber industry, 7
Lundgren, John A., 101
Lying-In Hospital, 67

MacArthur Foundation, 152
Make It Better, 154
Malott, Robert H. family, *144*, 150
Manning, Warren, 127, 202
Marshall, Tyler, Rausch architecture firm, 151, 152
Marsh speedwell (*Veronica scutellata*), *213*
Martin, Louis B., 172
Mather, Stephen T., 204
McCagg, Ezra, 9
McCauley, Lena M., 202
McCormick, Cyrus, Jr., 127
McCormick, Cyrus H., 13
McCormick, Edith Rockefeller, 127
McCormick, Harold F., 13, 127
McCormick, Harriet Hammond, 127, 202
McCormick, Robert, *12*
McCormick estate, *127*
McCormick Foundation, 151, 154
McCormick Place, 77–79; flower show, 20, 41;
    Windy City Harvest rooftop garden, *28*
McCrea, A. E., Mrs., 128
McDonald, Bert Schiller, Mrs., 18
McDonald, Mary Mix, 150
McNally, Andrew, 8
McNeil Foundation, 154
Mecklenburg, Roy, 79, 139, 140
Melzer, Kurt, 130–31
Men's Garden Clubs, 18
Merchant Club, 13, *13*
Merlin, Peter, *173*
Metzler, Richard and Barbara, 154
Meyer, Peter Morrow, 153
Mid-America Bonsai Society, 84
Midwest Bonsai Society, 50, 84
Midwest Daffodil Society, 84

Midwest Fruit Explorers, 84
Midwest Horticultural Society, 18
Millennium Seed Bank Project, 213
Mitchell, John J., 12, 13
Miyabe maple, *209*
Monet, Claude, *99*
Moninger Company, 202
Morton, Joy, 36
Morton Arboretum, 36, 110, 208, 216
Mount Greenwood Cemetery, 126
Mueller, Greg, 216
Municipal Science Club, 12

National Chrysanthemum Society, 10, 64
National Garden Club, 77
Navy Pier, 76–77
Negaunee Foundation, 214
Newberry, W. L., 5
Newberry Library, 7, 171
New York Botanical Garden, 32
Nielsen, Gertrude B., 151
Nolan, Arthur, Jr., 208
Nolan, Patricia, 208
Nolan, Peter, 208
Norberg, John, 41
Northern Illinois Gesneriad Society, 84
North Shore, 70; landscapes, *127*
North Shore Garden Club, 15
North Shore Iris and Daylily Society, 84
Northwestern University, 145, 215
nurseries, 5, 10, 62, 67, 132, 201
Nursery in Homewood, 132

Oehme, van Sweden landscape architecture firm,
    147, 151, 153, 154, 164, 196
Oehme, Wolfgang, 164
Office of Civilian Defense, 16–17
Ogden, William B., 4, 126
Olmsted, Frederick Law, 7, 8–9, 10, 32, 64, 126,
    127, 189
Olmsted, Frederick Law, Jr., 9
Orange Meadowbrite cornflower, *209*
orchids, *86*, *108*, 108–9, *109*
Orchid Society, 109
Ornamental Growers Association of Northern
    Illinois, 132, 208
Osaka Garden (Jackson Park), 139
Outer Belt Commission, 12, 35

Page, Russell, 165
Palmer, Bertha, 61; roses, 101
Park and Cemetery magazine, 127

Pathways Project, 192
Patio Garden Institute, 20
Pepoon, Herman S., 202
Periam, Jonathan, 9
Perkins, Dwight, 36, 37, 51, 204
Peshtigo, Wisconsin, 7
Peterson, P. S., 201
Peterson, William A., *12*, 12–13, 17
Peterson nursery, 10
Pettigrew, J. A., 10, 64, 126
Pfister, C. Eugene, 17, 18, 19, 130
Pfister garden tour, 20
Pfister Rose Institute, 128
Pinkerton, Allan, 41
Pink Profusion phlox, *209*
Plan of Chicago (1909), 4, 13–15, *14*; commission, 13
Plant Conservation Alliance, 217
Plant Evaluation Notes, 113, 210, 221
plant science, 201–34; commercial use, 202; pes-
    ticides, 204, 205; plant breeding, 208, *209*,
    210–11; plant evaluation, 208, *209*, 210–11;
    plants in peril, 212–13; selecting plants,
    205. *See also* Chicago Botanic Garden:
    research
Poehlmann, August, 17
Poor, Janet Meakin, *165*, 181, 208
Prairieblues series of Baptista, 211
Prairie Club, 12, 127, *127*, 202
Prairie Farmer, 5
Progressive Era, vii, 11–16, 35, 171–72; flower
    shows, 69–74; legacy, 74; role of children,
    189; role of women, 69
Prost, J. H., 71
Public Garden Management, 186
Puck magazine, 8
Pullman, George M., 41
Pullman, William Allan Pinkerton, 41, *44*, 48, 51,
    150; awards, 135; garden, *129*; resignation,
    135
Pullman Strike (1894), 11

Race, Nancy Zimmerman, 150
Rausch, Geoffrey, 48, 50, 110, 118, 136, *136*, 137
Raynolds, James D., 63
Reedy, June, 41
reforestation, 7
Regenstein, Joseph, Jr., 22, *22*, 173
Regenstein, Susan, *173*
Reinberg, Peter, 12, 37, 202
Republic Flow Meters, 186
rhododendrons, 210; American Rhododendron
    Society, 84

Rice, Ada L., 208
Rice, Daniel, 183, 208
Robinson, William, 126
Rogers, David, 84
Roosevelt, Franklin D., 37
Roosevelt, Theodore, 202
Rosehill Cemetery, 126
roses, 72, 101–7, *106*; blue, 101; Chicago Peace rose, 186, *187*; cultivars, 113; Grant Park, 186, *187*; heirloom, *107*; Krasberg Rose Garden, 118, *118*, *119*, *120*, *121*; named after Chicago leading ladies, 71; Pfister Rose Institute, 128; Rose Festival (1951), 106; tea roses, 106; "war of roses," 101, 106
Rothert, Gene, 185, *185*
Routzahn, Evart G., 70
Rowland, Pleasant T., 153, *164*
Rudd, Willis N., 71, 72, 99, 126, 202
Ryerson, Martin A., 13, *99*, 202
Ryerson Foundation, 182

Sabuco, John, 181
Saint Lawrence Seaway, 76
Sanders, Edgar, 126
Sauers, Charles G., 18, 42, *43*, 44
Saunders, William, 126
Schneider, George, 8
Schupp, Philip, 17
Scott Byron & Co., 152, 154
Searle Family Trust, 152
Sears Roebuck: "Fun in the Sun" patio, *132*
Second Regiment Armory, 65
Selfridge, Harry Gordon, 17, 108
Shaw, Sophia, vii, 146
Shaw Foundation, 151
Shedd, John G., 13
Sherman House hotel, 3, 9
Simms Family, 153
Simon, Andreas, 108
Simon, Seymour, 44
Simonds, John O., 135–36, *136*, 139, 206. *See also* Simonds and Simonds architects
Simonds, O. C., 11, 12, 98, 126, 202
Simonds and Simonds architects, 20–21, 36, 37, 48, 50, 110
Sinclair, Upton, 11
Sipe, Susan B., 189
Skokie Marsh, 31–32, *36*; controlled burns, *47*; fires, 32; lagoon system, 37–38, *39–40*; missiles, 32, *45*; mosquitos, 32; purchase by Forest Preserve, 37; soil, 32; water quality, 48

Skokie River valley, *35*, 230, *230*
Slater, John and Mary Helen, 154
Smith, Carl, 12
Smith, Ellen Thorne, 151
Smith, F. A. Cushing, 181
Smith, Hermon Dunlap, 151
Society of American Florists, 7, 63, 71
Southwest Central Community Counsel, 186
Special Parks Commission, 12, 35, 51
Still, Shannon, *215*
Stroger, John H., *173*
Sykora, James, 18
Szokol, Pam, 216

Taft, Loredo, 204
tallgrass prairie plant seeds, *213*, 220, *220*
Taylor, Georgiana M., 151
Taylor, Graham, 204
Taylor, John W., 151
Taylor, Roy L., 206
Thiele, Edward M., 153
Thiele, Pleasant Williams, 153
Thorne, Bruce (Mr. and Mrs.), 151
Thorpe, John, 9, 62, 64
Tonietto, Rebecca, *218*
Trenens family, 153
Tyznik, Anthony, 48

Uihlein, Edward G., 70, 108
University of Chicago, 101, 171, 172, 202; Botany Department, 202; field trips, 202, *202*
University of Illinois, 145; Department of City Planning and Landscape Architecture, 130
urban gardening, 130. *See also* Windy City Harvest
Urbs in Horto, vii, 4, *4*
U.S. Army Corps of Engineers, 154
U.S. Department of Energy, 216

van Sweden, James, 164
Van Valkenburgh Associates, 152
Vasumpaur garden of Western Springs, 20
Vaughan, J. C., 2, 10, 12, *12*, 18, 37, 63, 64, 99, 201; bulbs, *10*; garden, *16*
Vaughan General Hospital, 19, 183
Vaux, Calvert, 126
Versailles, 125
victory gardens, vii, 4, 16–17, *17*, *19*; children, 189
Visiting Nurse Association, 67
Vlasek, E., 15
Von Hofsten, Hugo: *Spring Winds on the Skokie*, 37
Voth, Paul, 101

Wacker, Charles, 12, *12*, 13, 15, 37
Wampanoag tribe, 125
Wanamaker, Minnie, 61
Ward, Aaron Montgomery, 34
Ward, Aaron Montgomery, Mrs., 101
Washburne, W. D., 37
Washington, George, 32, 133
Waud, Anne and Morrison, 152, 153
Weed, Howard Evarts, 128
Weese, Harry, 133
Weidenmann, Jacob, 126
West, Victoria Sackville, 165
White City. *See* World's Columbian Exposition (1893)
Whitnall, C. B., 70
Wildflower Preservation Society, 202, *203*
Wintz, Robert P., *44*
Windy City Harvest, 22, *26*, 27–28, *27–30*, *188*, 192, *192*, *193*; Lake County, *29*; McCormick Place, *28*; Roots of Success curriculum, 28; Washington Park, *27*
winged euonymous (*Euonymus alatus*), 113
Wirtz, Peter, 146
Wisconsin–Illinois Lily Society, 84
Women, Infants and Children (WIC) Centers, 192
women's club movements, 15
women's garden clubs, 15
World's Columbian Exposition (1893), vii, 8–10, 171; Court of Honor, 127; flower shows, 63–69; Horticultural Palace, 10, 64, *66*; landscape design, 127; Wooded Island, 127, 139
World's Columbian Exposition Horticultural Conference, 10
World's Fair of 1933–1934. *See* Century of Progress Exposition of 1933–1934 (Chicago)
World War I, 74–75
World War II, 183, 189

yards, 69–70, 131, *131*, 186; edibles in border, 130, *130*; front yard gardening, 130; landscape architecture, 130; outdoor entertaining, *132*; urban gardening, 130

Zimmerman, Elizabeth, 180